Auto Racing Titles from Potomac Books

Taking Stock: Life in NASCAR's Fast Lane
Edited By Monte Dutton

Rebel With a Cause: A Season with NASCAR Star Tony Stewart
By Monte Dutton

*At Speed: Up Close and Personal with the People,
Places, and Fans of NASCAR*
By Monte Dutton

INDY

The Race and Ritual of the Indianapolis 500

SECOND EDITION

TERRY REED

Potomac Books, Inc.
Washington, D.C.

Text Design by Susan Mark

Library of Congress Cataloging-in-Publication Data

Reed, Terry, 1937–
    Indy : the race and ritual of the Indianapolis 500 / Terry Reed.—2nd ed.
        p.   cm.
    Includes index.
    Rev. ed. of: Indy, race and ritual. c1980.
    ISBN 1-57488-907-9 (pbk. : alk. paper)
    1. Indianapolis Speedway Race—History.   I. Reed, Terry, 1937– Indy, race and ritual.   II. Title.

GV1033.5.I55R43   2005
796.7′2′06877252—dc22   2004022429

Paperback ISBN 1-57488-907-9
(alk. paper)

Printed in the United States of America on acid-free paper that meets the American National Standards Institute Z39–48 Standard.

Potomac Books, Inc.
22841 Quicksilver Drive
Dulles, Virginia 20166

10   9   8   7   6   5   4   3   2   1

Contents

To Bill Reed
ab ovo usque ad mala

Illustrations

Preface

The origin of this editorial project reaches at least as far back as 1974 when I was vacationing for a week or so at a resort called Buck Hill in the Poconos, and when by some fortunate confluence of circumstances I happened to make the acquaintance of Leon "Buffalo" Mandel, then editor of *Car and Driver* who had recently published a combined biography and autobiography of the recently sacrificed Peter Revson. Fortunate too was my having read the book with sufficient attention to satisfy Leon that I had completed my homework. We passed a memorable day at the two-and-a-half-mile triangular Pocono International Raceway where there happened to be a NASCAR race scheduled, and where he happened to introduce me to Roger Penske and Bobby Allison. On the return to Buck Hill we spoke fluent auto racing, a blood sport with which I was reasonably familiar since the age of nine. Within days I was in touch with Leon's literary agent, and in the process of writing (first in pencil, and then on a well-seasoned Underwood) the original edition of *Indy: Race and Ritual* (1980) that found its way into the hands and shelves of a few good readers, and opened doors that would otherwise have been bolted shut.

Pursuant to writing about the Indianapolis Motor Speedway and its 500-mile race, I went rather brazenly to the track, announced my intentions over lunch to skeptical track historian Donald Davidson, and then, as was the policy toward anyone who appeared to be seriously researching Indianapolis in those days, secured permission from the equally skeptical publicity director Al Bloemker to graze at will through IMS filing cabinets and randomly jot copious notes, even at times when I was the only person in the office. When David Arthur of Potomac Books surprised me by suggesting in the fall of 2002 that we prepare a re-edited, revised, and rewritten version of *Indy*, it became clear to me that, although in well over half a century I had accumulated at least twenty-five bookshelves of various Indianapolis Speedway data and material (bibliographies, computer files, addresses, telephone numbers, letters, interview transcripts, photography, racing programs, magazine and newspaper clippings, voice tapes, press releases), anything I wrote would be the work of many hands and that I would owe a profound debt of gratitude to a great many people who had experienced Indianapolis before and since.

I had long ago canvassed newspaper archives at the Indiana State Library, then located in the Indiana Statehouse, and pored endlessly over Peter DePaolo's *Wall Smacker: The Saga of the Speedway* (Thompson Products, Inc., 1935), Russ Catlin's *The Life of Ted Horn: American Racing Champion* (Floyd Clymer, 1949), Wilbur Shaw's autobiographic (albeit ghostwritten by Bloemker) *Gentlemen, Start Your Engines* (Coward-McCann, 1955), and of course Bloemker's *500 Miles to Go: The Story of the Indianapolis Speedway* (Coward-McCann, 1961). I also could little afford to ignore Griffith Borgeson's *The Golden Age of the American Racing Car* (W. W. Norton & Company, 1966). Bill Libby's *Parnelli: A Story of Auto Racing* (E. P. Dutton & Co., 1969), Anthony (Andy) Granatelli's *They Call Me Mister 500* (Henry Regnery Company, 1969), Jerry Miller's *Fast Company: The Men and Machines of American Auto Racing* (Follett Publishing Company, 1972), Ron Dorson's *The Indy 500: An American Institution Under Fire* (Bond/Parkhurst Books, 1974), Jerry M. Fisher's *The Pacesetter: The Untold Story of Carl G. Fisher* (Lost Coast Press, 1998), Bill Libby's *Foyt* (Hawthorne Books, Inc., 1974), and Ed Hitze's *The Kurtis-Kraft Story* (Interstate Printers and Publishers, Inc., 1974) that provided various insights on the track and its people. I reread such documents and reviewed again Jack C. Fox's indispensable 500-race chronicle entitled *The Illustrated History of the Indianapolis 500* (Carl Hungness & Associates, 1975), Clint Brawner and Joe Scalzo's *Indy 500 Mechanic: The Inside Story of Big Time Auto Racing* (Chilton Book Company, 1975), John and Barbara Devaney's *The Indianapolis 500: A Complete Pictorial History* (Rand McNally & Company, 1976), Bill Libby's *Champions of the Indianapolis 500: The Men Who Have Won More than Once* (Dodd, Mead & Company, 1976), Sam Posey's *The Mudge Pond Express* (G. P. Putnam's Sons, 1976), Paul Van Valkenburgh's *Race Car Engineering and Mechanics* (Dodd, Mead and Company, 1976), Phil Berger and Larry Bortstein's *The Boys of Indy* (Corwin Books, 1977), Sonny Kleinfield's *A Month at the Brickyard: The Incredible Indy 500* (Holt, Rinehart and Winston, 1977), Hal Higdon's *Summer of Triumph: The Life of Jimmy Caruthers* (G. P. Putnam's Sons, 1977), Dan Gerber and Heinz Kluetmeier's *Indy: The World's Fastest Carnival Ride* (Prentice-Hall, Inc., 1977), Bobby Unser and Joe Scalzo's *The Bobby Unser Story* (Doubleday & Company, 1979), Roger Huntington's *Design and Development of the Indy Car* (HP Books, 1981), Carl

Hungness's *Go! The Bettenhausen Story* (Carl Hungness Publishing, 1982), A. J. Foyt and William Neely's *A. J.: My Life as America's Greatest Race Car Driver* (Times Books, 1983), Jack Fox's *Illustrated History of Sprint Car Racing 1896–1942, Volume One* (Carl Hungness Publishing, 1985), Bob Gates's *Hurtubise* (Witness Productions, 1995), Gordon Eliot White's *Offenhauser* (Motorbooks International, 1996), Trevor Griffiths's *Grand Prix* (Motorbooks International, 1998), White's *Indianapolis Cars of Frank Kurtis: 1941– 1963 Photo Archive* (Iconografix, 2000) and *Kurtis-Kraft: Masterwords of Speed and Style* (MBI Publishing Company, 2001), Mark S. Foster's *Castles in the Sand: the Life and Times of Carl Graham Fisher* (University Press of Florida, 2000), and Gary Wayne's *The Watson Years: When Roadsters Ruled the Speedway* (Witness Productions, 2001).

Among serial publications, Indianapolis historians cannot possibly overlook Floyd Clymer's 1941 *Indianapolis Race History* that consists of reprinted Indianapolis race articles published in the first four decades of the twentieth century in *The Automobile, The Horseless Age, Motor Age,* and *Automotive Industries.* Commencing in 1946, Clymer's race yearbooks offer readers a literary opportunity to revisit Indianapolis as events were unraveling. The same is true with the invaluable yearbooks produced in more recent times by Donald Davidson and Hungness. Back issues of Walter Bull's *Illustrated Speedway News* weekly trade papers, as well as yellowed and brittle back issues of *The Bergen Herald,* which evolved into the *National Speed Sport News,* are immensely helpful, as are back issues of *Speed Age,* copies of *Auto Racing Memories and Memorabilia, Auto Racing, Coast Auto Racing,* papers of the *Emeryville Historical Society,* and certain issues of *The New Yorker, Indy Car, Car and Driver, Circle Track,* and *Open Wheel.* IMS race programs from 1911 forward are extremely telling, as are copies of the Indianapolis 500 old-timers newsletters, *The Alternate,* hard-to-find copies of *National Speedway Weekly, Speedway Sparks,* and *US Autosports.* For more recent data, IMS official press releases, especially its *Media Fact Book* series, its *Daily Trackside Report* compendia, and its annual *Record Book* (once prepared by *The Indianapolis Star* and edited and produced by IMS Properties, Inc.), are indispensable, as is Dick Jordan's recordkeeping from the United States Auto Club. No less useful are records and other data compiled at Championship Auto Racing Teams, Inc. Phil Harms's extraordinary transcripts of every Indianapolis-style race ever run is a critical reference for any motorsports historian. Of particular value has been Allan E. Brown's *History of America's Speedways: Past and Present* (Allen E. Brown, 2003) and *The Encyclopedia of Indianapolis,* edited by David J. Bodenhamer and Robert

G. Barrows (Indiana University Press, 1994), especially contributions by Patrick Furlong on automobiles and automotive history, and biographical information on IMS founders provided by Sheryl Vanderstel, Glory-June Greiff, Wanda Lou Willis, and Matthew Morris. I am particularly indebted to the Indianapolis Motor Speedway, especially Fred Nation, Donald Davidson, Deb Taylor, Ron McQueeney, Josh Laycock, and Eric Powell, for their prompt, good-natured assistance and encouragement, and to my friends and fellow travelers in racing, especially Mike O'Leary, Don Radbruch, Bob Watson, Nan Salih, Chris Economaki, Bob Jenkins, Mac Miller, Stan Sutton, John Cooper, Dale Fairfax, Howard Matre, Phil Rider, Deke Houlgate, Robin Miller, Gordon White, Shandon Vickers, Cliff Jacobs, Richard Deaton, Galen Kurth, two Jerry Millers, Bob Falcon, Shav Glick, Bob Kent, Dick Lee, Tom Schmeh, Mark Dill, Sandy Campbell, Al Isselhard, George Peters, Bill Reed, Bob Gates, Len Ashburn, John Mahoney, Denise Melilli, Kevin Cuddihy, John Church, and Dick Berggren, in addition to hundreds of others who know a thing or two about Indy, its race and its rituals, including several Indianapolis winners (especially Troy Ruttman, Rodger Ward, and Gordon Johncock) who, along with scores of others who had raced at Indianapolis, afforded me hours of interview time and other courtesies over the last half century.

Indianapolis Motor Speedway

ENCOUNTERING INDY

"In America any boy may become president. I suppose
it's just one of the risks he takes."
—Adlai Stevenson, public address, Indianapolis,
September 26, 1952

The beloved World War II Pulitzer Prize–winning war correspondent Ernest Taylor "Ernie" Pyle (1900–1945), born in Dana, Indiana, about sixty-seven miles straight west of the Indianapolis Motor Speedway, remarked that "I would rather win that race than anything in the world. I would rather be Ralph DePalma than president." The race to which he referred is of course the Indianapolis 500-mile classic run on or near Memorial Day eighty-eight times. Ralph DePalma, as every Indianapolis enthusiast knows, won the 1915 race at a speed of 98.5 miles an hour in a cream, red, and black Mercedes, and competed in nine other 500-milers on the fabulous two-and-a-half-mile brick course six miles west of the Indiana capital. The millions of enthusiasts who over the decades have been smitten with the seductive aura and mystique, and all the many arcane customs and rituals that the track and the race entail, will also understand the spirit with which Pyle made his remarks. Since 1975 the enigmatic race course has been listed on the National Register of Historic Places. Said an in-house publicity release from the 1990s, "the Indianapolis Motor Speedway is an American icon and the world's greatest racecourse." It also accommodates the largest single-day sporting assemblage in the world (the *Indianapolis Star* estimated in 2004 that there are 257,401 permanent seats) with an estimation (but never disclosed) of up to 425,000 people in attendance, the largest public address system in the world, the largest radio network in the world, and at certain times the largest traffic tie-up in the world. Prior to the 2003 race the Speedway announced that ESPN was dispatching its television coverage of the race to more than 200 countries (not excluding Africa, Asia, Australia, Latin America, New Zealand,

and the Middle East) and into what it estimated to be 325 million households. Joe Cloutier, who in certain respects resembled Donald Rumsfeld, and who from 1945 served variously as treasurer and later twice briefly as president of the IMS until his death in 1989, told *Indy Car Racing* magazine in 1985, "this race is so institutionalized that, if anything in this world is bulletproof, this is it." Allan E. Brown, who for almost twenty years has attempted to compile an annotated list of every auto racing track, exclusive of road courses, drag strips, and motorcycle trails, estimates that there are or have been some 5,905 speedways (meaning auto racing tracks that are in some sense or another round) on American soil. Notwithstanding, when anyone in the racing business says "the Speedway," it refers only to Indianapolis. "Every once in a while," said architect Paxton Waters, "I hear of someone wanting to build a track that exactly duplicates the Indianapolis Motor Speedway. I can't imagine that anyone would ever do it. Every new track owner wants to create 'the next IMS,' but most know that you can't get that simply by copying the layout of the track. A track has to develop its own history." Indeed, when some people think of race tracks, they think arbitrarily of two-and-a-half miles, a distance they identify with Indianapolis. The original Indianapolis plan, however, called for a three-mile course, a distance scaled back to two-and-a-half because of property limitations.

There have indeed been other two-and-a-half mile tracks. One was a beach course in Galveston, Texas, back in 1913. In 1928 there were some exhibition races at the two-and-a-half-mile Packard Proving Grounds in Utica, Michigan. There was also a two-and-a-half-mile track in Dodge City, consisting of airport runways, in 1949. The financially troubled and now-vanished Ontario Motor Speedway in California attempted to reproduce the IMS in the 1970s, except that it elevated its backstretch to improve sight lines. It did, at one time, designate IMS president and chairman of the board Anton "Tony" Hulman to become chairman of Ontario's board, as if to suggest that the Speedway had consented to having itself cloned for western American audiences. Ontario failed, one might say, because it had not developed its own *shtick*. The two-and-a-half-mile Daytona International Speedway that opened in 1959 has developed its own myth, but it is no Indianapolis nor was it intended to be. Nor was the three-cornered Pocono International Raceway that opened in Long Pond, Pennsylvania in 1969. When ground-breaking ceremonies were underway for Homestead-Miami Speedway in 1993, the concept was to build a mile-and-a-half, scaled-down Indianapolis Motor Speedway with short straightaways at both ends of the track. The short straights turned out to not be conducive to racing, and were subsequently eliminated.

Three-time Indianapolis winner Johnny Rutherford, during a moment of introspection, said recently that the Speedway is a place "to realize your dreams," saying too that dreams are "what this place is made of." Many (687 men and three women) have come to the IMS over the past ninety-six years to play out their dreams and stake their lives on the outcome. The MSN.com web site listed a visit to the Indianapolis 500 as one of the "Top 10 Things to Do Before You Die." Clark Gable came to the track at least three times and made a film entitled *To Please a Lady* there and elsewhere with Barbara Stanwyck in 1950. Tony Hulman's Yale classmate Rudy Valee stopped by the track. Crooner Mel Torme arranged booking in Indianapolis every May so that he could be on the scene. Comedian Eddie "Rochester" Anderson, a regular attendee at the Gilmore Stadium midget track in Hollywood, loved the Speedway and its people. One never knows who may turn up. Mickey Rooney was there. So were Messrs. Ford, Reagan, Bush (I), and Clinton. Since the track is a showplace, it attracts show people. Dinah Shore dropped by. So did Burgess Meredith, Ginger Rogers, Phil Harris, Roy Rogers, the Beatles, Jimmy Stewart, Jayne Mansfield, Shirley MacLaine, and Muhammad Ali. Indeed, various people have been conceived, born, and killed there. Although there is a prohibition against it, people have directed that their ashes be distributed at the track. In 1941, the *Indianapolis News* sportswriter Bill Fox, Jr. reminisced about a colleague who entertained exactly that wish. "My friend who was over there in the [grand]stand isn't around any more," Fox wrote. "He loved this race with his whole heart. He worshipped the drivers. Speed was his god of sports. He always left the press pagoda and went down to the first turn. He loved it down there. He inhaled the smoke down there as if it were perfume. Once he said to me, 'I'm a funny duck, I guess, but when I die I want the fellow who wins the pole position in qualifying that year to scatter my ashes down on the first turn on the first lap that counts in the 500-mile race.'" Folks have long cherished possession of the dozen or so different brand names of genuine Speedway bricks (nine inches in length, with a width of four inches, by three-and-a-half) that originated from The Wabash Clay Company that subsequently subcontracted to other brickmakers. The IMS required as many as 3.2 million such blocks to pave the course within sixty-three days in 1909.

Some Speedway aficionados collect autographs, snap thousands of photographs, roll miles of video tape. They cherish torn ticket stubs, tattered yellowed newspapers with race events, sound recordings of racing engines from bygone eras, voices of public-address people no longer among the living. Others collect silver and bronze pit badges, programs, commemorative drinking glasses, children's toy racing cars, even worn racing tires, pieces of rubbish, and shrapnel from out of garage-area trash bins. When the old Gasoline Alley yielded to a larger, more modern, if more faceless, facility in 1986, there were those who scarfed up the battered old dark green and white doors and reinstalled them in their homes and shops. People who might otherwise suspend a moose head or a tarpon from a den wall, instead mounted the tail of a memorable racing car or some racer's urine-stained fireproof driving suit. Some beg drivers for old helmets, stone pitted and insect blotched, that they preserve under glass. A fireman assigned for years to the Speedway's southeast turn was, as he directed, buried in his fire suit, possibly in anticipation of some infernal destination. Drivers too have been interred in their driving togs as if they were fittingly suited-up for some motor race in the afterlife. Tens of thousands have stalwartly planted themselves in Speedway grandstands on days when there was ostensibly nothing going on. Everyone has a Speedway story to tell, and the tales, some literal, some embroidered, are part of the bottomless cultural litany of the Speedway.

Most racing enthusiasts understand that while the Indianapolis Motor Speedway is by motor racing standards exceedingly old, other American race courses were older. Brown has unearthed several, among them the mile track at Narragansett Park at the Rhode Island State Fairgrounds in Cranston where there was a car race on September 7, 1896. Back home in Indiana there was a place called Fort Wayne Driving Park, another mile track, that staged a race on October 2, 1902. Three other notable miles appeared with the construction of the Michigan State Fairgrounds (1899) in Detroit, the Columbus (Ohio) Driving Park in 1903 (not at the Ohio State Fairgrounds), and the 1902 Lucas County Fairgrounds (later called Fort Miami Speedway) in Toledo. The Indiana State Fairgrounds mile dirt track on East 38th Street in Indianapolis has been in existence since 1892 when it was constructed on what was once the Voss farm, but first used for automobiles in 1903 when Berna "Barney" Oldfield turned a lap in a Ford Red Devil in excess of sixty miles an hour, a fairly smart clip on a bumpy clay track, even today. Quite likely, the mile, including mile-and-a-sixteenth, track format was intended for horse racing.

The four investors who put up $250,000 for the Indianapolis Motor Speedway project were Carl Graham Fisher (designated as president),

Arthur C. Newby (vice president), Frank H. Wheeler (second vice president), and James A. Allison (secretary-treasurer). Fisher (1874–1939) was an immensely imaginative, ambitious Citizen Kane whose life, sad in certain respects, took him from rags to riches and then back to rags. Much has been made of his Greensburg, Indiana birth; his poverty stricken youth; his leaving school (where he was perceived as a dunce) at the age of twelve to support his divorced mother and his two brothers; his selling candy, tobacco, and newspapers on Indianapolis trains; his astigmatism and quasi-blindness; his riding a bicycle on a highwire suspended between two Indianapolis buildings on Washington Street; his participation as early as 1901 in American and French automobile races; his bicycle shop; his race horses; his breach-of-promise suits initiated by at least ten disgruntled women; his Indianapolis auto dealership that included Fiat, Stoddard-Dayton, Baker Electric, Overland, Empire, Winton, Oldsmobile, and Premier; his envisioning a highway between New York and California and another between Chicago and Miami; his establishing of the Prest-O-Lite Storage Battery Company; his fifteen-year-old bride who regarded him as "crazy" (Fisher was thirty-five at the time of the nuptial); his helping establish the Hoosier Motor Club; his development of Miami Beach out of a subtropical wasteland; his grandiose plans for a Montauk, Long Island, resort; his divorce; his alcohol addiction; and his Miami Beach death (attributed to a gastric hemorrhage) at the age of sixty-five on July 15, 1939, when he was diagnosed also with liver cirrhosis. During the Depression Fisher had gained weight and lost everything else. "I'm beggar-dead broke," he said in his final days.

Fisher became acquainted with lifelong bachelor Arthur C. Newby (1865–1933), a man in most respects different from himself, except that they shared a momentous gift for promotion and at one time were in the bicycle business. Newby came from a farm near Monrovia, a few miles southwest of Indianapolis, and passed some of his youth in California. Newby then settled into a job with flour-milling machine builder Nordyk and Marmon (who later developed the Marmon automobile that in racing trim won the first 500-mile auto race in 1911) in Indianapolis, where he rose through company ranks in the old established way. His interest in bicycling prompted him to organize the Zig-Zag Cycling Club. He then joined other investors in establishing the Indianapolis Chain and Stamping Company that manufactured bicycle chains, and that survives today as Diamond Chain Company. Newby's interest in bicycle racing motivated him to build the quarter-mile board Newby Oval cycling track, erected in 1898, on the northeast side of Indianapolis, with future IMS partners Carl Fisher and Jim Allison. When his passion turned more toward motor racing, Newby collaborated with other investors in creating the National Motor Vehicle Company, producing both electric and gasoline powered automobiles. A National, as it was called, finished seventh in the first 500-mile race, and won the second with Indianapolis driver Joe Dawson aboard. Newby, in precarious health, died in 1933.

The municipality of Speedway, Indiana, today cherishes elementary schools named in honor of Fisher, Newby, Allison, and Wheeler. James A. Allison (1872–1928), like Fisher, ended his schooling at the age of twelve. He came from Niles, Michigan, to Indianapolis in 1880 when his father Noah founded a business called the Allison Coupon Company that was eventually subsumed by James and his two brothers, although Jim for a time initiated his own business called Allison Perfection Fountain Pens. It was not until 1909 that Allison joined Fisher in the formation of a literally explosive firm called Concentrated Acetylene that in turn altered its name to Prest-O-Lite and, in 1912, relocated across from the Indianapolis Motor Speedway on West Sixteenth Street. Simply put, Prest-O-Lite capitalized the demand for improved automobile headlamps. Allison, a talented entrepreneur, opened a machine shop on the Prest-O-Lite property that was eventually acquired by General Motors and became Allison Gas Turbine and Allison Transmission. Union Carbide then acquired Prest-O-Lite. Through the automotive business, Fisher became acquainted with Manchester, Iowa's Frank Wheeler (1864–1921) who had notable entrepreneurial successes before he came to Indianapolis, by way of California, in 1904, and joined creative forces with George Schebler, developer of superior internal combustion engine carburetors, to establish the Wheeler-Schebler Company. Stricken with diabetes, Wheeler used a pistol to end his life. Curiously enough, what had been the estates of Wheeler, Fisher, and Allison are now part of Marian College, established in 1851, on Indianapolis's Cold Spring Road, where they have become collectively known as the Marian College Mansions. The Wheeler place (built in 1912, sold in 1937 to William B. Stokely of Stokely–Van Camp) is still shrouded in magnolias, has a y-shaped hand-carved staircase, a Tiffany glass ceiling, and an oriental tea house. The 1911 Allison home has a forty-by-forty two-story grand foyer with hand-carved Cirassian walnut walls in leaf and berry motif, and a one-ton German chandelier. Pneumonia carried Allison off in 1928.

Those speculators built the Indianapolis Motor Speedway at a moment in American history when it appeared that Indianapolis could well become the nation's motor capital. There was every reason to think so, despite some cultural resentment toward horseless carriages. Said satirist Abe Martin in 1919, "a feller kin buy a suit o' clothes an' th' tailor'll make forty alterations an' keep it pressed fer a year, but th' feller that sells you a three or four thousan' dollar car never wants t' see your face agin." Maurice Abrahams's satiric 1913 song warned, "He'll have to get under, get out and get under, and fix up his automobile." Historian Patrick Furlong has estimated that "perhaps as many as 90 makes of automobile[s] and five of motorcycles were manufactured in Indianapolis, most of them in small numbers for a brief span of years." Writing in 1941, Theodore E. "Pop" Myers, then vice president and general manager of the Speedway, recalled that "Indianapolis was then [at the time of its construction] the center of the fast-growing automobile industry and these gentlemen [Fisher, Newby, Wheeler, Allison] were up to their necks in this growth." Besides the National, there came on the Indianapolis horizon the Atlas-Knight, the Brooke-Spacke, the Economycar, the Waverly Electric, the Ideal, the Empire, the Hoosier Scout, the Pathfinder, the Black, the White, the Overland that became the Willys-Overland, the Henderson, the Cole, the Mohawk, the Marmon, the Stutz, and the prohibitively expensive Duesenberg. The automobile manufacturing business blossomed during the teens and twenties, but certain unanticipated factors militated against land-locked Indianapolis as the great American motor mecca. Its niche automobiles became too much a cottage industry, although the Ford Motor Company would set up regional assembly plants at Indianapolis and elsewhere to build the Model T and, in time, the Model A. As Indianapolis found itself producing ever fewer cars for a dwindling market of affluent people, the 1929 American economic disintegration smothered what little was left of the city's automobile manufacturing business (Ford abandoned its Indianapolis plant in 1933; Marmon and Stutz both closed in 1934). Such an economic failure could not have been foreseen back in 1909, however. The object of building a huge speedway was to test and promote a new age of glamorous motorized transportation, and secondarily to evolve its automobile races into elaborate theatrical pageants. Over time, those priorities reversed. "One of the prime objects of this Speedway," a 1909 article in *The Automobile* read, "is to afford to the builders of automobiles, at Indianapolis, and in the vicinity, a place to try out new models before they are turned over to purchasers." It continued, "advanced models, prior to building in quantity, may also be given the hardest kind of service, within the shortest possible time." Said bluntly homespun philosopher Homer McKee in 1922, "Every man who steps into anybody's automobile OWES HIS LIFE TO AUTOMOBILE RACING." It was reassuring to think so, at least.

Apocryphal though it may be, legend has it that in 1907 Fisher was the first Indianapolis citizen to own an automobile, and that in time, anyone else who purchased one became part of some exclusive brotherhood. Legend also has it that a real estate trader named Lemon "Lem" Trotter was also an early and proud car owner, and as a consequence he and Carl Fisher became profitably acquainted. Trotter also implicated himself in some of Jim Allison's real estate transactions. As a result, Fisher charged him with finding enough land to construct a large motor racing track to be tentatively called the Indiana Motor Parkway Grounds. What Trotter uncovered was the Pressley farm, followed by the cornfield property of Kivi Munter, and still later the Chenoweth family acreage, west of Indianapolis. History tells us that Trotter negotiated a large portion for $200 an acre, and the balance of the property at $300. The five entrepreneurs (Fisher and Allison had a majority 60 percent interest) secured the options necessary to purchase the Speedway's original 320-acre plot, consisting of four eighty-acre farm tracts for $72,000, in 1908. Fisher, by the way, had attempted to do something of the same sort in 1906 when he contemplated construction of a five-mile track at French Lick in southern Indiana. The future of the Indianapolis Motor Speedway, however, was in the hands of men with a stake in the future of the American automobile. Fisher's limited career as a racing car driver on dirt tracks taught him, if little else, that he disliked them for their dust, their mud, and their inadequate guard railings. Circa 1908 Fisher, Newby, Allison, and Wheeler apparently visited the 2.75 mile track at Brooklands in Surry, England, to review the implications of a large race course. What interested Fisher was a relatively long, three to five mile dustless race circuit. The concept of a three mile track soon became a two-and-a-half-mile course instead, with the south chute but a short stretch from the horse and buggy traffic out on what is now West Sixteenth Street. At the time the consortium filed its articles of incorporation in 1909, they called their track the Indianapolis Motor Speedway.

Were one to "plug" the track surface these days in the manner that one plugs a golf green, the result would be multiple surface layers, the product of ninety-six pampered years. The original 1909 track surface consisted of a single layer of bitumen sealer, probably crushed stone and tar. Through the decades the racing surface has been redone repeatedly. The

Behind the scenes with the balloon platoon in 1978. On race day, hundreds of parti-colored balloons waft over the speedway at the start of the Indianapolis 500. *John Mahoney*

first auto race, run on August 19, 1909, was to have been orchestrated over three days. On the first, driver Wilfrid "Billy" Bourque and his mechanic Harry Holcomb (both from Springfield, Massachusetts) died "within the hour" (said the *Automobile Trade Journal*) when they veered off course on the main straightaway and overturned during the running of a 250-mile race won by Bob Burman. On the third day there were three more deaths when a car driven by Charles Merz "shed a tire" and veered into a group of spectators. Merz's riding mechanic Claude Kellum was dead along with Homer H. Joliff of Franklin, Indiana, and James West of Indianapolis. Another man suffered a compound fracture of his right arm, a broken nose, and a few scalp wounds. The contest was to have been 300 miles, but after the casualties began to mount it ended at the 235-mile mark. "The race was declared no contest," according to an eyewitness account, "and the great Indianapolis Motor Speedway trophy will be raced for again."

The IMS management deemed the accident problem was in the

track's surface, and the solution to that problem was to pave it with bricks, 500 carloads of them. Crews reported that in the most productive nine-hour day, workers dropped 140,000 bricks into place. Journalist Thomas Fay waxed poetical about bricking the track, saying "that there is nothing new about brick may be readily shown; they were used in the Tower of Babel; about this time, so it is recorded, they were also made by the children of Israel, in Egypt, under the Pharaoh." Workmen completed the project in time for another series of races scheduled, for some reason, on December 18, not the most likely of dates. Indiana has been known to experience Siberian inclemencies. Nineteenth-century settlers recorded that in the winter of 1820–21, for example, snow blanketed central Indiana from early November to the first day of March.

To no one's surprise, temperatures hovered around zero degrees on December 18, 1909. To everyone's surprise, the races, sanctioned by the American Automobile Association, ran as promised and the crowd turnout was respectable, albeit consisting of what one observer called "the substantial sort, to whom a little detail like zero weather would have but small influence in the face of the expected performance." Prior to the races there was a pro forma starting line ceremony during which Indiana Gov. Thomas Marshall, assisted by his "private" secretary Mark Thistlethwaite, ceremoniously lowered into place the final Speedway brick, purported to be fashioned from coin silver plated with gold and weighing fifty-two pounds. More recent investigation has it that the gold brick was fashioned at the Wheeler-Schebler carburetor factory not from gold, but from a mundane amalgam of brass and bronze, and that it unaccountably vanished from the Speedway office on North Capitol Avenue during World War II, never again to turn up. Some of the races for motorcycles and automobiles, in the meantime, were in effect straight line runs over a specified distance such as a half and quarter-of-a-mile. Other events used the whole race track. "Drivers suffered intensely from the cold," a report read. "Despite the fact that they wore heavy gloves and had their faces protected by woolen bandages they were almost frozen during the trials. When they stopped their cars they could scarcely move their bodies and frequently had to be lifted out." The track events of 1910 consisted of short heats run over the three last days of May, concluding with a 200-mile car race. It was, said one reporter after surveying a throng estimated at 60,000, "probably the largest crowd that ever watched a similar event in this country." The track scheduled more races in July, and still more over the Labor Day weekend. Someone, and it is not clear who, suggested that in 1911 it would be better to stage one grandiose 500-mile race on its (then) 328 acres rather than put together shorter events run over a three-day succession as was done in 1910.

On Tuesday, May 30, 1911, the Speedway consisted of forty-one buildings in the form of garages, aerodromes, aviation sheds, clubhouses, cafes, restaurants, office buildings, oil houses, and machine shops. Its grandstands and box seats were able to accommodate 40,000, and the open areas another 160,000. "Big Four" trains from Union Station and interurban cars carried passengers to the Speedway's main gate at the rate of 30,000 an hour, while there was room enough on the grounds to park 10,000 automobiles. Taxis ran passengers to and from the track for a dollar. There were special telephone and telegraph connections—enough, said one bulletin, to "connect the Speedway with the city and the principal cities in the United States." There was a forty-acre tree grove at the northwest corner of the track where, the bulletin continued, "picnic parties find a delightful place to hold forth." There were sanitary facilities at all parts of the track, and automobile and foot bridges for crossing it. Without a public address system, the Speedway dispatched scoreboards and announcers to different parts of the course to keep spectators apprised about the race's progress. For security, the track enlisted the Speedway militia, a squad of special police and plainclothed officers, part of whose obligation was to dissuade spectators from wandering on the race course. Every one of the forty-car field was to be timed every ten miles (four laps) with an electrical device called the Warner Horograph. Said another notice, none other than Charles H. Warner "operates the machine himself for this great race." The Speedway estimated 2,000 participants on race day to include racing teams, accessory representatives, concession employees, guards, and scorers. F. A. Payne, proprietor of the Busy Bee restaurants, was the track's concession manager. A nickel bought a Cracker Jack, salted or jumbo peanuts, a cigar, or a glass of buttermilk. A dime covered the cost of lemonade, an ice cream cone, a better cigar, a pack of cigarettes, a "bread ham sandwich," a cheese sandwich, a cup of coffee, or a package of candy. A quarter bought two cigars, a chicken sandwich, or a box lunch. Fifty cents purchased a bigger box lunch, and a dollar would buy a chicken dinner. Women were, according to contemporary reports, commonly assumed to be wearing Nemo corsets at the track. That fall, if it continues to matter, Yale and Harvard ended their annual football encounter in a scoreless game.

At Indianapolis, out-of-towners had accommodation choices such as the eight-year-old Claypool Hotel at Washington and Illinois streets (which eventually closed after a 1967 fire); The Denison, built in 1880 and closed in 1920, at Ohio and Pennsylvania; the English Hotel and Opera House on Monument Circle (then called Monument Place); the Gem Hotel (James T. Managhan, proprietor) on West Ohio; the Grand Hotel at Illinois and Market; Hotel Colonial at New York and Illinois; Hotel Edward on South Illinois; and the Spencer House (billed as "the only hotel in the city thoroughly equipped with fire escapes") opposite Union Station on Illinois. Others put up for the race at the Grand, the Kingston, the Linden, the Lorraine, the Oneida, the Plaza, or the Princeton. Milling around those hotels on the night before the race was Richard J. Snowhook, the *Chicago Record-Herald* staff correspondent who observed that "race-mad" fans were "laying wagers to-night on the probable death toll" of tomorrow's race.

The first 500, that one writer obliquely called "the greatest automobile race ever run so far in the history of the industry," got under way with a flourish, with the cars lined up five deep in eight rows between which were 100-foot intervals. Carl Graham Fisher, predictably, paced the starters at forty miles an hour behind his Stoddard-Dayton. At precisely the ideal theatrical moment, he pulled to the left on the main straight while dapper starter Fred "Pop" Wagner flourished the starting flag and a ceremonial bomb exploded. Six hours and forty-two minutes later the winner was Ray Harroun, a twenty-nine-year-old native of Spartansburg, a few miles southeast of Erie, Pennsylvania, who had started twenty-eighth (starting positions were decided upon the date of entry in addition to a stipulation that every car must exceed seventy-five miles an hour for a quarter of a mile) and won the $10,000 first prize (out of a $25,000 total payout) with an average speed of 74.59 miles per hour. Harroun, driving the only one-man car (a deep yellow Marmon Wasp with a pointed tail) requested relief for thirty-five laps by relying upon a pinch-hitting driver named Cyrus Patschke. Harroun had won a 200-mile race at Indianapolis the previous year, but he never raced at Indianapolis after capturing the first 500, partly because he considered himself an engineer rather than a driver. Historian Donald Davidson discovered Harroun and his wife Mary fifty-six years later living in a trailer court on the southern fringes of Anderson, Indiana, where the 1911 winner explained that, aside from a short career with race cars, he served as a dental technician, a hat salesman, a chauffeur, and a naval combatant in the Spanish-American War. He was the alleged inventor of such indispensable amenities as automobile bumpers and fenders, bomb trailers, and bubble cars. His friends knew him as "the little professor," and sometimes as "the Bedouin" because of his supposed Arabic heritage. Harroun, who was perhaps more Irish than Arabic, died on January 19, 1968.

The 1912 race continued to line up as in 1911, except that a car now had to demonstrate that it could run at 75 miles an hour for an entire lap. Adhering to a fairly arbitrary formula that allocated a certain amount of breathing space to every participant, the 1912 race started thirty-three cars (customary in most recent years) and mandated that every car carry a riding mechanic. The winner this time was Joe Dawson, a local driver relieved by Don Herr (once employed as a National test driver, he owned a fleet of taxis with 1919 Speedway winner Howdy Wilcox) between laps 108 and 144, at the wheel of an Arthur Newby National, a locally manufactured car. National never again pursued competition events, however. The heartbreak of the day, aside from those who hit walls and overturned, was Ralph DePalma who led 196 laps, broke a piston, and found himself reduced to pushing his white Mercedes across the finish line with the aid of an Australian mechanic named Rupert Jeffkins. DePalma finished a disappointing eleventh after commanding the race. Said a writer for *The Horseless Age*, "a moan went up from the spectators, who appreciated the misfortune of the Italian." Dawson led for the final two laps, with an average speed of 75.93 miles per hour. Tenth-place finisher Ralph Mulford, permitted to remain on track as long as he pleased, limped home after staying out for eight hours and fifty-three minutes. Finishing twenty-first that year was rookie Eddie Rickenbacker (sometimes spelled *Richenbacher*), arguably America's greatest fighter pilot who downed twenty-six German planes in World War I, and who in 1927 would own the Indianapolis Motor Speedway.

Visitors to the 1913 race were greeted, oddly enough, by a five-story, open-sided pagoda, replaced in 1926 with another after the first burned to the ground. There were thirty-one entries, with twenty-seven of them starting the race. The winner was twenty-eight-year-old, fun-loving French rookie Jules Goux, who surpassed second-place runner Spenser Wishart by almost two-and-a-half miles an hour, encouraged, no doubt, by a benevolent spectator who reportedly furnished the Peugeot driver with no less than six pint bottles of good chilled champagne that brought him to his pits six times for mechanical service and supplementary refreshment. Goux credited the bubbly for his victory, proclaiming unequivocally that "sans le bon vin, je ne serais pas été en état de faire la victoire." Ventured J. C. Burton, "the gallant Gaul seemed anything but fatigued," and indeed called for a seventh bottle that he unabashedly "drained the contents [of] at one gulp." Indeed, Burton continued, Jules Goux "termed it a nectar, a nerve-sustaining potion that quickened the mind and eye, conquered fatigue and spurred on supreme desire." The French, who more or less invented auto racing, cleaned up at Indianapolis in 1914, when it was estimated to have been viewed by more than 100,000, sweeping the first four positions, with Rene Thomas winning the race at a record average speed of 82.47 miles per hour in a Delage, followed seven minutes later by Arthur Duray in a Peugeot, Albert Guyot in another Delage, and Goux in another Peugeot. The first American to cross the line on that Saturday Decoration Day was the noted daredevil-at-large Barney Oldfield who managed to salvage fifth at the switchboard of a Stutz. "Today has been a bad day for America," wrote a crestfallen Edward Schipper. "Our hopes have been crushed to earth one after another. One by one our idols were shattered." Even so, said an unidentified journalist, "a thunder of cheers burst out from every throat when Barney Oldfield brought the first American car across the line." The race started thirty cars, the lineup determined by a random drawing the night prior to the race.

Ralph DePalma, bitterly discouraged after coming close to a win in 1912, compensated in the rain-postponed 1915 race with its $50,000 purse by defeating twenty-three other contestants and establishing a new 500-mile record speed of 89.84 miles per hour in a Mercedes. There were forty-one entrees in 1915, all of them two-man cars with no more than three cars of a single make permitted to start. There was an 80 mile per hour minimum single-lap qualification speed, and cars were numbered in accordance with their starting positions, with car No. 1 on the pole, meaning on the inside front row. Spectator seating at that time consisted of an arrangement of grandstands on the outside of the track that began at the exit of the northwest turn (where there was a pedestrian catwalk) extending to approximately the middle of turn two, the southeast. DePalma, a former bicycle racer, was a grandstand favorite "of distinguished appearance," as one piece of hype phrased it, "courteous and even temperament, with the sunniness and warm-heartedness of Italy ever shining in his countenance." Ernie Pyle, recall, said that he would rather be Ralph DePalma than president.

World War I, known also as the Great War, acquired its destructive momentum from the June 28, 1914 assassination of Arch Duke Francis Ferdinand at the hands of a Serbian nationalist in Sarajevo. Before it ended in

1919 it cost an estimated ten million lives. For a variety of reasons, some valid, some less so, Carl Fisher decided to telescope the 1916 500-mile race into a 300-miler with a duration of 120 laps. The 1915 race had taken more than five-and-a-half hours to run its course, and something or somebody advised Fisher that a three-and-a-half hour contest was quite long enough to satisfy the attention span of most customers. Possibly so, but thereafter he reestablished 500 miles as the race's gold standard of duration. With a war raging in Europe, he anticipated less foreign competition, although as it turned out the 300-miler went to a Frenchman (Dario Resta) in a French car (another Peugeot), all the same. Wishing to play down the race's reduced distance, the official program called its event the "Sixth Annual International Sweepstakes Race," whereas the 1915 programs had called the contest the "Fifth International *500-mile* Sweepstakes Race." Only twenty-one cars started the 300-miler, before which each car cruised noisily around the race course one time to introduce it to the crowd, figured at 83,000.

Conspicuously absent was Ralph DePalma, who had communicated to the Speedway through business manager Theodore E. "Pop" Myers (who had hired on with his secretary and auditor Eloise "Dolly" Dallenbach in 1911 as an "auditing director" and would remain a Speedway employee until his death in 1954) that he expected a large cash advance, known in racing parlance as "deal money," for entering in 1916. Myers, a man circumspectly cast in the Horatio Alger mode, was willing to consider, but Carl Fisher flatly turned the idea down. On Saturday, September 9, 1916, the Speedway presented what it called the "Harvest Racing Classic" that consisted of races progressively staged as a twenty-miler, a fifty, and finally a one hundred. Johnny Aitken, who was pit chief for Joe Dawson when he won in 1912 and for Jules Goux in 1913, this time engineered a win for himself in all three fall challenges. Despite a short field of cars (some of the Peugeots were owned by the Speedway), despite close finishes, despite the contrite reappearance of Ralph DePalma who said that he would not only race but race any car that the Speedway designated, and despite a plethora of marching bands to brighten the occasion, the Harvest Auto Racing Classic seemed not to have engaged much spectator enthusiasm. Said one attendee, "Indianapolis appeared to have been surfeited with entertainment, the State fair having closed yesterday, for there did not seem to be over 10,000 to 12,000 present at the races."

Racing enthusiasts would have to wait until May of 1919 for the revival of racing engines at the Indianapolis Motor Speedway. Carl Fisher may have had reasons other than the Great War for shuttering the track until 1919. Always on the alert for what he believed to be lucrative challenges, Fisher did not long remain in one place if it could be helped. He had grown gradually weary of operating the Indianapolis Motor Speedway and of finding a suitable buyer to take it off his hands. Then too, he had bigger fish to fry. He was in the process of building Miami, Florida, out of a tangled, steamy wilderness of snakes and other vipers. Meanwhile, it was business as usual for championship automobile racing, which simply found other venues. There were fourteen races in 1916 in places like Sheepshead Bay, Uniontown, Cincinnati, Chicago, Des Moines, Santa Monica, and Los Angeles. Even without Indianapolis there were twenty-two events in 1917, some of them run on the same day in the same place, and sixteen more in 1918, including a 250-miler on the board track at Cincinnati on May 30, a day traditionally reserved for the Indianapolis 500. While this was going on, Fisher allowed the Speedway to be deployed for what might be construed as more serious purposes, such as an aircraft maintenance depot and a farm that, according to record, nurtured forty-eight acres of oats, forty acres of wheat, and twenty acres of timothy, a spiked plant used for making hay. After the war the Speedway conceded that it "took its toll of human lives during its wartime dress as a landing field," but that, on balance "the value of its very existence at the beginning of the hostilities far overshadows the sadder side of the track's history." The only cars on the race track were Marmon passenger vehicles undergoing a final tune-up before sales delivery. It was at this time that a cash-strapped Frank Wheeler unloaded his stock in the Speedway to Jim Allison, who believed in the track's bountiful future. Prest-O-Lite sold in 1917, and rather than invest profits in the Speedway, Fisher instead devoted it to his new subtropical Eden.

After the Treaty of Versailles, the Indianapolis Motor Speedway returned to life, contemplating another 500-mile race not on Memorial Day, but on Saturday, May 31. The date adjustment came as a result of lobbying that held it unpatriotic and disrespectful to present an auto race on a day when America should be solemnly remembering its war dead. By that time there was another protracted war raging, this between American and European automobile makers. Prophetically, the Speedway's 1913 official program devoted five paragraphs of counsel on "How to Pronounce the Foreign Names." American Howdy Wilcox won the 1919 race in another, albeit Speedway-owned, Peugeot, meaning among other things that European technology had won Indianapolis for five years running, on a track intended to showcase American automotive ingenuity. A 1914 Stutz advertisement attempted to make the familiar case for the race track as a development arena, saying that "out of every important racing event has grown a better and truer Stutz," although the company never succeeded in carrying off an Indianapolis win. Studebaker Corporation soft peddled that notion in 1912, claiming that "it is no trick to tune a motor so that it will do from 70 to 100 miles an hour on a race course. That doesn't tell you much about its real merits." In another, rather micro-war, the Indianapolis Motor Speedway had warned its ticket holders to stay clear of bootleg program publishers and vendors. In 1919, car numbers were assigned on race morning to frustrate such nefarious trade.

That same year the track took somber notice of former competitors whose lives had been lost, in and out of racing: Johnny Aitken, died of influenza, 1918. S. F. Brock, killed in a submarine disaster off the English coast, 1918. Georges Boillot, killed in action with the French Aviation Service, 1915. David L. Bruce-Brown, killed in practice for the Vanderbilt and Grand Prix, Milwaukee, 1912. Bob Burman, killed, Corona Road Race, 1916. Billy Carlson, killed, automobile race, Tacoma, 1915. Joe Cooper, killed, automobile race, Des Moines, 1915. C. C. Cox, killed, automobile race, Sioux City, 1915. Harry Grant, died of burns, Astor Cup, 1915. Harry Endicott, killed, automobile race, Jackson, Michigan, 1913. Hughie Hughes, killed, auto race, Uniontown, 1915. Harry Knight, killed, automobile race, Columbus, Ohio, 1912. Billy "Bunny" Pearce, killed, automobile race, Sioux City, 1911. Lewis Strang, killed, promotional tour, Blue River, Wisconsin, 1911. Spencer Wishart, killed, Elgin Road Race, 1914. Paul Zuccarelli, killed, French Grand Prix, 1913.

The 1919 race that called itself the Liberty Sweepstakes had problems of its own. Arthur Thurman died at the north end of the track, while Louis LeCocq and his mechanic Robert Bandini died at the south end. One of the Speedway's most bizarre deaths began when a wheel came loose from Louis Chevrolet's Frotenac on the main straightaway, and tore loose a timing wire, an end of which whipped murderously back into the throat of fellow driver E. T. Shannon, severing his jugular. Shannon, whom one writer described as having been nearly decapitated, nevertheless drove another lap, hemorrhaging all the while, then arrived at his pit box before collapsing. Chevrolet, in the meantime, continued on to finish tenth, while Shannon's riding mechanic E. E. Rawlings continued the race as driver, ending thirteenth after completing the full 500 miles. The thirty-three drivers who raced in 1919 did so after a qualification procedure requiring them to execute a single lap with an 80 mile an hour minimum. In 1920 the 80 mile an hour requirement was still in force, but the qualification run extended to four laps, with first day qualifiers placed ahead of subsequent days, as it is today. There was also a lap prize money feature wherein the lead car would earn a $100 bonus for each lap. In a nod toward the French Republic, itself in the midst of a protracted World War I recovery, Carl Fisher agreed to a 183 cubic inch maximum piston displacement limit in accordance with the international Grand Prix Formula. Part of Fisher's intention was to make the Indianapolis 500 an international contest to be called the Eighth Annual International Sweepstakes Race. "The race this year," a Speedway press release said, "will be a Franco-American affair." But the entries totaled a meager thirty-two, all of them two-man cars. When it flagged off, it had twenty-three contestants, eleven of whom were still in motion when the event ended. This time it was an American car (the first since Joe Dawson's victory with a National in 1912) designed by a French-American named Louis Chevrolet with a French driver in the person of his brother Gaston Chevrolet, an outlaw bad boy who, having been scored third after he believed he was second in a 1917 race on the Cincinnati board track, left AAA ranks in the company of Barney Oldfield, Earl Cooper, and Louis Disbrow to hit the western dirt tracks. The technical significance of the 1920 race, said Lambert Sullivan of *Motor Age*, lay in the principle that "light cars can be built which are in every way the equal of their heavy brothers of the present."

There was no Gaston Chevrolet at Indianapolis in 1921, his having been killed at the Beverly Hills wooden track the previous November, less than six months after having won the 500-mile race. Said the Speedway in memory of its fallen champion, "To Him Alone Among All The Winners Of The Indianapolis 500 Mile Race, The Great Starter Has Given The Checkered Flag. He Died, As He Would Have It—AT HIS WHEEL." Hot tempered and vision-impaired Tommy Milton, filling in for Gaston Chevrolet, won by two laps, this time in a Frontenac (so named after an eighteenth-century French colonial governor) prepared by Gaston's brother Louis. To be on the safe side, Milton spent the night before the race replacing rod bearings. Second place went to Lafayette, Indiana's dirt-tracking Roscoe Sarles who, according to the Indianapolis Motor Speedway (with a freshly hired, sprightly Hoosier publicity man named Steve Hannagan), had "taken more spills than a drunken paper hanger." Sarles's final spill happened on September 17, 1922, in Kansas City, another board track, when he rocketed through the guard railing, descended an estimated fifty feet behind the banking, and died in his burning car. But Indianapolis in 1921 continued to have entry problems. There were only twenty-five, twenty-three of which started the race, and only eight of which lasted 500 miles. It was DePalma's race to lose, his having started on the pole at a four lap average of 100.75 miles per hour and leading 108 laps before a connecting rod reportedly snapped.

It was all Jimmy Murphy, a Milton protege, in 1922. Milton started twenty-fourth in a white car named after himself, and ended there. Murphy, fresh off a Grand Prix win at Le Mans (the first such achievement for an American), started first and finished there, with a record speed of 94.48 miles per hour. He had lost an exhaust valve in practice the day before, and had the problem hurriedly repaired for the race. The day began with intensified theatricals. Barney Oldfield, wheeling a National, prepared to pace the field. A multitudinous band, purported to be of 1,000 pieces, strutted down the straightaway, along with several men bearing radio transmitters that electronically conveyed the music into untold American homes. "How the world does move," said one onlooker. When the race got underway, a balloon bearing the American flag wafted overhead. A huge catwalk stretched across the track, from which starter Eddie Ricken-

Ray Harroun, circa 1910. Although he would later win shorter races at Indianapolis, after capturing the first 500-mile race in 1911, he never returned to the contest as a driver. Harroun preferred to think of himself as an engineer, which indeed he was for the Marmon Motor Car Company. In 1918, he and a cousin unveiled the Harroun Motor Company in Detroit. Assumed, even today, to have come from Middle Eastern origins, the Harroun family actually emigrated from Ireland. *Ed Hitze*

backer waved a red flag to start the event. In those days great puffs of white oil smoke poured from the cars under acceleration. Twenty-seven racers from an entry list numbering thirty-two took the flag. The twenty-seventh was a chap named Jack Curtner who, though born in Indianapolis, was better known for ably presiding over the Speedway Pool Hall in Greenville, Ohio. He drove a red Fronty-Ford that had been crashed before the race by another chap named Tommy Mulligan. The car never ran a qualification run and, since the track could well use another car to swell the field, received permission to start on condition that it not compete for prize money. There have been drivers since who, because they wanted to start the race badly enough to do so at their own extreme expense, agreed to drive *pro bono.* But the 1922 race was a Duesenberg Day, with Duesies finishing in six of the first nine positions.

The 1922 Duesenbergs were racing with between 181 and 183 cubic inches of piston displacement. For 1923, however, engines were limited to 122 cubic inches and permitted to burn leaded Ethyl gasoline at the request, and possibly the behest, of Dayton, Ohio's extraordinary Charles Franklin Kettering, who had also developed a synthetic aviation fuel. By the end of his life Kettering, as if to leave his indelible stamp upon the world, accumulated 140 patents and collected thirty honorary doctorates. Racing cars, however, were now mandated as single seaters, meaning that their smaller engines were at least compensated by a weight reduction, always a significant aspect of auto racing. It developed in the race that the springs that were serviceable enough with heavier racing cars were a bit too stiff for the lighter ones. The uncomfortable result was that cars danced over the track from intense vibration while drivers fought for control. Twelve of the twenty-four drivers who started the race, including winner Tommy Milton, who sat out laps 103 to 151 when Howdy Wilcox took the helm, called for relief drivers. All in all, there were twenty-three driver changes. Indianapolis in 1923 drew about 150,000 spectators who, from all accounts, seemed to be enjoying themselves, even if the contestants that year decidedly did not.

By early June, however, the Chicago publication *Motor Age* ran a story headline that read, "Future of the Motor Speedway in Doubt," earnestly explaining that the track had for some time quietly been on the auction block, and that Carl Fisher, who had just built himself a shack on Long Island, had called a meeting of automobile manufacturers whose interest in the track appeared to be waning, and other involved parties, to determine not how the track should be developing, but whether it should develop at all. Meanwhile, certain problems emerged after the 1923 race. The late Speedway publicity man Al Bloemker wrote that Perry Faulkner, commander of the state's American Legion, spearheaded a bill that prohibited commercial sports on May 30. Fisher had, in fact, postponed the 1919 race in response to just such pressure. The measure passed both houses of the state legislature, only to be vetoed by Gov. Warren McCray on counsel from his attorney general, U. S. Lesh, who deemed the matter unconstitutional. Fisher's public position was that the track's first calling was scientific, with its entertainment aspect "entirely secondary." The article also averred that Jim Allison and Arthur Newby were disinclined to continue operating the IMS. Fisher furthermore estimated that the track and its grounds would be needing $200,000 for improvements. It came to pass that certain figures in the automotive industry, among them Henry Ford (who insured every driver's life for $10,000 in 1924), did what they could to keep the track and its race on wheels. Indianapolis newspapers reacted favorably to the Speedway's function in automotive technology, and in attracting visitors and their money to the capital city every May, whether they are interested in motor racing or not. Journalist Clyde Jennings noted "the number of people who picnic back of the stands and, as far as one can judge, do not see any part of the race and do not care about it."

Some saw the race, and indeed took an absorbed interest in its outcome, however. Joe Boyer, for instance, liked the 1924 race so much that he drove two cars in it. His original mount for the day was the No. 9 Duesenberg that, fitted out with a newly developed centrifugal supercharger (Duesenbergs were the first American machines to be so equipped at the Speedway), assumed the lead for two laps until a key sheared off in one of the supercharger's gears, whereupon Boyer faded from competition. This left L. L. (Lora Lewis) "Slim" Corum and Pete DePaolo as the only viable vestage of the three-car Duesenberg team. When Corum stopped on his 111th lap, Fred Duesenberg, straw hat and all, replaced him with Boyer, and barked unambiguous instructions to "put that ship out in front or burn it up." Boyer took the No. 15 Duesenberg for the final eighty-nine laps and, as per instructions, won the race at a 98.234 track record. The car with which Boyer began the day fell into the hands of Thane Houser, who held it at bay for 177 laps before he popped the wall at the south end of the course. Of the twenty-two cars that started the event, fourteen completed it. Joe Boyer perished at the Altoona, Pennsylvania, board track that Labor Day weekend. If nothing else, however, Indianapolis had been a triumph for team players. The track itself, however, underwent an administrative team shakeup. After Carl Fisher stepped aside to become a director, Jim Allison was president-designate, and A. C. Newby its vice president. There was something to be said for team players. IMS publicity man Steve Hannagan argued that auto racing "harbors less enmity and better fellowship than is displayed on any college campus. For these men do not harbor the animosities so seemingly necessary to college competition."

In 1925 America's interest gravitated toward the contentious Scopes Trial, and its literary bounty brought forth memorably enduring pieces like John Dos Passos' *Manhattan Transfer*, F. Scott Fitzgerald's *The Great Gatsby*, Sinclair Lewis's *Arrowsmith*, and Eugene O'Neil's *Desire Under the Elms*. In that same literary season Terre Haute, Indiana, born Theodore Dreiser published his *An American Tragedy*. Standard Oil instituted its eight-hour working day in 1925, and Firestone selected the Indianapolis Motor Speedway to introduce a newly developed balloon tire that, said the company, its dealers would be more than happy to install on a passenger car "quickly and at low cost." In March, Carl Fisher more or less insisted that a coterie of his Speedway driving stars (Louis Chevrolet, Pete DePaolo, Harry Hartz, L. L. Corum, and Tommy Milton, among them) appear in Miami where, under heavy publicity surveillance, they were encouraged to race boats and be entertained at the Cocoloba Kay Club whether they liked it or not. On race day, 1925, the track gloated about drawing a crowd larger than had ever witnessed "Babe Ruth knock a home run, seen Jack Dempsey knock out a challenger or seen Red Grange make a spectacular end run on a football field." Although there was no Rickenbacker waving the starter's flags, there was a Rickenbacker automobile pacing the race with a Rickenbacker at the wheel. Pete DePaolo did the balance of the leading with an eight-cylinder, 121.8 cubic inch Duesenberg, leading 115 laps, although he sat out between laps 106 and 127 receiving medical attention to his blistered hands that he said had been taped "in prize-fighter fashion," while he left the driving to Norman Batten. When he jumped back into the car, he was riding fourth. At the end he had established a 500-mile record speed of 101.127 miles per hour, making him the first winner to exceed the 100 mile per hour mark. So too, Dave Lewis's second place Junior 8 Miller was the first front-drive car to race at Indianapolis. Following the race, DePaolo recalled, "a young fellow dashed up and said 'Hey, Pete, do you want to talk on the radio? A big manufacturing company will pay you $100 a minute for it.' I replied, 'Boy, where is that microphone!'" DePaolo eventually walked back to a private home in Speedway City that he had rented for the race month, and drew a tub of hot water while his wife poured him a "good shot of grape brandy." Continued he, "I started yelling in cowboy fashion, and our good friend, the landlady, rushed upstairs and asked Mrs. DePaolo if anything had happened to me. My wife answered, 'Yes! He just won the big race.'"

A day later, the track's pagoda burned to the ground. Behind the scenes, Tommy Milton retired from racing while he was still alive and healthy after thirteen years in combat. Quoting Kin Hubbard, creator of the philosopher Abe Martin, Milton repeated the cliche that "there are no ex-aviators or ex-automobile race drivers." Carl Fisher, ever more interested in his Miami project and ever more weary of coping with the Speedway, asked Milton whether he might care to purchase it. Fisher claimed that both he and Allison had quite enough of running the track. He may well instead have wanted to unload it, the better to create another speedway, this one near Miami, a location that could support auto racing in the winter months. In typical Fisher fashion, he engaged 1911 Indianapolis winner Ray Harroun to design it, he secured the American Automobile Association to sanction it, and he named a race after himself. Milton begged off from buying the Speedway, saying that he had no experience in promoting, and that furthermore he was more interested in investing in Fisher's Montauk Beach undertaking. It was a bad choice. In a catastrophe prophetic of Fisher's own eventual downfall, the Miami track known as Fulford literally blew away with the breezes in September of 1926 after having run only one auto race.

For 1926, the Speedway again reduced the number of allowable cubic inches of displacement, this time to 91.5. A new pagoda stood high and proud, replacing the one consumed by fire. Thirty-three cars answered the flag for the first time since 1919, and all were powered by straight-eights. By early morning, rain clouds began to collect over the track. By race time, however, portly Seth ("they say I'm the traffic cop for the world's fastest street") Klein, red starting flag in hand, prepared to set the show in motion. The race went to dirt-tracking, California-riding, mechanic Frank Lockhart, whose fate it was to die in a highly publicized crash on Daytona Beach on April 25, 1928. Lockhart's one big Indianapolis opportunity came when designated driver Peter Kreis fell ill, and when Lockhart qualified back in twenty-second position then led ninety-five laps in a race that was halted by rain for an hour and five minutes and ruled complete on the leader's 160th lap when he was two circuits ahead of second place Harry

Hartz. No question, it was one of Indianapolis's long-shot finishes. Writer Clarence Phillips could not but conclude that "pre-race predictions do not always mean much," adding that "the prophets failed to include Lockhart in their ticket. They also overlooked [Cliff] Woodbury [like Frank Lockhart another dirt track specialist], who finished third and ran one of the most consistent and headiest races of the day."

To all appearances, Lockhart (who entered his own car) was on his way to a second consecutive victory in 1927, starting on the pole position with a new four-lap standard of 120.100 miles per hour and leading 110 laps until a connecting rod disconnected in his 91.5 inch Miller engine on lap 120, relegating him to eighteenth. Instead, the chase went to another dark horse rookie named George Souders who had started (thanks to owner William S. White) in the twenty-second position in a gray and black Duesenberg with fewer than ninety inches of displacement and tenaciously held on to his No. 32 (the same number that had won the first Indianapolis 500 with Harroun in 1911) and won by an amazing margin of nearly four minutes over Earl DeVore. The day was extremely hot, probably the reason why every driver between finishing positions second and seventeenth had called for a relief driver. Souders, a Purdue dropout, had, after the death of his father migrated to Texas where he found employment as a mechanic and entered some dirt track races. After a near death accident on the Michigan State Fairgrounds in Detroit that left him unconscious for six months, Souders wisely bailed out of racing, and lived until July 1976.

In the middle of August, 1927, Eddie Rickenbacker, who had arranged financing, purchased the Indianapolis Motor Speedway for $750,000, designated himself president and board chairman, retained Pop Myers as vice president and general manager, retained Fisher and Allison as directors, added Omar Rains as a third director, kept Hannagan as publicity head, brought E. D. Moore on board as treasurer, and Paul Davis as secretary. Meanwhile, as Hannigan pointed out, "drivers come and drivers go." One of Rickenbacker's first gestures as president was to authorize William H. Diddel to design and build what Rickenbacker may have envisioned as the World's Greatest Golf Course on the World's Greatest Race Course, with nine holes in the infield where an aircraft landing field had stood in 1917 and 1918, and nine holes adjacent to the backstretch on the east side of the grounds. The holes at one time carried names of Speedway luminaries, to wit: one (Ray Harroun), two (Joe Dawson), three (Ralph DePalma), four (Dario Resta), five (Howdy Wilcox), six (Gaston Chevrolet), seven (Jimmy Murphy), eight (Tommy Milton), nine (Peter DePaolo), ten (Louis Meyer), eleven (Frank Lockhart), twelve (Billy Arnold), thirteen (Pop Myers), fourteen (Bill Cummings), fifteen (Mauri Rose), sixteen (Tony Hulman), seventeen (Cotton Henning), and eighteen (Wilbur Shaw). The course, known originally and ambiguously as The Speedway Golf Club, came with an artificial watering system ("no dusty, Graham cracker fairways," a publicity sheet read) and a Tudor style clubhouse.

First-time starter Louis Meyer from Huntington Park, California, the first of the Speedway's eventual three-time winners, triumphed for the first time in 1928, driving a Miller entered by Phil "Red" Shafer with Wilbur Shaw (another future three-time winner) originally entered in the saddle. It was, incidentally, the same car that Tony Gulotta had used to finish third in the previous year's race. Because promised sponsorship money from A-C Sparkplug's Albert Champion dried up unexpectedly, and because Shaw could not immediately raise other money to replace it, Meyer appealed to wealthy Alden Sampson (grandson of an Ohio steam tractor originator) who agreed to finance the car, and Meyer, for the race. This left Shaw (who had been relieved by Meyer the previous year) without a car for this, his second assault on Indianapolis, but he secured AAA permission to execute a qualification run on race morning in a car known as the Flying Cloud Special. It had been rebuilt in Louis Chevrolet's race shop after having been wrecked and rolled the previous Saturday by 1925 winner Peter DePaolo who, incidentally, sustained injuries but was borne on a stretcher into (rather than out of) the Indianapolis Motor Speedway for the race. One commentator reported that "Pete appeared in good spirits but soon after the start returned to the hospital." Shaw completed only forty-two laps.

When Steve Hannagan remarked that drivers come and drivers go, he had in mind people like Philadelphia's chunky Ray Keech, who hit 207 miles per hour over the sands of Daytona Beach in 1928, won the 1929 race at Indianapolis, and was dead two weeks later in that same Miller-powered Simplex Piston Ring car after a horrifying incident at the mile-and-a-quarter Altoona board track near Tipton, Pennsylvania. Keech hit a ribbon of steel guardrailing that another car had torn loose after losing control. Keech overturned several times, paused at the top of the banked track, exploded, and finally stopped at the base of the turn. The AAA declared Louis Meyer the winner. That year marked the end of Ray Keech and the end too of ninety-and-something cubic inch engines. At Indianapolis Keech had run a two-stop race that appeared to belong to Meyer, who led sixty-five laps to Keech's forty-six before killing his engine during a pit stop, rejoining the race seven minutes later and settling for second almost two miles an hour behind Keech.

Before the 1929 race was run, Rickenbacker made an executive decision to start forty (rather than thirty-three) cars in 1930, return to two-man cars, and liberalize engine specifications. His plans, in retrospect, were right on economic target, except that no one but a clairvoyant economist could have forseen the country's financial collapse in October of 1929 that in its depth left sixteen million people unemployed by 1933. Rickenbacker's objective was to reduce racing's cost, a subject always under discussion but seldom acted upon, and to rekindle automakers' interest in racing competition. Instead of continuing with expensively developed supercharged overhead cam 91.5 cubic inch Miller eights, 1930 Speedway entrees were permitted, even encouraged, to bring forward engines with four- (e.g. Coleman F. D., Clemons, Miller, Fronty), six- (Buick, Chrysler Eighty), eight- (Duesenberg Model A, Studebaker, Maserati, duPont, Stutz) and even sixteen-cylinder (Sampson, Maserati) mills with piston displacements ranging from 100 to 336 cubic inches. The new rules of engagement outlawed superchargers on four-cycle engines. There were other regulations specific to valves, carburetors, and weights. Said one technical commentator, "Some of the new engines are strictly racing designs whereas others are tuned-up or rebuilt stock car engines, generally mounted in racing chassis although in a few cases stock cars were entered with but minor changes." When entry forms arrived at Speedway offices early in 1930, there was indeed every legal specification represented. Notwithstanding, the first two finishers in that year's race were still Miller powered.

Detractors then and now have misleadingly referred to the 1930s liberalization of championship car engines as the "Junk Era," and sometimes as the "Junk Formula." The term *junk* alluded to the relative sophistication of a stock block engine compared to a Miller or a Duesenberg. The formula did, however, bring new engines into racing, improve car counts, stimulate innovation, and help preserve automobile racing from extinction during the Depression. But stock block cars were not winning races at that time. Moreover, by the end of the 1931 racing season, only Altoona, of the original twenty-four board speedways, was still in business, thanks to the economic collapse and the immense maintenance costs that plank tracks entailed. Altoona's final race, and therefore the last board track event ever run, was on September 7, 1931. Jimmy Gleason won the twenty-five mile event in a Duesenberg, with Zeke Meyer second in a Hudson. Five of the six races in the constricted 1932 season were on the mile dirt tracks at Syracuse, Detroit (used twice that year), Oakland (prior to the building of the paved Oakland Stadium) and Roby, Indiana. Miller engines won them all, with stock block cars generally bringing up the rear.

In 1930 Indianapolis was abuzz with the heartrending Depression Era story of the Rain Baby, an infant abandoned beside Bluff Road on a rainy, cold evening, and not discovered until 4:30 the following morning. The child was taken to an Indianapolis hospital for care and treatment, while police managed to solve the mystery of the child's origin, tracing it to a twenty-one-year-old divorcee from Bloomington, Indiana, who told reporters that she left the child because she had no home, no food, and no money. Two days later someone found a second infant abandoned in the back seat of an automobile parked behind the air conditioned (a rarity in those times) Indiana Theatre on Washington Street where a traveling vaudeville troupe entertained the mounting pre-race crowd. Elsewhere, the Bandbox movie house featured a "Men Only" double bill consisting of *Does White Slavery Exist?* and *Pitfalls of Passion*—both for twenty-five cents admission. Despite dark economic days, the race's attendance was about 170,000, 12 percent above the previous year. Aeronautics authorities predicted about 150 aircraft, bearing race fans from across America for the eighteenth running of the 500-mile race. A party of Flora, Illinois, youths copped first-in-line honors out on West Sixteenth Street near the Speedway's main pedestrian gate. They were a dozen post–Jazz Age men beneath the age of twenty who positioned their automobiles in line on Monday, and devoted the balance of the week to frolicking before Friday's race.

When the track opened on race day the boys from Flora were among the first through the portals. Since 2:00 that morning there had been continuous bus service for ten cents in fare, while trains shuttled passengers to the track from Union Station for thirty-four cents, round trip. Indianapolis streets were alive with motor traffic. Wrote one reporter, "Nobility, society, and labor rubbed elbows at the eighteenth running of the American auto derby." The nobility to whom he referred was Baron Rothschild. The weather was clear as Speedway owner Rickenbacker appeared at the front gate at the wheel of an imposing, spit-polished, sixteen-cylinder Cadillac, and rolled his window down long enough to issue a terse statement to the waiting press, notebooks in hand. "Ninety-five miles an hour will win the race," he said confidently, almost arrogantly. Up went the window and in went Captain Eddie, motoring toward the infield. Prohibition, enacted in 1919, and aimed at the august goal of national sobriety, would not be repealed until 1933. Consequently, the area in and around the Speedway was amply stocked not with intoxicating spirits, but with law enforcement officers in quest of illicit booze. "Hip flasks, kegs of beer, and iced quarts will be targets of dry enforcement agencies at the Speedway Friday during the 500-mile classic," police chief Jerry Kinney announced. "The police will watch bus, railway, and traction stations, and the unloading terminal across from the Speedway entrance." The *Indianapolis Star* also warned that "federal agents probably will follow their usual custom of wandering about the grounds pursuing riotous parties."

Although forty starting positions were available at Indianapolis in 1930, thirty-eight cars took the flag on a Memorial Day that turned into a Billy (Richard William) Arnold runaway after he started on the pole with a new record speed of 113.263 miles per hour, assumed the lead on lap three, and remained there for the balance of the day in a Harry Hartz front-drive powered by a five-year-old eight-cylinder Miller bored out to 151.5 inches. Arnold stopped only once, on lap 111, to fill up with gasoline, oil, and water and to replace his back wheels. So far ahead of second-place finisher Shorty Cantlon (using a four-cylinder Miller marine engine) was he, that in the seven minutes that separated the two at the finish, Arnold had time to accept the checkered flag, cruise around the track, unbuckle, kiss a few babies, and still see Cantlon hit the tape. Despite his lead, Arnold had steadfastly refused to slow down, even when car owner Hartz went trackside and threatened him with his fist. Arnold finished the full distance in all three of his Indianapolis 500-milers. "What did you want me to do?" Arnold is alleged to have said to Hartz afterward, "get out and walk?" There is a story afoot that publicity man Al Bloemker repeated, to the effect that Arnold came to Indianapolis that year not fully recovered from an accident at the Salem, New Hampshire, track. What turned out to be the winning car at Indianapolis was originally assigned to Ralph Hepburn. Arnold stopped by Hartz's garage daily, saying, "Gee, Mr. Hartz. That certainly is a beautiful car!" He, with the grandest paycheck of his life, seemed similarly cavalier about the disappearance of his svelte Chrysler roadster that someone sacked from the 1500 block of North Illinois Street on the day before the race. "Tell the guy [who stole it] to come around to my room and I'll give him the certificate of title," said the reigning idol of Indianapolis. The thief never accepted the cordial invitation, for while Billy Arnold made the rounds of post-race parties, police discovered his missing car at Twentieth and Meridian streets, and returned it that evening.

The 1930 race put to rest any notions of formula equivalency, with six Millers and one Duesenberg copping the first seven finishing positions. Eighth in a Studebaker, that reportedly cost between $1,500 and $2,000 to build, was Russ Snowberger. Some of the stock block cars were showcasing their stock characteristics. The Stutz that L. L. Corum nursed home to tenth was fitted with a cigar lighter. In another somewhat comical instance, mechanics discovered a broken carburetor when Chet Miller stopped his Fronty Ford on his ninety-second lap, roamed the Speedway infield until they discovered a Model T with no owner in evidence, borrowed part of the carburetor, installed it on the racing car which ran another sixty-eight laps, then hurriedly reinstalled it on the Model T, the owner of which was none the wiser. In a rather inscrutable decision about scoring the 500-mile race, the Speedway decreed that, instead of crediting drivers who fell out of the race on the distance they covered, for this race, they would be scored in the order they fell out of the hunt.

Baby faced Arnold's winnings amounted to more than $20,000 of the $97,000 total purse paid out to contestants. He was in an expansive mood following the grind, but luck did not fall his way in 1931. In one of the stranger incidents in Speedway history, Arnold unwittingly played a role in the death of a child outside track boundaries. Arnold's was the fastest qualification in the race at 116.080 but he was obliged to start eighteenth because he did not register his time on the opening day of trials. Attempting to pull off his second Speedway win, he raced to the front by lap seven, and was still in front by several circuits on lap 162 when the rear axle snapped and his car went into a spin. Then Luther Johnson, riding sixth, struck Arnold's car on its left side, damaging the frame and destroying four carburetors that in turn exploded. The force of impact sent Arnold, his car enveloped in flames, over an inner railing. At that moment one of Arnold's rear wheels came loose, vaulted the wall, continuing across what is now Georgetown Road that runs parallel to the track's main straightaway. The wheel then struck eleven-year-old Wilbur Brink, playing in his own front yard. Delivered to a hospital, the boy subsequently died. Arnold, meanwhile, crawled out of his car shortly before it would have been too late, with two pelvic fractures, a broken nose, a laceration that required thirty sutures to his right thigh, and severe burns on his left thigh. His riding mechanic Spider Matlock fell out of the car, suffering from a broken shoulder along with scratches and bruises.

Researcher Galen Kurth has uncovered contradictory documentation on Arnold that raises new questions about the 1930 winner's identity. Widely believed to have been born into a Chicago family of Czechoslovakian immigrants, supposedly in 1911, it therefore follows that he won Indianapolis at the age of about nineteen when, according to his second wife, he probably did not have a driver's license. One of his obituary notices claimed that Arnold had taken a bachelor's degree at the University of Illinois and a Ph.D. from a place called Michigan Institute of Technology. The notice further claimed that Arnold had served with General Eisenhower in World War II, and left that campaign as a "one star general." To the contrary, Kurth determined that Arnold was the second child born in 1905 to Canadian-born blacksmith William Henry Arnold and schoolteacher Anna Harrison, that he apparently entered military service under his father's name, and that he used that name on his 1976 military grave marker in Oklahoma City. If one is willing to believe that he was both a Ph.D. and a general in the Army Air Corps, it remains unclear why he settled in Oklahoma, sold lumber and automobiles, and, for a time, managed a hardware store and built luxury homes.

Be that as it may, the 1931 race had attracted seventy entries, as compared to forty-two the year before. Harry Hartz entered Billy Arnold in the same front drive Miller, but he also entered a Duesenberg for a driver with the unlikely name of Fred Frame, thirty-six, who continued on to second place behind Louis Schneider, the twenty-three-year-old former Indianapolis motorcycle cop who won the race in 1931. Best of show among stock block contestants was again Russ Snowberger's budget priced Studebaker that placed fifth. The remainder of the first eight finishers drove Millers and Duesies. When *Motor* magazine published coverage of the 1931 race in its July issue, its focus was primarily upon the plight of the less than "pure" racing cars in contention. "8 Semi-Stock Cars Finish 500-mile Grind," said the headline. "Although perhaps not evident at first glance," the article claimed, "the semi-stock cars made a very impressive showing. So much so that some of the dye-in-the-wool special race car enthusiasts are beginning to ask themselves whether for next year it would not be wise to build their cars of stock units." Noteworthy also was the run of Dave Evans with a blue and white Cummins Diesel in a Duesenberg chassis that soldiered from wire to wire without a pit stop, finishing 13th. That feat repeated itself when Cliff Bergere brought the Noc-Out Hose Clamp Special to fifth in 1941, when Jimmy Jackson captured sixth in the Howard Keck Special in 1949, and when Johnny Mantz earned seventh in an Agajanian Special, also in 1949.

There was even some thought that stock blocks might prevail. In 1932 a Studebaker driven by Cliff Bergere ran third, and behind him in fifth was Snowberger, this time in a Hupmobile. In sixth was Zeke Meyer in another Studebaker. Hudson entered two cars, Hupmobile one, and Studebaker four, having discovered a way to race on a budget. Lest there was any doubt about the Depression's severity, however, there were all too obvious empty seats at the Speedway in 1932, and the total prize payout for the race shrank from $70,000 to $40,200, a decline of 42.5 percent. It crossed Rickenbacker's mind to suspend the race until the economy recovered its health. Henry Ford saved the lap prize fund from disappearance by pledging $5,000 to keep it alive. More telling, however, was the reality that Fred Frame's 181.8 cubic inch, eight-cylinder winning machine was originally the car that Tommy Milton built for wealthy driver Cliff Durant in 1928 at a cost exceeding $100,000. Hartz had substantially rebuilt it, with no costs spared.

For a variety of reasons, drivers seemed uncharacteristically on edge in 1933, and were ostensibly set off psychologically by Howdy Wilcox (a driver using the same name as the 1919 winner) who, though he had finished second in 1932 and had qualified for the 1933 event, learned that he has been denied medical clearance to participate because of a diabetic complication. Supposedly, the thirty-nine others who were about to race declared with their signatures on race morning that if Wilcox was not permitted to compete, neither would they. Five minutes prior to the race Rickenbacker appeared before the assembled drivers (who had been threatened with suspension from the American Automobile Association) and announced the Wilcox car, a Gilmore Special owned by Joe Marks, would start the race in last position if it had a different driver. Marks hired rookie Mauri Rose, who later won the race three times, and who lasted forty-eight laps until a timing gear retired him. People were starving everywhere in 1933, but the Wheeler restaurant chain—with three Indianapolis locations and others in Lafayette, Logansport, Lebanon, Frankfort, and Richmond—awarded the race leader at 300 miles with a year's meal ticket. Said a Wheeler's advertisement, "Pay attention to what you eat, but more to where you eat it." Elbert "Babe" Stapp was the first recipient, succeeded by Rose (1934), Petillo (1935), Louis Meyer (1936), Shaw (1937), and Jimmy Snyder (1938). Meyer, the 1928 winner, prevailed again in 1933, his seventh attempt at victory circle after leading seventy-one laps. When he crossed the finish line, Meyer held nearly a six-minute advantage over second-place Wilbur Shaw. There were forty-two cars that started the race, of which fourteen did the distance. That month, accidents claimed the lives of five participants, three of them drivers and two mechanics. A year later, in 1934, an exclusive club organized for men who had driven the entire race distance in excess of 100 miles an hour without relief assistance. Champion Spark Plug Company organized it as the Champion 100-Mile-An-Hour Club. The first four positions that year were powered with Miller engines, while positions five through ten were make up of stock block engines, one Buick and five Studebakers.

In his thirteen Indianapolis races (record books show only twelve, overlooking his rookie year as a relief driver for Wilbur Shaw in 1927), Meyer finished the event seven times, and would win for a third time (the first man to do so) in 1936. He died at ninety-one in October 1995 after having lived for years a few miles south of Las Vegas in Searchlight, near the California border. Meyer, who with his colleague Dale Drake founded Meyer and Drake, builders of the Offenhauser (the origins of which date to 1921 in the form of the Miller 8 developed to disarm Duesenberg) and other specialty racing engines, sold his part of the business and thereafter became a distributor for the Ford Motor Company's Indianapolis car engine. The program was eventually turned over to A. J. Foyt who moved the engine development program to Houston where what was known as "Ford" became instead "Foyt."

Millers claimed the first four spots in 1934, a year that produced a first-time winner in "Wild Bill" Cummings in his fifth Indianapolis assault, this time entered in a car owned by Chicago labor organizer Mike Boyle, affiliated with the International Brotherhood of Electrical Workers, and prepared by Harry Charles "Cotton" Henning. Cummings, a former grocery delivery boy, hit the finish line twenty-seven seconds ahead of Mauri Rose in a black and white Miller. Boyle became the preeminent Speedway car owner of his day, and won the race two more times, both with Shaw, in 1939 and 1940. Together with Henning, Boyle put cars on the track that led some 448 laps of Indianapolis competition in the decade beginning in 1931. In 1934 Cummings was driving a red, white, and blue No. 7, with the seven painted in red as earnestly advised, so Davidson recounted, by an anonymous tippler at Charlie Hasse's bar on Washington Street, south of the Speedway. Cummings was thereafter inclined to credit the number and its color to the win, and in time opened a bar of his own that he named The Lucky Seven. The 1934 race was decidedly unlucky for

Peter Kreis and his riding mechanic Bob Hahn, who were killed at the south end of the track, and for 1932 winner Fred Frame who crashed in practice and never joined the thirty-three car field, quite possibly reduced to that number because of on-track disasters the year before when the race was open to forty-two contestants.

The 1935 chase was likewise anything but safe. Johnny Hannon, the 1934 eastern "big car" champion, died in practice, and Harmon, Illinois's Clay Weatherly died in the race. They drove the same car, entered by Leon Duray, who had driven to second place in the 1914 race. Killed also was Hartwell "Stubby" Stubblefield and his riding mechanic Leo Whitacker. Pittsburgh-born Californian Kelly Petillo, in and out of serious trouble with the law most of his adult life, won the race in a particularly difficult way. It began when he established a new qualification record of 121.687 on the opening day, only to be disallowed because he exceeded the maximum fuel allotment. Returning to the track a second time, he blew the Offenhauser engine in his red and cream Gilmore Speedway Special to smithereens, delivered the broken engine to a machine shop for repair, reinstalled it, and settled for a second qualification run of 115.095 that caused him to start the race in twenty-second position. Petillo led over half the rain-slowed race to win it by forty seconds over Wilbur Shaw, who thereby finished second for the second of three such occasions. Owing to

Indy racers were once unceremoniously towed to the track on open trailers. Pictured here is the 1936 Gasoline Alley arrival of owner-driver Chet Gardner's light blue and red Duesenberg that started sixteenth and finished thirtieth that year after it fell out of competition with an oil leak. *Ed Hitze*

the disproportionate number of accidents involving first-year drivers, the Speedway developed a program, still in use, to screen newcomers before they were permitted to take to the track. Henry Banks, a six-time Indianapolis starter and 1950 AAA National Champion, was the first suppliant to seek and find approval under the new driver examination regimen.

Wider and more uniformly banked turns greeted drivers in 1936, and miraculously no one tested the corner walls during the race, although Mauri Rose, Tony Gulotta, and Ralph Hepburn collided with them earlier in the month. Most of the aggressive wall-smacking gathered momentum in the post-World War II period. Publicist Steve Hannagan, whom Carl Fisher had assigned to his Miami project, found replacement in Joe Copps, the former's long-time assistant at the Speedway. It was in 1936 that Louis Meyer, mechanic Lawson Harris at his side, became the Speedway's first three-time winner, and although there was talk of someone, anyone, winning four times, it seemed hardly possible until A.J. Foyt amassed wins in 1961, 1964, 1967, and 1977, followed by Al Unser, Sr. in 1970, 1971, 1978, and 1984, and Rick Mears in 1979, 1984, 1988, and 1991. Shaw, who led fifty-one laps and who was in control at the 200 mile mark, might well have been a four time winner, speculation has it, had not hood rivets come undone and obliged him to stop twice in the Gilmore Special that he had entered himself. He finally scored seventh, although in his actual running time he was three-and-a-third miles an hour quicker than Meyer's Miller-powered Ring Free Special. Only one stock block engine, Mike Boyle's ninth place Studebaker, finished among the top ten. Second in the race was the miraculous three-time National Champion Eylard Amandus "Ted" Horn, son of a Cincinnati concert hall musician, whose Miller-Hartz Special won the 1932 race with Fred Frame on board. Horn never did win Indianapolis, but he won almost everything else. He was third at Indianapolis in 1937, 1941, 1946, and 1947, and fourth in 1938, 1939, 1940, and 1948, and therefore never finished higher than second nor lower than fourth. Horn completed 1,799 laps out of a possible 1,800 in nine consecutive races. His single missing lap got away from him in 1940 when rain prompted the chief steward to end the race after the first three cars were flagged. Horn died on the third turn of the mile dirt track at DuQuoin in southern Illinois after a left front spindle broke on Sunday, October 10, 1948, a chilly rain date that drew a light spectator crowd.

In the twenty-fifth 500-mile classic witnessed by an estimated 170,000, (a goodly proportion of which was turned out in its Sunday best) Wilbur Shaw and what he called his "pay car," that he had crashed in a

Long Island road race the previous year, found revenge on the loose rivets of 1937 by winning the first of his three times, but not by much. Aware of falling oil pressure in his 255 cubic inch Offenhauser, he throttled back and led Ralph Hepburn to the stripe by a thin 2.16 second margin, good enough for a new race record of 113.580 miles per hour. "My oil supply was all but exhausted," he said later. "My right rear tire was ready to blow at any instant. My tired arms felt as if they were ready to drop off. My right foot was completely numb. I wasn't even sure it was attached to my body." This had been his ninth attempt at Indianapolis. All of the first ten positions were powered by Millers or Offenhausers (so named for Fred Offenhauser who, as Miller shop superintendent, gathered up Miller specifications when the company ceased operating in 1933, and gave the engine his name after reorganizing the company in 1934) except tenth-place finisher Louis Tomei in a Studebaker. Both he and riding mechanic John "Jigger" Johnson suffered burns from leaking oil (cars that day were permitted to burn commercial gasoline and limit themselves to twenty-five quarts of oil) on a race day that took its toll in high oil consumption and crankcase temperatures that exceeded 300 degrees Fahrenheit. Louis Meyer, who hung on for fourth in a Boyle Miller, said that he was able to run faster than Shaw, but had to stop four times and wait for the car to cool enough to add water to the radiator before rejoining the fray. Hepburn had required relief because of the intense heat, and turned the driving over to Bob Swanson between laps 108 and 167. Following the race Shaw declared that "This is the happiest day of my life outside of my wedding day," after which he embraced his wife of eight years, a woman named Cathleen "Cass" (nee Stearns) whom he preferred to call "Boots." Shaw's first wife and child had died years before in childbirth. After winning, he repaired to the Gilmore accessory booth for a few minutes of celebration when, on the other side of a wire fence, there appeared his old nemesis, 1931 winner Louis Schneider who, in Shaw's words, "made some sneering remark about being a 'lucky so-and-so.'" Continued Shaw, "His 'smart crack' touched me off like a skyrocket. I went over the fence like a monkey, landed on the other side of it and hit Louis right on the nose faster than I can tell about it." Shaw let it be known that he was going to indulge in a two-hour nap, then invite some friends to stop by his home in the 500 block of East 31st Street. The following day he was back out at the track. Later, Wilbur and Boots posed contentedly with one of the Borg-Warner Corporation's Norge Refrigerators. The photo appeared in an advertisement that quoted the 1937 Speedway champion saying, "After my experience in last year's race, I wouldn't be without a Norge refrigerator at home or at the track." The ad went on to say that in 1938 there would be thirty-six Norge refrigerators at the track so that during pit stops drivers could open the fridge and grab a chilled helmet before moving back to battle. Revelers in town for the 1938 race danced to the music of Art Berry and his orchestra at the Atrium Cafe, "where everybody meets," in the lobby level of the Claypool Hotel. On the night before the 500, Borg-Warner Corporation threw its annual bash at the Indianapolis Athletic Club. On the night following the race, the Indianapolis Chamber of Commerce sprung for its annual awards dinner at the Riley Room in the Claypool. Few drivers turned up at the first event, and somewhat more at the second.

Eddie Rickenbacker, always accommodative to rule adjustment as necessary, eliminated fuel regulations, decreed a 274 cubic inch displacement for normally aspirated engines, and 183 inches for supercharged ones. Gone forever were two-man cars and riding mechanics. Not long after the 1937 race, Rickenbacker and Myers met with Ted Allen of the AAA Contest Board at Manhattan's New Yorker Hotel to iron out rules changes for the 1938 race. Both Rickenbacker and Myers served on that very board, and Rickenbacker had once been chairman. "We had arrived at the definite conclusion," Myers wrote later, "that the International Racing Formula would be the thing to benefit American racing." By 1938 the Speedway's back straightaway was coated with asphalt, while the front straight remained the vibration producing brick. Chunky Floyd Roberts from Van Nuys, California, was in town with his red, black, and silver Burd Piston Ring Special, a Louis Wetteroth chassis with a Miller engine wrenched by retired driver Lou Moore, to race in the fourth of his eventual five 500s. He predicted he would win, and did. He also started on the pole with a new 117.200 record, and held the lead for ninety-two laps, as did Jimmy Snyder who fell out at 149 laps with a failed supercharger. Rex Mays led the other sixteen laps. Junk formula or not, the first eleven finishers were powered by Millers and Offenhausers that together won Indianapolis thirty-nine times, versus the third-most winning engine (Cosworth) with its ten wins. A year later Floyd Roberts died when he broke his neck on the Speedway's backstretch, having been thrown from the same car he had used the previous year. Roberts, who made a reputation for himself on Los Angeles's Legion Ascot Speedway, was the first Speedway winner to die at Indianapolis. The second, in 1955, was Bill Vukovich. In 1939 the track was asphalted everywhere but the main straightaway. Wilbur Shaw, the 1939 champion, won again in 1940, having, as Roberts had in 1938, boldly predicted that he would. It was the first time since 1919 when Howdy Wilcox won in a Peugeot that a foreign chassis, an Italian Maserati painted in maroon and cream Boyle colors, won at Indianapolis. Its engine was a fairly conventional alcohol-fueled 178 cubic inch straight-eight blown by two Roots-type compressors drawing upon two dual carburetors. It was also the first time that a rear engine car (this one equipped with independent suspension), the George Bailey No. 17 silver and red Miller Special, ever competed at Indianapolis. It was, as they say, the wave of the future. Beginning in 1967, every car to race at Indianapolis carried its engine in the back.

Shaw drove the same Boyle Special to Victory Lane in 1940, thereby establishing himself as the Speedway's second three-time winner, and its first back-to-back champion. Rose would duplicate a back-to-back in 1947

Indy prerace in 1939. Roscoe Turner (left) was a celebrated airplane racer who maintained a hangar at the Indianapolis airport and once took to the sky with a lion as passenger. World War I ace and Congressional Medal of Honor recipient Eddie Rickenbacker (right) drove in the 500 four times and later owned the Speedway as well as Eastern Airlines. *Ed Hitze*

and 1948, Bill Vukovich in 1953 and 1954, Al Unser in 1970 and 1971, and Helio Castroneves in 2001 and 2002. Shaw's win was rendered considerably easier by light rains that fell during the last quarter of the race that, instead of halting competition, caused officials to continue under the yellow flag to the finish line. There were twenty of thirty-three starters still in competition at that point. The 1940 race was a healthy mixture of racing engines, of which nineteen were four-cylinder, four were six-cylinder, nine were eight-cylinder (four of them Maseratis and three Alfa Romeos), and one was sixteen-cylinder (the supercharged Sampson carried to sixth by Bob Swanson). Shaw himself had been handicapped from winning in 1935 when light rains caused officials to freeze competition between laps 177 and 190 of the full 200, relegating him to second in the Pirrung Miller. In 1940, all drivers were scored according to their standing at the 150 lap (375 mile) point when the yellow flag appeared. Race day began with a fifty-four degree temperature at 8:00 A.M. The rain held until 1:15 P.M. The 1940 race also finished under darkening geopolitical clouds. In 1936, Italian dictator Benito Mussolini had overrun Ethiopia. The Munich Pact of 1938 had resulted in Germany's taking over parts of Czechoslovakia. In August of 1939 Adolf Hitler invaded Poland, then Norway and Denmark. In 1940, Pop Myers penned an essay that ended by saying, "this year the Indianapolis Motor Speedway welcomes back this foreign competition which has had such a healthy influence in not only allowing us to compare racing motors but to foster international sport and friendship which is so rare but so welcome in these dark days of world strife." At Indianapolis, an advertisement for Bowes Seal Fast sparkplugs began with the words, "Who cares what Hitler says today? Our eyes are on the Old Speedway!"

America could no longer look the other way, however. Prophetic of the war years that loomed, Gasoline Alley garages ignited in flames on race morning, 1941. A cold drizzle had engulfed the track the night before. Said one unidentified reporter, "the story is that [George] Barringer's crew was filling the gasoline tank and that heavy fumes from the fuel crept along the floor to a garage a couple of doors down Gasoline Alley where somebody was using a blow torch." There was one fire truck on the Speedway grounds when the conflagration broke out, then other trucks from the Indianapolis Fire Department arrived through an emergency gate but had difficulty arriving at the front lines because of race day spectators who mobbed the site. Before the fire was under control, half of one garage building (there were two at the time) was destroyed, taking with it fuel, spare parts, tools, crew clothing, and pocket cash. The IFD did indeed save

A grimy but elated Wilbur Shaw greets well wishers in 1940 after becoming the first three-time Indianapolis 500 winner. *Ed Hitze*

the day, even though there was some confusion in locating hydrants, or there might well have been no race at all.

The race began, two cars short, more than an hour after the 10:00 A.M. advertised start. One of the cars did not race anyway. The No. 28 Tom Joyce 7 Up Special, entered by Ed Walsh of St. Louis and driven by second-year man and future (1957) race winner Sam Hanks, had crashed the day before the event, leaving Hanks seriously injured. The car destroyed in the fire was the No. 35 Miller Special, a four-wheel-drive supercharged car driven by George Barringer who would ultimately die in a double fatality accident at Atlanta's Lakewood Park dirt mile track along with 1946 Indy winner George Robson. The winner this time was cantankerous, pipe-puffing, Columbus, Ohio-born Mauri Rose, thirty-five, who triumphed for the first of his three victories in a circuitous manner. He began the day in a Lou Moore Elgin Piston Pin Special, a 183 inch eight-cylinder Maserati that retired from the chase after sixty laps, just in time to greet Floyd Davis who was riding in fourteenth in another Moore entry. Davis came in on his seventy-second lap and relinquished his car to Rose who hit the road and hit the pedal, running eighth at 250 miles, fourth at 375, second at 400, and first from the 425 mile mark to the end of the day. Rose's other two Indianapolis victories in 1947 and 1948 were choreographed by Lou Moore as well. In the meantime, Wilbur Shaw's quest for a fourth win on the

At dawn on race day in 1941 Gasoline Alley exploded in flames. "For years," Wilbur Shaw wrote, "it had been like a bomb, with only a single spark needed to set off all of the fuel and oil stored around the place." On the right is Al Putnam's orange and black Schoof Special that finished twelfth later in the day. World War II precluded any further racing at Indianapolis until 1946. *Ed Hitze*

bricks came to a painful ending on lap 151 when the spokes in his right rear wheel disengaged, sending the Boyle Maserati into a spin and into the wall tail first in the southwest turn, puncturing the fuel tank, and emptying fifty gallons of methanol. "Only God," Shaw commented later, "knows why it didn't catch fire. If it had, it doesn't take much imagination for anyone to realize what my fate would have been—because I was paralyzed from the waist down." Shaw's first concern was spending the rest of his life in a wheelchair. Hospital investigation, however, showed that his injury amounted to a compression fracture. Shaw's seeming paralysis, meanwhile, gradually disappeared. The root cause of the accident was traceable to the morning garage fire when water from fire hoses erased a chalk mark Shaw had made on a wheel that he had examined and did not trust to be properly balanced. The wheel ended up on the right rear of the

Driver Mauri Rose (left) and Floyd Davis won the 500 in 1941 on the day the garages burned. They lean here on the famous Borg-Warner trophy that has a curious history of its own, it once having fallen into the hands of some fraternity boys who pulled off its removable top and filled it with beer. *Ed Hitze*

car, then disintegrated. Shaw passed ten hospital days of convalescence and then returned home where he contemplated another attempt at a fourth win. What he could not know was that his driving days were over regardless of his decision. The Japanese attacked Pearl Harbor on December 7, 1941. The Indianapolis Motor Speedway would close for the duration.

TURN ONE: THE SOUTHWEST

*"Life is a gamble at terrible odds—if it was a bet, you
wouldn't take it."*

—Tom Stoppard, *Rosencrantz and
Guildenstern Are Dead*

"**A**uto race fans must forego their favorite thrills," a July 1941
Washington dispatch read, "in order that rubber may be con-
served for the nation's armed forces." That news bite noted also
that the American Automobile Association, then the country's foremost (if
not unrivaled) motor competition sanctioning body, had indeed preemp-
tively cancelled its race programs back in February. "One of the principal
objectives of automobile racing," said a May 9, 1942, bulletin from the
AAA Contest Board, "is to provide a testing ground for advances in automotive design and essential equipment; such efforts will temporarily lose
much of their value since the automotive industry is being fully converted
for war production." In the meantime, racing car drivers and mechanics
directed their attention to participating somehow in either, maybe both, of
two raging war theaters, one in the Atlantic, the other in the Pacific. American racing hero Rex Mays, so said one racing trade paper, had by 1943
directed his patriotic energies toward piloting military aircraft, although
he apparently never departed America's shores to do so. "The California
Comet who hurtled sleek racing cars to the gold and glory of two national
championships," the article proclaimed, had "taken to the air" with the
Army Air Force.

Mays's fondness for aeronautics was no eccentric aberration. Racing
drivers have traditionally harbored a passion for taking wing. The first-
ever competition at the Speedway was, in fact, a gas-inflated balloon race
wherein a person named Charles Walsh, dangling from a bubble he called
the "Hoosier" (the meaning of which is still under disputation), wafted all
the way to Westmoreland, Tennessee. The Speedway reported in 1911, the

year of the first 500-mile race initially called the "International Sweep-stakes," that it possessed "the largest enclosed aviation park in the world, and the finest balloon park in the world." The Speedway's 1919 official program contained an article attributed to Lt. Col. J. G. Vincent on "The Influence of Aviation on Motor Cars," intended for reading by "automobilists." World War I flying ace Eddie Rickenbacker, who bought the Speedway in 1927, also purchased Eastern Airlines which, by 1939, operated 5,328 miles of passenger, air mail, and freight routes. English-born George Robson, the 1946 winner, passed the war years machining aircraft parts with his younger brother Hal, who also raced at Indianapolis. Sam Hanks, who would win in 1957, was employed by Lockheed Aircraft Corporation when war broke out and earned a commission in 1943 as a first lieutenant in the U.S. Army Air Force. Billy Arnold, the 1930 Indianapolis winner, flew B-17s over Europe during World War II. Henry Banks, another English-born racing champion, navigated a light plane from western Michigan to Milwaukee by following the shores of Lake Michigan. Dennis "Duke" Nalon, identified best with the powerful Novi Indianapolis cars, passed the war years maintaining Rolls Royce fighter plane engines. George Connor, fourteen times an Indianapolis competitor, was an enthusiastic flyer before it was fashionable, even before Lindbergh traversed the Atlantic, and after retirement assisted in the development of Ford airplane engines. Oklahoma driver Jimmy Reece was an Air Force plane mechanic. In later years, headline Indianapolis drivers like Rodger Ward, A. J. Foyt, Lloyd Ruby, Jan Opperman, and Rich Vogler were licensed to fly, although they did not necessarily do so in an orthodox manner. One might even infer that racing car drivers are disappointed aviators. Janet Guthrie, whose father was an airline pilot and whose hero was Charles Lindbergh, flew twenty-three types of aircraft prior to being Indianapolis's first female contestant. Airplanes, though, have exacted a heavy toll on auto racing that, needless to say, carries significant dangers of its own. A disheartening number of Indianapolis drivers (Mack Hellings, Wilbur Shaw, Joel Thorne, Eddie Johnson, Graham Hill, Al Holbert, Al Loquasto, Chip Mead, and the second Tony Bettenhausen) died in plane disasters not necessarily of their own making. "When my time comes," the fatalistic Shaw remarked, "I don't believe it will make any difference whether I'm flying in an airplane in bad weather or sitting at home in a comfortable easy chair." He and his two companions died on October 30, 1954, when, in bad weather, their single-engine private plane crashed near Decatur, Indiana.

After the capitulation of Germany and Japan that ended World War

The freshman class at Indianapolis after the resumption of racing in 1946. On the far left is long-time flagman Seth Klein. Left to right on the back row are: Bill Sheffler, Tony Bettenhausen, Jimmy Wilburn, Danny Kladis, 1946 winner George Robson, and Charlie Van Acker. The front row consists of Jimmy Jackson, Duke Dinsmore, Hal Cole, and Luigi Villoresi. *Ed Hitze*

II in 1945, the government-mandated prohibition on automobile racing was at last lifted. Pre-war racing cars, safely retired from Speedway action between Pearl Harbor and V-J Day, subsequently rolled out of storage, dusted off, and cranked up as if awakened from some protracted hibernation. Dapper pole-vaulting Yale man Anton "Tony" Hulman (class of 1924, hair parted down the middle) purchased the track for a reported $750,000 (the same dollar figure that it sold for in 1927) in November of 1945 from warrior celebrity and gifted fund-raiser Eddie Rickenbacker. In 1946, however, the Indianapolis Motor Speedway was a dilapidated mess. "It stood unattended, in silent deterioration," wrote the alliteratively curmudgeonous former Indianapolis sports writer Al Bloemker, "at the whim of winds and the weather." Racing's people inexorably turned up at the track's decrepit Gasoline Alley, towing such technologically outdated but still lethal chariots as the black and ivory Bowes Seal Fast Special that Mays had wheeled to second place in 1941, the Jimmy Snyder record-setting Thorne Engineering car from 1939, the Floyd Roberts 1938 winning Wetteroth chassis, and the 1941 pole-winning Maserati that fractious Mauri Rose had driven for Oklahoma-born racing car builder and former driver Lou Moore, whose mother, quite incidentally, claimed to be a fifth cousin of Thomas Jefferson.

Those of the racing fraternity who survived military service were all the more eager to resume the frenzied freedom of motorized competition that itself constituted another war zone. It was to be sure a dangerous existence, but not nearly as hazardous as being targeted by enemy mortar. Newark, New Jersey-born Mike Nazaruk, who finished second at the 500 in 1951, for example, had always been, despite the earnest efforts of his widowed Ukrainian mother, the bare-knuckled Dead End Kid who, after enlisting in the Marine Corps, engaged in hand-to-hand combat amid the howling firestorms of Iwo Jima, Bougainville, Guam, and Guadalcanal. He liked to say that he was one of eight men in his outfit not to come home in a body bag. No amount of carnage that the bloody post-war open-wheel racing era could dish up in Hell's own kitchen could match the sustained violence that Nazaruk knew in the Pacific. "He was a character," remarked one of Nazaruk's companions, "and he was a brave son of a bitch. Too brave." Nazaruk, needless to say, managed to kill himself in a race car, as did a staggering proportion of the men with whom he competed. It happened on a Sunday May Day afternoon in 1955 at the infamous circular-mile Langhorne dirt track located halfway between Philadelphia and Trenton.

Out in balmy California, meanwhile, an exciting new generation of mostly brash, hard-edged hotrodding youngsters like Johnnie Parsons, Troy Ruttman, Bill Vukovich, Bob Sweikert, Pat Flaherty, Sam Hanks, Rodger Ward, Jim Rathmann, and Parnelli Jones, each of them accorded at least one Indianapolis win, bravely and resolutely strapped themselves into racing cars of all descriptions, then raced the floodlit western states' short tracks, sometimes as many as eight times a week. Frank Kurtis, whom racing historian Gordon Eliot White has aptly called "the son of a Croatian blacksmith" whose "designs set the standards for the cars of the late 1940s and 1950s," fabricated those cars by the hundreds at his Los Angeles shops. There were plenty of willing drivers to take the wheel. America was eager after dark years of economic depression and armed conflict to create a new and productive future and have a little fun doing

The remarkable Anton "Tony" Hulman, who died in 1977 at age 77, saved the Indianapolis Motor Speedway from obliteration when he purchased it from Eddie Rickenbacker in 1945. Hulman, a 1924 Yale graduate with an engineering degree, relentlessly nurtured the track. *Ed Hitze*

it. Automobile racing, as old as automobiles themselves, was part of the cultural mix.

Aspiring drivers such as these western Americans earned a reputation as a loose band of unfettered gypsies who asked little more from life than to be free and footloose in postwar America, armed with a helmet, goggles, and a roadmap, wending their way to the races, eating and sleeping on the run, and growing cheerfully accustomed to living contentedly out of a suitcase full of sport shirts, and bedding down in a pickup truck. One prevalent motive was to reclaim their freedom and to acquire enough experience on the sometimes shabby and dangerous quarter- and half-mile tracks with the ultimate intention of driving in the 500-mile race where the big money and big reputations were made. To race at Indianapolis was the gold standard, a place to certify one's self as a serious, committed auto racer. This customary apprenticeship was gradually undermined by those racing aspirants who bought their way into Indianapolis cars and, having relatively little on-track experience, hoped for the best. To be sure, the prospect of injury and death in those postwar days was grim. Of the thirty-three men who competed at Indianapolis in 1950, for example, nine (more than one in four) would eventually die as a consequence of racing mishaps. Fifteen of the thirty-three starters (more than 45 percent) in 1951 met their end in racing accidents. On July 29, 1951, the American auto racing community lost three cherished members within about twenty minutes on one hot Sunday afternoon. By some bizarre coincidence, those three had been the slowest qualifiers at that year's Indianapolis 500. All died during qualification attempts, all were on half-mile tracks, all on the first turns of those tracks, and all were dead at the scene. Cecil Green and Bill Mackey (William C. Grietsinger, Jr.) sailed backfirst over the low guardrailing at the steeply banked half-mile bowl near rural Winchester, Indiana. Sometime bank teller Walt Brown, the eldest of the three, perished at the muddy Williams Grove dirt oval near Harrisburg, Pennsylvania, after a deceptively routine looking tipover in the car that had won the 1941 Indianapolis 500. Racing people continued to sacrifice substantial numbers of their promising young men in the 1940s and 1950s until they gradually acknowledged that such common sense precautions as fire-repellant driving suits and overhead cage protection could reduce and often prevent injuries, fatal and otherwise, to a fraction of what had been. Said one grizzled survivor of the postwar racing battlefields, "We felt that if a driver thought he needed all kinds of safety paraphernalia, he probably had no goddamned business in a race car in the first place."

On August 3, 1955, the American Automobile Association, with its commitment to promoting automotive safety, had enough of auto racing, and thereafter administrated no more racing events. At a meeting designated at the Indiana State Fairgrounds a month later, a temporary committee convened, consisting of Speedway owner Tony Hulman; Tom Marchese, the promoter of the Wisconsin State Fairgrounds mile track; George Ober, an Indianapolis magistrate; Bob Estes, a California racing car owner; Herb Porter, a cantankerous mechanic and engine builder; Arthur Herrington, the former chairman of the AAA Contest board; and articulate Duane Carter, who at that time had competed eight times in the 500-miler. Together they formed the United States Auto Club to fill the vacuum left in the wake of the AAA's sudden departure. USAC remained the sanctioning body for the 500-mile race until the Indianapolis Motor Speedway instigated its own in-house racing series called the Indy Racing League, which conducted its first 500-mile race in 1996. Even then the USAC remained to administer the race under IRL regulations until the IRL had its own people in place in June 1997 at the Texas Motor Speedway.

Although American oval track racing car drivers have tended to be

The inimitable Rex Houston Mays earned two second-places in a dozen Indy starts. His refusal to wear a seatbelt resulted in his death at Del Mar, California on November 6, 1949. *Ed Hitze*

temperamentally cut from the same bolt (independent, fun-loving, ego-centric, generally unflappable, politically conservative, assertively post-adolescent), those who race at Indianapolis have at the same time evolved in recent years to fit the template of respectably literate, well-coifed sporting gentlemen who, although they may not have passed their finest ephebic years in tweeds and ivied seminar rooms, can at least comfortably hold their own in civilized company. Quotable Eddie Cheever, Jr., the 1998 winner who was born in Phoenix and raised in Rome, can express himself ably in English, French, and Italian. That is more than sufficient for Indianapolis's south side. Indeed, since racing in all its aspects is business, drivers with a glossy public relations facade have a far better than average probability of driving the more sophisticated, potentially winning machinery at the Speedway, although driving at ridiculous rates of speed is only part of the job description. Contractual obligations mandate their suffering fools pleasantly, orating at respectable suburban high schools and dowdy Rotary luncheons, albeit more than one driver has at least privately bristled at having corporate public relations people control his life.

Alas, with the passing of front line Indianapolis drivers whose identities were defined by barbarous grammar, carious teeth, gritty fingernails, and greasy coveralls, so passed much of the engrossing B movie theatricality of the Indianapolis track and its participants in the days when big-time racing in America was far more a low-budget, shade-tree operation rather than some foolish corporate advertising and public relations pop. There are things to be said in favor of old timers. One of the last of the old breed of roving race car chauffeurs was a craggy character named Travis "Spider" Webb, known familiarly to some as "Webbie," a Joplin, Missouri, native who departed to his eternal reward in January 1990. Webbie won the American Automobile Association–sanctioned middle west big car championship in 1948 at a time when he was viewed by some as little more than a roughnecking roustabout. Fond of life's infinite varieties, he turned up at Indianapolis (where he competed on six occasions between 1948 and 1954) accompanied by one blonde, one brunette, and one redhead. Webb had a portable bar conveniently at the ready in the trunk of his car. "We had very little money to spend in those days," Webb disclosed shortly before his death. "Lou and Bruce Bromme [his Indianapolis car owners] would call on Meyer and Drake [California manufacturers of the Offenhauser racing engine] and gather up whatever used parts for our engine that they could. If somebody left a bad set of pistons or a crankshaft he thought was going to break, why, we'd buy them and use them in our car. We came to the Speedway with one engine, and that meant that we'd run it as little as possible. I'd take two practice laps in the car and then try to qualify it. If you call yourself a driver," Webb continued, "you don't need more than five laps of practice at the most." Not withstanding, Webbie was beset by more problems at the Speedway than most of his contemporaries who raced there as much. In 1949, for example, his temperamental Grancor Special failed to budge from the starting line, resulting in a last-place finish, and a paycheck of $1,555 that had to be divided several ways. That said, Webbie claimed to have set aside a good proportion of his race track winnings, purchased heavy equipment, and carved out the third Los Angeles zoo.

Were he with us today, Spider Webb might well posit that the quintessence of Indianapolis is best discovered in its four turns, each of them a quarter-mile in length. Were it possible to piece the four corners together, they would therefore constitute a mile circle. Straightaways are merely straight. "Indy is a fine payday," twenty-two time Speedway driver George Snider told reporter Linda Mansfield recently, "but I didn't like the big long straightaways; they just took too much time to get down." The front and back straightaways require an experienced driver only to keep his car pointed dead straight ahead. Granted, without today's immense wing-driven downforce, the enormously powerful Indianapolis cars of the 1970s flirted briefly with harrowing straightaway speeds of 245 miles per hour, all the while keeping well away from the walls and away from other people's on-track pirouettes. But Indy's turns are notoriously subtle, tricky, treacherous—and lethal. They have eaten Indy's best for lunch, and will continue to do so. No drivers, even those who have won Indianapolis multiple times, have yet claimed to have mastered the Speedway, and but few drivers have evaded hard, bone-rattling contact with the unforgiving walls of its four turns. Racing cars have always, and without warning, broken loose and careened, as if impelled by some overwhelming magnetism, into an immovable and unforgiving concrete retaining wall as if lured into catastrophe by the seductive Lorelei of Germanic legend. In the turns the high-speed running groove narrows, and with that narrowness usable track width diminishes. The closer a car comes to the wall at the track's apex in the north and south chutes, the more track it uses and, theoretically, the faster it goes. While all the track is a stage, the footlights shine brightest where the track bends and develops its maximum pitch of nine degrees and twelve minutes, and where cars that moments before ran as much as three abreast on the straights must suddenly accommodate each other by falling into a whirlwind that skims through Indy's treacherous corners. The spectacles unfolded in those bends are sometimes choreographic, sometimes catastrophic, but never are they less than spellbinding. Viewed from high above, the Indianapolis Motor Speedway resembles far more a two-and-a-half-mile rectangle than an oval. The entire Speedway acreage, including the championship golf course located both inside the track and to the east of it, a motel, various trackside suites, utility buildings and the like, is 559 acres.

Modern race tracks tend to be variously oval, often D-shaped, and they are relatively easy to drive, allowing as they do for cars to be raced in any of several spacious and forgiving lanes. Not Indianapolis. Its four sixty-foot-wide bends are sudden and severe. There is nothing unusual about them at a distance. "Until I became a racing driver," said former driver Sam Posey who finished fifth at the Speedway in 1972, "I never understood Indy at all . . . to someone as absorbed as I was in the world of Grand Prix, the Indy 500 seemed stupid and boring. For example, the track has only four turns, all identical; the Nurburgring (venue of the German Grand Prix) has a monumental 176 turns, all different." Time was, however, when racing people doubted whether because of the severity of its four left turns, the track could be driven in excess of 100 miles an hour. Drivers have in more recent decades likened the Indianapolis experience to driving substantially above 200 miles per hour—into a closet. To complete the whole 500 miles means 200 laps at four turns per lap, coming to 800 turns in all, not counting one or two pre-race pace laps and cooldown laps at the end.

The current one-lap track record is 237.498 miles per hour, set by Dutch-born two-time Indianapolis champion Arie Luyendyk in 1996. A four-lap qualification run therefore means sixteen turns to negotiate. Indianapolis's turns are named and numbered. Once a car passes the starting line in a southbound direction it reaches the first turn, also known as turn one and occasionally as the southwest turn. When a car leaves turn one it briefly passes eastbound over an eighth-mile (660 foot) section called the south chute and into turn two, the southeast. After a car passes through the southeast it is suddenly northbound on the five-eighths-mile (3,300 foot long), fifty-foot-wide backstretch. That leads into turn three, the northeast, that feeds into another eighth-mile straight section called the north chute. It leads westbound into turn four, the northwest, that in turn empties into the fifty-foot-wide southbound main straightaway.

Driving at breakneck speeds around the Indianapolis Motor Speedway is attempting to play at hare and hounds with the immutable laws of physics. In recent years cars have tended for aerodynamic reasons to run at approximately the same rate of speed on all parts of the track, be they straight or curved. Consequently, the driver might like to drive faster on the straightaways, but because of aerodynamic drag and horsepower limitations, it is not possible. The downforce that retards motion on the straightaways presses the car to the track in the turns and thereby reduces the number of wall encounters. That is the tradeoff, the *quid pro quo.* Crews "trim" the car so that it runs faster on the straights, but that makes them less secure in the corners of the track. Some drivers call for their cars to be the most trim toward the last few laps of the race. Most drivers do their utmost to transform the track from rectangle to oval by entering the turns as early and as low as permissible, allowing the car to peak out at the apex of the turns in the south and north chutes. The trick is to run at maximum speed and, obviously, to keep from connecting with the wall. This, as they say, is easier said than done. In the seventies, cars ran at blinding rates of speed on the straights, got off the pedal as they approached the turns, used quite a bit of braking, and got through the corners any way possible. The drivers of the powerful front-drive Novi cars of the forties and fifties exited turn four so fast that they needed to back off the throttle near the starting line.

Accidents happen because cars are going too damned fast; because a driver's job is to take the car to its edge, and even over the edge; because driving in "dirty" air (artificial turbulence caused by other vehicles) upsets the car; because there's insufficient downforce to press the car to the track; because the track is slippery from oil and other fluid accumulation; because wind gusts blow the car out of control; because the driver isn't paying attention; because the driver has insufficient experience; because the driver has suddenly to evade some accident; because the driver should have his eyes examined; because the driver should have his head examined; because the driver has been told to go faster than he has a mind to; because the driver is using too little of the track; because the driver is trying to use more track than exists; because the driver is frightened half to death; because the driver is not frightened enough; because the tires are not wide enough; because the tires are made from too soft a rubber compound; because the tires are made from too hard a rubber compound; because tires are not up to operating temperature; because the tires have improper "stagger" (inflation-adjusted circumference); because a tire is losing inflation pressure; because a tire is cut; because a pit man did not secure a wheel during the last pit stop; because the car's "setup" (a combi-nation of aerodynamics, weight distribution, ride height, and so forth) is off the mark; because an engine blows to smithereens; because the car's body parts are falling off; because the car will not steer; because the car wants to spin out; because the car's fuel load is adversely affecting its bal-ance; because the car is one total design flaw; because a chickadee hit the windshield; because the track is too congested with cars; because the track is outdated and therefore unsuited to high-tech racing cars; because high-tech racing cars have not figured out a way to drive a lap without hitting something quite obdurate.

Because, because, because.

More eyes have been transfixed upon activity deep in the number one turn, the southwest, than in any of the other three turns. Since the south-west is at the end of the main straight, it is the turn closest to the Speed-way's busiest pedestrian gate, situated on the tumultuous intersection of Georgetown Road and West Sixteenth Street. On race day, thousands con-verge there, keeping at least ten ticket handlers amply occupied. Across the track at the southeast turn there once stood an apparently timeless, low, elongated sign that carried the stern admonition, A BOTTLE ON THE TRACK MAY CAUSE A SERIOUS WRECK WATCH YOURS. Behind that rambling message, especially during the 1970s, was a delectable sector of the infield known as "The Snake Pit," so designated in honor of its free spirited denizens' penchant for unabashed displays of nudity (on balmy days), partial nudity (on chillier days), cannabis inhaling (anytime), and beer guzzling (almost anytime). Speedway management took a properly dim view of such counter-cultural misbehavior, and eventually disbursed these guests, after which they in their hasty diaspora temporarily resettled half-heartedly on the inside of the fourth (northwest) turn, from which (possibly out of boredom, possibly out of incipient maturity) they eventu-ally decamped. Had it been 1924, for instance, there would have been an on-site magistrate and lockup at the track for implementation in just such cases.

Before the 1966 and 1968 erection of massive new aluminum grand-stands called the Southwest Vista outside turn one, there stood two smaller seating arrangements designated as grandstands B and E, over which, from the starting line there afforded a reasonably clear view of a Speedway, Indiana landmark, a smokestack situated at what once was the Prest-O-Lite plant, originally a headlamp and battery factory brought to this location in 1912 by James Allison, Carl Fisher, and a third partner. The

Waiting for the track to dry in 1974, these spectators engaged in the noble and ancient art of streaking to while the hours away. *John Mahoney*

now-vanished smokestack, left long standing after Prest-O-Lite closed, dominated the local landscape like some Vesuvius of the Plains, belching black smoke toward midtown Indianapolis. It served another worthy purpose in its time, namely for Speedway drivers who looked at the smoke's direction to surmise the direction and velocity of prevailing winds, factors that could well affect the handling of cars traveling at enormous speeds.

Until 1956, when workmen layered fresh asphalt on the turns of Indianapolis, there was a persistent problem at the southwest, over and above the hazards of driving around it at whiz bang speeds. At the entrance there is, as there always has been, a crossway for pedestrians and motor traffic when the track is closed to racing activity. At that time, motor traffic wore a scarcely perceptible dip in the track surface. Howdy Wilcox, the 1919 winner, testified after that race that one of what he called his "biggest problems" happened to be "that number one turn at the bottom of the stretch." Said he, "There's a bump in it, and you got to go high on the bank. Hit it, and you could land in downtown Indianapolis." Although it was not visible to the naked eye, its presence was all the more obvious at ever increasing speeds in a racing car. Post-war driver Freddy Agabashian

The famous Snake Pit in turn one at the IMS was always a gathering place for revelers and other free spirits, until track management succeeded in disbanding it. *John Mahoney*

from Walnut Creek, California, remembered it well: "You had to watch yourself in turn one because of that bump in the track," he recalled, "and once you passed over it there was still another dip in the track just a little bit ahead." Movietone newsreels of cars rounding the southwest revealed images of racing cars seeming to bounce, possibly even lurch, as they negotiated the corner. To Spider Webb, that bounce could, with the astute application of a little English, be parlayed to tactical advantage. "I would let up on the throttle as I came through there" he said. "It would sound as if I was off the gas at that point, but that's not true; I was just easing back a little bit. I tried to drive through there in exactly the same place every time. I'd catch the bump, which always pitched the rear end of the car out toward the wall. If you came into the southwest in just the right way, it would cock your front wheels to the left and help you set up for the turn."

If Spider Webb actually did play the dip in turn one to his own favor, he was one of the few who polished the technique. That same dip caused a number of his predecessors and successors inestimable grief. Back in

1913 for instance, a driver named Jack Tower misnegotiated the southwest, and overturned in the south chute after exiting the turn. Tower broke a leg. His mechanic Lee Dunning broke some ribs. Tom Rooney had much the same unpleasant experience in 1916, veering into the wall at nearly the same place and breaking a hip. His riding mechanic Thane Houser (whose son Norm Houser raced at Indianapolis in 1949) sustained serious, if unspecified, injuries, but later drove in the 1926 event. In 1919 Louis LeCocq and rider Robert Bandini were killed upon exiting the southwest. "The race was not one of bloodless aspect," journalist Darwin Hatch wrote, explaining that LeCocq and Bandini died because the gasoline tank on their Roamer exploded. "The car overturned and the two men were killed instantly and their bodies cremated under the burning car." Christian Lautenschlager, the only man with a riding mechanic in 1923, smacked the wall down there on his fourteenth lap with his Mercedes, but no one paid much attention. "There is," averred journalist Clyde Jennings, "a curious lack of thrills in this event." That same Thane Houser relief driving for Joe Boyer on Friday, May 30, 1924, bopped the same wall, fortunately without injury. Earl Cooper crashed there while leading the 1925 race, and in 1927 car owner Henry Kohlert, taking over for his driver Freddy Lecklider, hit the wall in the southwest turn after colliding with irrepressible pipe-smoking Hollywood stunt-artist Cliff Bergere who, as part of a 1923 motion picture assignment, leapt four and a half stories from a window in the Long Beach City Hall and into a catch net. Bergere, who had also been gamely lowered upon a horse's back by a rope ladder suspended from an airplane, motored on to ninth place at Indianapolis, while Kohlert overturned and was dumped on the track where he sustained reportedly serious injuries. How Bergere who, according to Speedway's publicity department spoke English "with the precision of an Oxford graduate" survived all this, is a mystery. He died in 1980 at the age of eighty-three.

The aforementioned Spider Webb began his eventful racing career in 1928, the same year that Louis Meyer, a young and ambitious California mechanic, enjoyed the first of his three Indianapolis victories. Twenty-nine sad-looking cars started the 500 that year, and the trackside pit area consisted of groin-high wooden enclosures that resembled hog pens at the Chicago stockyards. Benny Shoaf, who had begun the day from twenty-sixth position, also finished there after his mighty Duesenberg banged the southwest wall with considerable force on his thirty-fifth lap. Fortunately, he escaped the confrontation with only minor injuries. Ira Hall's Duesenberg also came out second best in an altercation with that same wall on his 115th lap. Hall, incidentally, became the sheriff of Vigo County, Indiana, home to the Terre Haute Hulmans. Earl DeVore, in a striking chrome-plated car appropriately called the Chromolite Special, was the next turn one casualty when he connected with the concrete after 161 laps. It was DeVore who, sad to say, died at sea in November of 1928 with 114 other people (including fellow Indianapolis driver Norman Batten) among the 328 on board a vessel called the SS *Vestris* that had departed from New York and forever disappeared roughly 300 miles off the Virginia Capes. DeVore, Batten, and their Miller racing cars were en route to winter racing in Brazil and Argentina when the *Vestris* capsized. Batten is perhaps best remembered for having stood up in his burning Miller racing car at Indianapolis in 1927 long enough to protect others from harm. His courage won him a Carnegie Medal.

While Louis Meyer enjoyed his somewhat unanticipated second Indianapolis win in 1933, one of the forty-one other cars chasing him was a Studebaker-powered Universal Service Special driven by Westville, New Jersey's Malcolm Fox, who slowed momentarily behind another car in the southwest turn on Fox's 123rd lap. Riding behind Malcolm Fox was Les Spangler in a Miller Special owned by Harry Hartz, himself now securely enshrined in the pantheon of racing immortals. Spangler's machine drove over Fox's right rear wheel, bolted through the air, and came to rest right-side-up on the turn one inner apron. Wrote *Motor* magazine's Harold Blanchard after he returned from the accident scene, "Spangler and his mechanic G. L. Jordan were so badly crushed and mangled that their friends had some difficulty telling which was which." Fox and his passenger-mechanic Bert Cook, meanwhile, spun several times, climbed the wall, and suffered a fresh round of relatively superficial injuries. "It might have been us," said Fox after the accident, "but I guess we were lucky."

Blanchard the scrivener was back at the Speedway with *Motor* magazine in 1934 when, during a practice session driver Pete Kreis and his riding mechanic Art Hahn, aboard another Miller-Hartz Special, hurtled over the retaining wall in the southwest and wrapped themselves around a tree that blossomed among some private homes on what is now Speedway property. Only the tree survived. Remarked the speculative Blanchard after he had surveyed the two pieces of the car after they arrived in the garage compound, "Members of Gasoline Alley at the Speedway have been greatly mystified as to the cause of this accident. Kreis was a capable driver, steering parts had recently been X-rayed and were assembled by unusually competent mechanics. In consequence, there is uncertainty as to whether something went wrong with the car or did Kreis faint?" Internationally known as a board track driver, Kreis had been a factor in Frank Lockhart's 1926 win at Indianapolis when Kreis fell ill with influenza and surrendered his Miller to his California riding mechanic Lockhart who qualified it 20th and had assumed the lead when the race ended because of rain on the leader's 160th lap.

Allegedly because Wilbur Shaw's Lion Head Special lost the better part if its six-and-a-half gallon oil capacity on the track in the 1934 race, even the early stages of the contest were run on a decidedly slippery racecourse. Participating in his fifth consecutive 500, Chet Miller and his mechanic Eddie Tynan were running well behind the leaders when their poorly handling Bohnalite Ford began to spin through the southwest turn. After having looped once toward the inner wall, it left the apron and spun twice more, finally moving up and over the outer barrier. Witnesses reported that the car executed a complete mid-air somersault and then returned to earth right-side-up fifty feet east of the Stevens home where, during the month of May some drivers roomed and enjoyed Mrs. Stevens's twenty-five-cent lunches. Chet Miller remained all the while in the cockpit, but Eddie Tynan was hurled into a tree where he received what one reporter dismissed as "a few minor scratches." Miraculously also, the Bohnalite Ford was reported only "slightly damaged" in spite of having its hindquarters disengaged. The Stevens's backyard was minimally disrupted.

A little less than a year later, on May 21, 1935, Hartwell "Stubby" Stubblefield and mechanic Leo Whitacker rammed the southwest barrier during a time trial run. Both were killed. That was the year when, in the interest of everyone's safety, the Speedway installed electric traffic lights and made helmets mandatory. Prior to the 1936 race (when Meyer became the first driver to win three 500-mile races, and the first man to gulp the now traditional milk in Victory Lane) the Speedway management had altered the configuration of the turns, the outer few feet of which were banked more steeply than the usual brick running groove. The original idea, presumably, was to provide a little margin of catch-banking to offer stability to any unfortunate wayfarer who strayed from the usual running line. Although this supplemental banking was paved with the best of intentions, it was bordered by a retaining wall of nine-inch-thick reinforced concrete extending thirty-three inches above the race track. Behind that wall was another, this one more deeply recessed in the ground. The inner wall, however, was perpendicular to the ground, but not to the contour of the turns. The result was that some perfectly good men in some perfectly good cars launched out of the park. Mishaps involving Malcolm Fox, Les Spangler, Pete Kreis, Chet Miller, Stubby Stubblefield, and a fated group of other unfortunates were abetted by a ramp effect at the periphery of the turns, and by the retaining walls that, far from retaining much of anything, were encouraging cars to vanish over the side. Small wonder that, in subsequent years, drivers learned what they could about piloting aircraft.

Before the 1936 race, however, turn banking was at least uniform in slope, striking a maximum pitch of nine degrees and twelve minutes. Newer reinforced concrete walls superseded the old ones and tilted toward the track itself. Meanwhile, the inside retaining walls that had introduced more problems than they solved were removed and replaced by an oiled dirt safety apron. When this happened the Speedway's original brick surface, aside from a symbolic "yard of brick" that still survives at the start-finish line, vanished. Come what may, new asphalt and new walls did not prevent Frank McGurk, reaching for his second Indianapolis start, from crashing his Belanger Special in that selfsame southwest turn. Mechanic Albert Opalco died, but McGurk, who received treatment for serious injuries, returned in 1946, and crashed again. "Ride 'em, Speed Boy, ride 'em!" wrote sixty-two-year-old hometown Indianapolis versifier William Herschell in 1934. "Turn back the burning miles;/ There's gold galore/ Behind your chore—/ Plaudits and women's smiles!"

Seldom has the story of any Indianapolis 500 been rehashed as many times as the 1947 race that developed into a memorable confrontation between that disagreeable little man named Mauri Rose and his smiling if somewhat paranoid teammate, the ice and rollerskating champion Bill Holland. Both men, before they were done racing, amassed outstanding Indianapolis résumés. Holland earned a first and three seconds in his first four starts. Rose won three times in fifteen attempts. Both had their career problems. Holland was blackballed from AAA racing in 1951 because he allegedly participated in an "unsanctioned" Miami race to benefit a boys' club. On September 20, 1931, Rose and an accomplice named William "Shorty" Wolf were jailed for arsonous complicity after someone set fire to the New Bremen, Ohio, track grandstand after they and certain of their cohorts became sufficiently disgruntled with the track's management that they incited a riot. But in 1947, Holland and Rose were both driving cigar-shaped metallic Blue Crown Spark Plug Specials superintended by Lou

Moore who had finished second and third place at the Speedway. Rookie Holland had taken the lead with Rose in second place, when team owner and manager Moore displayed an ambiguous "OK" sign on a large chalk board to both drivers, ostensibly instructing them to hold their positions and finish one-two. Moore then erased the "OK" and replaced it with a similarly ambiguous "E-Z." Holland took the directive seriously and eased back, whereupon Rose managed to forge ahead, overtake Holland, and win the race, much to Holland's eternal disgust and regret. In 1950, Holland would again finish second, that time to Johnnie Parsons, when rain halted the race at 345 miles. Holland grumbled that the race was never restarted and run to its 500-mile conclusion, which indeed it could have been, because the AAA conspired to prevent his winning a second time.

There were thirty cars in the 1947 race, and Holland had started in eighth position, in the middle of the third row. Directly in front of him, starting fifth, was William "Shorty" Cantlon, the second-place finisher in 1930, who was making his eleventh and, as circumstances turn out, final start. A compulsive worrier and a popular underdog, the aging Cantlon (Wilbur Shaw knew him as "Runt") confided to reporter Russ Catlin before the race, "I'm going to win this one." Ominously, his orange and black Automobile Shippers sixteen-cylinder Miller stalled twice as it tried to leave the starting grid and join the other twenty-nine contestants. Holland too had every intention of winning, and was in the lead with thirty-nine laps down. But as he began to execute his arc into the southwest on his fortieth circuit he momentarily lost control and slid into the grassy area below the track's paved surface. Mud and turf flew as Holland, an experienced and highly successful Pennsylvania dirt-track driver, struggled for control and darted back on the track just as Cantlon arrived on the scene attempting to avoid Holland, but instead striking the wall head-on before hitting it a second time with the car's tail section. His car then spilled oil that streamed down the track. Holland, by that time, had recovered control and motored on. As Holland passed the accident site the next time, he waved. Rescue workers, in the meantime, had removed Cantlon, with his crushed chest and his broken leg, on a stretcher. His wrecked car, strange to say, remained on the race course for the balance of the afternoon. Shortly thereafter came a public announcement that Cantlon had become the fifteenth driver to die at the Speedway.

George Connor, who had fallen out of competition prior to the accident had, as some drivers did in those times, moseyed down to the southwest turn to see the balance of the race play out. What he saw, or believed he saw, was Holland bump the back of Cantlon's car prior to Cantlon's driving into the southwest wall. He also saw a dent in the front of Holland's Blue Crown Special. Connor well knew, as Holland no doubt did, that to be physically involved in a major accident meant among other things, that one had to bring his car into the pits for a safety inspection. This did not happen. Connor surmised that Lou Moore's E-Z signal flashed on a chalkboard to Holland was indeed intended to reign him back to second place. Had the dent been uncovered in the Speedway's coveted Victory Lane at the entrance to the southwest turn, it might well have resulted in Holland's disqualification. It would likely also have disqualified him from placing second. Connor further claimed that at the end of the 1947 race, someone threw a blanket over the front end of Holland's machine, quickly hustled it back to a garage in Gasoline Alley, and then propped Moore's large chalkboard in front of the car to shield it from inquiring eyes.

Connor's observations remain conjectural. Apparently no AAA race observer saw Holland drive into Cantlon. Nor did any other race contestant protest the outcome of the race, as was often done. In an article entitled "The 1947 500," published in *Speed Age*, then the leading American motorsports magazine, the purported author Wilbur Shaw managed to say nothing about the race or the fatality. There is, however, a familiar and often published photograph taken after the 1947 race that shows Holland leering at Rose with a combination of disgust and contempt written across his visage. Whether Holland was absorbed at that moment with his losing the race, the Cantlon fatality, the unexpected Rose victory, or some other pressing issue, will never be known. Rose died in 1981, Holland in 1984.

Among the throng present on the afternoon when Shorty Cantlon died was an Indianapolis man named George Metzler. Those who recall his presence in Gasoline Alley remember him best as a slender, likable person, albeit another local fellow named Jack Dixon who played a role in bringing Metzler to the Speedway as a driver was inclined to say that Metzler was slender, yes; likable, no. Said Dixon, "he was both overbearing and bull-headed." As for Metzler's mechanical abilities, Dixon remembers a time when Metzler installed left hubs on the right side of a racing car, and right hubs on the left. "If he had driven on the track that way," said he, "the wheels would have come off." Others remember him as a mediocre driver, a man sometimes ruefully referred to as a "fill-in" at a traveling auto racing roadshow on a day when there were insufficient drivers to stage a respectable auto race. More significantly, Metzler possessed an attitude bordering on arrogance, not necessarily unusual among the many hundreds of similarly motivated young men who since 1909 had converged on the Speedway to establish an identity and a reputation, even before there was a 500-mile race. Metzler wanted to race at Indianapolis in the worst way. His story was to end amid noise and confusion in the track's southwest turn.

St. Joseph's Cemetery, established by Indianapolis's German-Catholic congregation in 1860, is located on South Meridian, the road that divides the city's east and west. Close to the intersection of South Meridian and Pleasant Run Boulevard lies the once unmarked grave of George Metzler, scarcely a hundred feet from the motor traffic that snarls this sector of Indianapolis's foundering south side. Metzler's life illustrates a good deal about the American racing mentality and temperament. A local kid, he was born into a working-class German-Catholic family in 1912, the year that local bachelor Joe Dawson won the second running of the 500-mile race. As a ten-year-old he stood in the Speedway infield and watched San Francisco's Jimmy Murphy, driving his own No. 35, dominate a field of twenty-six cars, composed mainly of Duesenbergs and Fontenacs, to win the race at slightly over 100 miles per hour from the pole position. After eleven years of public education, he followed the example of his uncle Edwin Metzler, who participated at Indianapolis as a riding mechanic with Deacon Litz in 1936 and Russ Snowberger in 1937, and who in his later years devoted himself to preparing cars for the great race. In 1932 Metzler turned up at Syracuse, New York, to compete in a scheduled 100-mile AAA Indianapolis car race on the state fairgrounds dirt track known as the Moody Mile. The race ended because of rain on leader Bob Carey's eighty-first lap, but Metzler was too slow to participate. In 1935, in the midst of the Depression, George Metzler was twenty-three years of age, married, and determined by a combination of economic necessity and temperamental inclination, to try his luck racing automobiles. One week before he saw Kelly Petillo, later convicted and sentenced to a prison term after using a blade to attack a woman at Indianapolis's Hotel Roosevelt, set a new 500-mile record exceeding 115 miles an hour, Metzler persuaded a local car owner Dale Chastain to let him drive his big car on the half mile tracks of Indiana and Ohio. Lacking wheels and tires, Metzler appealed to his friend John Byrne, an Indianapolis machinist who stabled racing cars of his own, for a loan of needed parts until Metzler earned enough to replace them.

At least as far back as 1915 the International Motor Contest Association and the Central States Racing Association maintained a cluttered calendar of parsimoniously paying races, many of them staged on half mile dirt county fair tracks better suited to horse racing and tractor pulls. In that nomadic tradition, Metzler who had married and fathered a son, sought to improve his financial life with earnings by racing with a ragtag group under the direction of Dan Sheek, an eccentric tool and die making son of a Greenwood, Indiana country doctor who claimed to have delivered 1,500 babies. Dan Sheek's racing outfit was known as the MDTRA, the Midwest Dirt Track Racing Association, known more popularly as "The Kerosene Circuit," consisting of a large contingent of mostly Indiana men with a hell-fired penchant for throwing caution, and themselves, to the winds. Among their swelling number were such irrepressible roughnecks as Harry King, Carl Scarborough, Orville Epperly, Wayne Padgett, Hank Schlosser, Wayne "Speed" Wynn, Cliff Griffith, Norm Houser, Joe Ray, Eddie Zalucki, Bobby Grim, and Joie Chitwood. Nor did they all survive. Between 1938 and 1949 (allowing for the suspension of auto racing during the war years) the Midwest Dirt Track Racing Association killed off about a dozen of its members. Its racing confined itself to a radius not exceeding 125 miles from Indianapolis's Monument Circle, to places like Greenup and Paris, Illinois; and Rockville, Mitchell, Bloomington, Franklin, Columbus, Scottsburg, Logansport, Greenfield, Muncie, and Montpelier, Indiana. Arguably the worst of these bullrings, known to some as "The Track with 1001 Turns," was the notorious (if entertaining) Jungle Park, located a few miles north of Rockville, Indiana, near the Illinois state line. Jungle was a thorough-going nightmare. "Whoever laid out the track originally," wrote Jerry Miller of the Marion, Indiana, *Chronicle-Tribune,* "was either a comedian or a sadist. Just looking at the oblong half mile of hard brown dirt convinced you it was the devil's work. Every foot of the track was bad, first twisting up, then down, then to one side, with uneven, pitched turns at each end."

By December 7, 1941, George Metzler had divorced and remarried. His new bride was a quiet, red-headed Indianapolis girl named Marjorie. At the war's outbreak he was drafted into the United States Army where he survived over twenty months fighting the Japanese, and a bout with malaria. Returned to Indianapolis in 1945, he used an army cash bonus to rent an apartment for himself and his wife in an aging, two-story frame dwelling at 32 South Dearborn Street. Behind the apartment loomed the P. R. Mallory electric plant where, in spite of an overwhelming number of employment applications from other returned servicemen, he found work as a machinist. Metzler still felt the residual effects of malaria that prevented his immediate return to dirt track racing, but he managed to raise enough money to purchase a big car and hire Cliff Griffith to race it on the half-mile tracks. By the spring of 1946, however, Metzler registered with the American Automobile Association and competed in what was reputed to be the most demanding of all American racing circuits, the one the AAA organized in the middle west, with its most frequent ports of call at Dayton and New Bremen in Ohio, Winchester, and Fort Wayne (and later) Salem in Indiana. Predictably, he found the going difficult. The competition, then dominated by such short track warriors as Jackie Holmes, Spider Webb, Elbert Booker, and Johnny Shackleford, was as arduous as it was dangerous. But because the AAA was then the autocratic governing body for the Indianapolis 500, and would remain so until in 1955 the United States Auto Club succeeded it, Metzler had little choice other than to join the AAA party and become visible in its racing circles by demonstrating that if he could not win races he could at the very least worry the competition.

Dayton, Salem, and Winchester (only the latter two tracks survive) were the most terrifying of tracks, no less for the spectator than for the contestant, so much so that a certain contingent of seasoned drivers who, after all, made their livings and their reputations by going fast, would not have raced there under any inducement. All the tracks were paved (albeit Winchester's surface was such that one was never quite sure whether it was or not) half-mile steeply banked saucers, over which spindly open wheeled cars rocketed a squirrely path on narrow wire wheels at dizzying speeds with precious little protection for anyone on the premises. Winchester alone has claimed so many lives that historians have lost accurate count. Spider Webb remembered a conversation with George Metzler on a hot afternoon at Winchester in 1946. "Johnny DeCamp [another driver] had walked over to the infield at the bottom of the first turn to see how the other cars were running that Sunday afternoon. He hadn't been there long before Metzler came over to us and said that he hadn't too much experience on the high banks. Then he asked us what the best way to drive the track was. I just told him to put his foot down hard on the accelerator and hold on real tight. He nodded and walked back to the pits."

Affable Jack Dixon of Indianapolis had driven at Winchester in 1918, crashed, returned home on a freight train with his teeth knocked out, a thumb nearly severed, and his leg wickedly fractured. He had long since wisely abandoned driving in favor of car building. He and former Wilbur Shaw riding mechanic Fred "Skinny" Clemons, his partner since 1927, fielded cars in Illinois and Indiana, and for a time employed as their driver, English dental student Alfred Moss (grand prix racer father of Stirling Moss whose career ended in a near-fatal crash at Goodwood, England in 1962). Clemons Motors raced a car at Indianapolis called the Hoosier Pete Special with Rickliffe "Rick" Decker at the wheel in 1930. Dixon and Clemons built another car in 1941, but the war prevented their racing it. Clemons died in 1945. Dixon brought the car out of storage in the winter of 1946 with the intention of running and selling it at Indianapolis in 1947. In the meantime, there remained a short, six-race 1946 season, the final two races of which were scheduled at Milwaukee on September 22, and Goshen, New York, on October 6. Dixon accepted the recommendation of fellow car owner Harry Wade to hire Metzler as driver. At Milwaukee, Metzler qualified thirteenth in a skimpy fourteen car field and scored eleventh after hitting a wall on the fortieth of the race's 100 laps. At Goshen among an even skimpier field of ten, Metzler was fifth fastest and then hit another wall on lap fifty-nine and scored eighth.

Dixon submitted the $125 Indy 500 entry fee ($100 of which was to be refunded to the entrant by the Speedway if the car made a bona fide attempt at qualification) by the April 15, 1947, deadline. The Speedway's official entry blank pledged a total of $75,000 in prize money, with $20,000 to the winner and $10,000 to the second place finisher. Among the 1947 rules was a continuation of the long-standing proviso (prudently instituted in 1930) that "the Chief Steward [the person who, more than any other individual, supervises the conduct of the race] shall have the right to require drivers to prove their ability to drive on the Indianapolis Motor Speedway. These demonstrations," the supplementary regulations continued, "shall be for a distance of at least ten laps at each of the following speeds: 85, 95, 105, and 115 miles per hour."

The chief steward designated for the thirty-first running of the 500-mile race was articulate Tommy Milton, eight times a starter and twice (1921 and 1923) a winner at Indianapolis, who eventually took his own life in Mount Clemens, Michigan, in 1962. One of Milton's paramount concerns was the screening of rookie drivers in his own rookie year as chief steward. "The problem of educating drivers to make safely the jump from hotrods or midgets to major league racing," Milton wrote in one of his AAA post-race reports, "is both serious and difficult." Part of Milton's way of dealing with George Metzler and his fellow Indianapolis freshmen was to dispense with the stern lectures he described as "chalk talks," in favor of what he called "the personally conducted tour plan." The idea, said Milton, was to invite "four or five candidate drivers" to a passenger car tour of the track. The chauffeur was to be "a top flight driver whose Indianapolis record would engender respect and confidence."

Metzler and Dixon towed the unsponsored No. 55 car to Gasoline Alley and deposited it in garage twenty-four where, owing to Dixon's illness, Metzler single-handedly performed most of the mechanical work. He took his personally conducted tour with three other rookies. When the track opened on Thursday, May 1, he logged as few laps as possible for fear of damaging the only four-cylinder Clemons engine Dixon owned. Metzler began the ritual driver's test, successfully completing the 85, 95, and 105 phases without apparent difficulty. After one lap in the 115 range, however, dyspeptic sounds developed in the engine, meaning that Indianapolis 1947 had ended for Metzler and his motor.

Dixon and Metzler were still at the Indianapolis Motor Speedway when Mauri Rose won the 500-miler over his beleaguered teammate Bill Holland and collected the traditional Victory Lane kiss, delivered this time by Mrs. Horace Schmidlapp, more gracefully known as actress Carole Landis who, with some heartfelt reluctance, arrived in the city to bang drums for her most recent Hollywood epic, entitled *Out of the Blue*, with George Brent and Turhan Bey. On the second Sunday after Indianapolis, Metzler time-trialed at a slow 27.28 seconds over the high banked Dayton Speedway in his own No. 56 Fronty (Ford) powered car that he had rechristened the "Dixon Special." Feeling an obligation to redeem his inauspicious Indianapolis debut of the previous month, he was out to rescue what he perceived as his damaged reputation. Nobody in racing likes to look bad at Indianapolis. The skies over Dayton, Ohio, were heavily overcast when he grabbed a tow rope for the start of the first eight-lap heat race of the afternoon. Lined up with him were Spider Webb, George Connor, Norm Houser, and veteran campaigner Elbert "Grandpappy" Booker, the forty-five-year-old 1946 AAA midwestern big car champion who appeared to be not a day over seventy. Booker, who had made an unsuccessful attempt at Indianapolis in 1946, found employment at a place called Briggs Body Company in Detroit, and usually arrived at race tracks with his wife and three children. When starter Ken Fowler (retired from racing after his Indianapolis start in 1947) green flagged the first heat, Booker fell into place behind Metzler and began threading his way through noisy traffic. Moving alongside Metzler on lap six at the midpoint on the backstretch, the two brushed wheels, sending Booker's No. 34 Jewell Special into the guardrail. He sailed an estimated 100 feet through the air, finally coming to rest with his destroyed racing car on top of him. Booker died en route to St. Elizabeth's Hospital. There is a photograph of the overturned racing car, behind which is a small boy wearing a baseball cap, possibly eight or nine years old, dissolved in tears, viewing the wreckage. Unscathed, Metzler loaded his car back on its trailer and started back toward Indianapolis on Highway 40.

Racing people have always placed great value upon resilience, watching and waiting for one of their number to buckle back in a racing car after a serious accident. Metzler did not disappoint, and was behind the wheel of the same car a week later at Winchester where he won the fourth ten-lap heat race of the afternoon. Returned to Winchester again on August 10 and September 21, he placed out of the money on both occasions. Jack Dixon entered him in the final two events at the Springfield, Illinois, mile

The ill-fated George Metzler, a veteran of service in the South Pacific during World War II, wanted more than anything to drive at Indianapolis. He died there instead, in 1949. *Ed Hitze*

dirt track on September 28. On October 12 he was back at the Dayton track, placing eighth in the ten-car feature race of the afternoon. By that time, Jack Dixon had sold his car to Lee Glessner, a used car dealer and pinball czar from Wheeling, West Virginia. Glessner hired a mechanic named Bob Johnson whom he directed to remove the Clemons engine and replace it with a quite tired 270 cubic inch Meyer and Drake Offenhauser. At Springfield Metzler was flirting with the big leagues, racing against such immortals of American auto racing as Tony Bettenhausen, Ted Horn, Bill Holland, Rex Mays, George Connor, Paul Russo, Walt Brown, Myron Fohr, and Jackie Holmes. There he started sixteenth in an eighteen car field, and hung on until the car stopped running at fifty-five laps, relegating him to eleventh. Moving on to rain-delayed Arlington, Texas, they lasted twenty of the race's ninety-five laps, and salvaged twelfth among only fourteen starters. On December 18, Metzler's shop, containing his racing car and about $10,000 in machine tool equipment, went up in flames. He was uninsured.

In the spring of 1948 Glessner returned the $125 Speedway entry fee at the same time Metzler became the father of a second son. Short of money and help, Metzler again assumed responsibility for the car's preparation, but without success. Mechanical problems developed, and the car never took to the track. Glessner disposed of the car, brought Metzler to Wheeling, and set him to work repairing and selling used cars. He was to be accorded one final chance at Indianapolis in 1949.

The 1936 seventh-place finishing Shaw Gilmore Special—a two-seater that Wilbur Shaw had driven—returned to the Speedway five more times, finishing in the top ten on five occasions. He won the Indianapolis 500 with it in 1937 and brought it home second in 1938. Mauri Rose drove it to eighth in 1939, Billy DeVore was eighteenth in the car in 1940 (the year that Shaw became the first man to win back-to-back at the Speedway), and Frank Wearne was eighth in both 1941 and (when the car was owned by Tulsa's Ervin Wolfe) 1946. George Barringer was killed in the car on the first lap of the 1946 100-mile dirt track event at Lakewood Park in Atlanta, when a pileup also claimed the life of British-born 1946 Indianapolis winner George Robson. Paul Russo carried the car to twenty-eighth place at Indianapolis after crashing it on the main straightaway. The same car, with a new body provided by Pennsylvania dirt track driver Mark Light, was in the 1948 500, driven by Joie Chitwood and removed from the race on lap 138 with a leaking fuel tank that relegated Chitwood to seventeenth. After that it fell into the hands of Lee Glessner who purchased it for

George Metzler to drive at Indianapolis. Metzler enlisted his temporarily unemployed Uncle Edwin to serve as chief mechanic, while Metzler himself concentrated upon passing the elusive driver's test he failed in 1947. Soon after Glessner remitted the now-doubled ($250) entry fee to the Indianapolis Motor Speedway, Ed Metzler resigned before he began working. Missouri-born "Cotton" Henning—master mechanic and strategist who had four Indianapolis wins to his credit with Peter DePaolo in 1925 when they were the first to average over 100 miles an hour, Bill Cummings in 1934, and Wilbur Shaw in 1939 and 1940—had died the previous winter, leaving the three-car Maserati team owned by a group of mostly Indianapolis bankers calling themselves Indianapolis Race Cars, Incorporated, or I.R.C., in need of a manager and chief mechanic. Although Ed Metzler landed the assignment, problems between him and the I.R.C. organization developed as the stresses of May mounted and led to his departure. It was too late, however, for him to be much aid in readying his nephew's car for the 1949 race, and the burden of car preparation fell again upon George Metzler himself.

Uppermost in his mind was the driver's test. Putting as little stress on the frayed Meyer and Drake engine as possible, Metzler resumed testing on May 5, 1949, a Thursday. The 1949 rookie class at the Speedway was unusually abundant with talent. Norm Houser, Johnny McDowell, Tommy Mattson, Ralph Pratt, George Fonder, Kenny Eaton, Bayliss Levrett, and Dick Frazier all passed inspection, as did future Indianapolis winners Troy Ruttman (1952), Pat Flaherty (1956), and Jim Rathmann (1960). The remaining rookies encountered problems of various kinds. Byron Horne crashed on the south chute on the eighth lap of his 115 mile per hour test segment, and suffered injuries so extensive that Speedway physicians scarcely knew how to evaluate his condition, although he ultimately survived. Randall Beinke (sometimes spelled "Banky") failed to complete his test, as did midget car champion Leroy Warriner, Bill Taylor, Lindley Bothwell (remembered as an old man in a 1914 twin-seated Peugeot), and Frank Burany, another midget car specialist who late in life became a helicopter traffic reporter for WTMU in Milwaukee.

When Metzler's turn came a corps of experienced drivers took their places at various points around the race course to assess his every move on the track. Among his examiners were some of the most notable names then on the American racing scene: George Connor, Bill Cantrell the hydroplane racer, Billy DeVore, and the great Rex Mays. They were assisted by Lee Wallard (1951) and Sam Hanks (1957) who would one day win Indianapolis. Ike Welch, the chief observer, required Metzler to rerun the entire test he had begun in 1947. He eased the car through the 95 mile per hour portion, passed, and advanced the car to 105. Passed again. Metzler increased his lap times to 115 miles per hour, then turned a single lap at 119. Signaled back to the pit area, Metzler took the news from Welch (after minutes of muffled deliberation with his men) that he had passed the first ritual hurdle that an Indianapolis rookie must clear.

But Metzler had mouths to feed and bills to pay, making it necessary for him to race his big car over a few short tracks before running the Indianapolis 500. Time spent on the short tracks, however, was time spent away from the listless Glessner Special that would need to find another seven miles per hour to qualify for the race. On Sunday, May 8 he appeared at Winchester in the No. 25 Ray Beasley-owned Hal (so named after Dayton, Ohio's engine and cylinder head conversion developer Harry Hosterman). Turning the track at 23.175 seconds, Metzler was assigned to the third heat race of the afternoon, but retired after five of its eight laps were down. Back to Indianapolis.

Time was not in George Metzler's corner. Despite numerous adjustments to the Glessner car, it would not exceed the 119 mile per hour lap recorded during the driver testing program. The front end "pushed," meaning in racing parlance that the car resisted turning, and the engine balked. The rains came as they do so persistently during an Indiana May. Missing the opening day of qualification runs on Saturday, May 14, Metzler stood by himself in the grassy area inside the southwest turn as Duke Nalon posted a four-lap average of 132.939 in a screaming white eight-cylinder Novi Special to win the pole position for the thirty-third running of the Indianapolis 500, sharing the front row with sophomore Jack McGrath and Rex Mays, both of whom were killed on western mile dirt tracks on November sixth in different years. On Sunday the rains visited again, washing all track activity away. Weather was clear on Monday when Metzler returned to the track, but with no improvement in speed.

One more weekend for qualification rounds remained. When Saturday, May 21 arrived, the car was still not delivering sufficient speed. The next day was the final opportunity. Metzler had despaired of making the 1949 Indianapolis 500 starting field. Another AAA big car race, this one scheduled at Salem, was also scheduled for Sunday, May 22. Beasley and Metzler loaded their race car under a black Indiana sky and motored south toward Salem on State Route 31. Arrived at the track, Metzler made a qualification run of 24.97 seconds over the steeply banked saucer that had opened for business the previous year and managed to have its first fatal accident occur on the first turn of the first lap of the first race on the first day it scheduled races in 1948. Before the day ended, Metzler's earnings came to a grand total of $50: $15 for the heat race, and $35 for his participation in a consolation race for slower participants. Beasley waited at the Salem pay window for their money, and returned to find Metzler brooding in the front of his pickup truck. Back to Indianapolis they went.

By the time the pair reached Columbus, Indiana, where Metzler competed with the outlaw MDTRA group, rain began to fall on the truck's windshield. At Indianapolis, as they were shortly to discover, it had been raining sufficiently all day to rain time trials out for the second time that month. Tommy Milton issued an official AAA bulletin and had it posted in Gasoline Alley: Qualification runs would resume on Wednesday, May 25 and again on Saturday, May 28. Metzler had two more opportunities to make the race.

More discouragement. On Monday and Tuesday his speeds did not improve. Still no luck on Wednesday morning. He watched as other drivers attempted qualification runs. On Thursday he padlocked his Gasoline Alley Garage, threw some clothes in a bag and drove straight east to Wheeling, West Virginia, for an eleventh-hour conference with Glessner, who listened sympathetically to Metzler's description of how the engine was not pulling and how a new set of pistons might provide the seven or so miles per hour necessary to make the race. Glessner dispatched Metzler back to Indianapolis Friday morning with instructions to acquire the pistons from Meyer and Drake and install them overnight. He promised to be at the Speedway on the morning of Saturday, May 28 to lend what support he might toward Metzler's qualification run.

Metzler arrived at the track late on Friday afternoon after five hours on the road, bought four new pistons and took them to a grocery store in Speedway, Indiana where he weighed each one on a butcher's scale. At ten that evening his old friend Johnny Byrne looked in on Metzler's Gasoline Alley garage. "He had that car in a blue million pieces," Byrne recalled thirty years later. They were all over the garage floor. I mean *everywhere*. George told me that he had to get the pistons in by morning, that it was his last chance ever to run at Indianapolis. He said that if he didn't make the race this time, nobody would ever hire him to run there again. I thought he was a pretty decent mechanic, but he was working alone. I felt sorry for him. I finally went home to bed, but George kept working.

George Metzler got no sleep on the night of May 27, 1949. He had left at about 1:00 A.M. to commiserate with some night-owl friends over a round or two of beers at Mates White Front, an oft-times rowdy dive frequented by racing people on West Sixteenth Street near the southeast corner of the Speedway grounds, and then returned to the track to reassemble his engine. When he lowered the Meyer and Drake back inside car No. 67, it was 9:00 in the morning. An abundant crowd had by this time besieged the Speedway gates for this, the final day of qualification runs. Tommy Milton had decreed that the track should open at 10:00 A.M. for a final practice session prior to the end of qualifications for 1949. AAA observers were dispatched to their posts around the two-and-a-half-mile course. Down in the southwest turn, sitting before a green trackside observer's table situated between grandstands B and E, were Paul Johnson of Anderson, Indiana, and his companion Harold Murphy of Chicago. Both men, fitted out with radio communications, were in touch with other observation posts around the Indianapolis Motor Speedway. A prevailing wind from the northeast blew smoke from the Prest-O-Lite stack toward St. Joseph's Cemetery, and ruffled a printed directive from Milton that lay in front of Johnson, who secured it to the table with an empty Coca-Cola bottle. "Don't use the word *tire* in your reports," Milton's instructions read. "It may sound like *fire*."

The 500-mile race was a short two days away, and the final five positions in the great Memorial Day classic were still open as several cars took to the track for this final practice session. Bachelor rookie Bill Cantrell motored his No. 74 Kennedy Tank Special into the first turn, followed by Freddy Agabashian (replacing Hal Robson) in the I.R.C. Miller No. 15. Over in the infield a Hollywood crew busied itself gathering footage for Mickey Rooney's *The Big Wheel*, a United Artists auto racing picture to be released later that year, financed partly by prize fighter Jack Dempsey and directed by Edward Ludwig, although Rooney had made the film without ever visiting the Speedway. Cincinnati's heavyweight boxing champion Ezzard Charles roamed the pit and garage areas signing autographs. For Indianapolis television this was day one, as WFBM-TV broadcast some forty minutes of final Speedway qualifications, calling its program "Crucible of Speed."

For Metzler, the pressure was greater than ever. Not having slept in twenty-eight hours, he still had not found speed at Indianapolis. Under do-or-die conditions like these when racing at Indianapolis could mean the beginning—or the end—of a career in racing, drivers had been known to assume some extraordinary risks to make this, the most prestigious automobile race in the world. The Speedway was everything. To win Indianapolis was to attain sports immortality, comparable to winning the Kentucky Derby, the Super Bowl, the U.S. Open, or the World Heavyweight title. Furthermore, long shots had been known to win the Indianapolis 500. Jules Goux won as a rookie in 1913. So too did Rene Thomas (1914), Frank Lockhart (1926), George Souders (1927), and Louis Meyer (1928). Lee Glessner, just arrived from Wheeling, stood by in the pits as Metzler grimly donned his helmet, the same helmet he had worn on the half-mile big car dirt tracks. His freshened Meyer and Drake melodiously barked into life and warmed its oil for a minute and a half. Moving out of the pit lane slowly, Metzler guided the car low in the southwest turn to make room for other cars that were by this time building speed. He waved briefly to Murphy and Johnson. After three warmup laps he moved the Glessner car wider into the track's running groove, turning laps at 112, then 118, then 120. Glessner himself took charge of the pit chalk board. Other cars were turning the track faster. Levrett was running at 130 miles an hour, easily enough to qualify for the race. Veteran Chicago tough guy Emil Andres, looking toward his ninth Indianapolis start, was running in excess of 126. Other entrants had resorted to desperation tricks that were causing speeds to rise. Some had lowered their rear axle ratios for greater acceleration out of the turns. Others replaced carburetors with fuel injection systems that showed greater potential for hotter lap times. Metzler found his car lacking in straightaway speed, and was attempting to compensate by driving harder and deeper into the turns, especially the southwest where the nearly imperceptible dip caused him to lose control momentarily when he passed over it.

Paul Johnson glanced at his watch. It was 10:49.

On Saturday evening when qualifications were complete and the field filled for the running of the 1949 Indianapolis 500, Ike Welch wrote a summary report of the day's activities. Levrett, Cantrell, Agabashian, Andres, and Manuel Ayulo, the gentle Peruvian, had earned starting positions in that order. Welsh continued his report to the AAA Contest Board: "May 28th at 10:50 A.M. driver George Metzler lost control while passing hump in turn #1, headed toward the apron, over-corrected and struck wall twice, seriously injured, car wrecked badly."

The 1949 Oldsmobile Rocket 88 pace car had sped to the accident scene bearing an anxious contingent of American Automobile Association officialdom that included Milton, Welsh, and metallurgist Sol Silberman. Lee Glessner ran on foot to the southwest turn, followed by an ambulance and a gaggle of newspaper reporters and cameramen. At the accident site was Speedway superintendent Clarence Cagle and a safety patrolman. Metzler had hit with immense impact. Unconscious, he was lowered carefully upon a gurney and hurried to the infield hospital where Margorie Metzler waited. A wrecker towed the No. 67 Glessner Special, its front end flattened, and its body buckled as far back as the cockpit, back to the garage compound. Inside the Speedway pressroom, a reporter for the *Indianapolis Star* composed the Metzler story in time to make the Sunday morning deadline. "The grim battle for places in the field took its toll," he wrote. "Metzler took his car to the track a few minutes before qualification runs to nudge just a few more miles per hour out of it so he could go to the starting line later. The car skidded down into the dirt inside of the track and then darted up and almost head-on into the wall as Metzler fought for control."

At the track hospital Dr. E. Rogers Smith, an Indianapolis neurologist who was one of several physicians who treated Wilbur Shaw after his 1941 accident in close to the same place in the track and who would supervise the activities of some 237 physicians and nurses on race day, waited for Metzler's arrival. Despite his evaluation of Metzler's injuries (a crushed right chest, severe brain damage and probable ruptured spleen, Smith predicted "a fifty-fifty chance to recover" to *Star* reporters clustered in front of the hospital security gate after Metzler had been hurriedly transferred by ambulance to Indianapolis's midtown Methodist Hospital. Metzler's critical condition notwithstanding, the Sunday *Star* reported that "his injuries were not as serious as those of Byron Horne of Scenery Hill, Pa., who crashed a few hundred feet from the same spot on May 2 and is still in the hospital." In Gasoline Alley, morning talk centered upon a *Star* allegation that Metzler "had been riding without a safety belt," a theory that Glessner, who had seen his driver exit pit lane on his final run, denied. After the accident cleanup there followed two more turn one incidents. Jimmy Daywalt, a Teamsters organizer from Wabash, Indiana, spun in the same place that Metzler had, but gathered the car up. After that it was Henry Banks, fearing that he was about to be bumped for the 1949 race—which he was—who lost control, supposedly because he ran over debris left on the track from the Metzler mishap.

George Metzler remained unconscious and in critical condition on

Sunday, May 29, at Methodist. At the Speedway, Tommy Milton and Wilbur Shaw conducted the annual drivers' meeting, admonishing all thirty-
three contestants to exercise all possible caution on race day. Hydroplane
racer and perennial Indianapolis 500 enthusiast Guy Lombardo arrived
with his royal Canadians for a dance engagement at the Indiana Roof.
"Race fans from the East have been rolling in on Highway 40 in a steady
stream." wrote Wieland Brown of *Speed Age* magazine. Out on West Sixteenth Street, a sideshow featuring "Hitler's personal armored pleasure
car" drew the abundant pre-race crowd inside its tent. When darkness
descended on the Indianapolis Motor Speedway, Brown observed "pick-
pockets, prostitutes, professional gamblers, and other practitioners of
frowned-upon vices."

The Indianapolis dailies carried no report on Metzler on race day,
May 30. At 4:00 A.M., just at dawn's first light, an aerial bomb exploded
high in the atmosphere over the track, signaling the opening of public
gates, and rattling window panes all over Speedway City. Said Mark Murphy, a correspondent for *The New Yorker*, from his perch on the Chinese
pagoda that then stood at the starting line on the inside of the track, "The
scene was like one of those old photographs of the opening of the Cherokee strip." "The eleven gates to the track had been opened the instant the
bomb detonated, and through them poured a torrent of cars—clanking
wrecks, brand new machines, trucks, and midget foreign makes. They
roared into the infield, churning up a vast cloud of dust, blowing their
horns, and in general raising a clangor that was indescribable." Crews
pushed thirty-three cars into position prior to the playing of "Taps," and
then Metropolitan Opera singer James Melton began his rendering of
"Back Home Again in Indiana," a melancholy pastoral originally called
simply "Indiana," once an upbeat number composed in 1917 by James F.
Hanley, with lyrics by Ballard McDonald, now rendered as a nostalgically
lachrymose anthem. A third of the 1949 starters were rookies. By day's
end, forty-one-year-old Bill Holland, the roller-skating-rink proprietor
from Reading, Pennsylvania, would glide his car into Victory Lane and
collect $51,575 in first-place money after having taken the lead at the 150-
mile mark in a Blue Crown Spark Plug Special.

Metzler died on Friday, June 3 at 1:22 A.M. His funeral commenced
the following Monday at the G. H. Herrman Funeral Home and continued
to St. Catherine Church where a priest averred that because Metzler had
devoted his life only to pleasure, he had reaped the penalty. The priest did
not accompany the funeral party to St. Joseph's Cemetery where Metzler

was buried in a No. 30 Monarch Vault in lot seventeen. One of the pallbearers was fellow driver Cliff Griffith. On Thursday, June 23, Carroll F. Durrell of the AAA Contest board disbursed a $1,500 death benefit claim check to Marjorie E. Metzler at 32 South Dearborn, Indianapolis, Indiana.

To be sure, George Metzler was neither the first nor the last casualty of the southwest turn, although he was assuredly one of the lesser known. Others were to follow in his wake. In 1953, for example, fifty-three-year-old Chet Miller, who had vaulted the wall there in 1934, died in the same turn when he lost control of one of the ill-fated Novi Specials. He had been an enormously popular, greying senior driver at Indianapolis and the proprietor of an upholstery shop in Glendale, California. He drove sixteen Indianapolis races, the first of which was in 1930, and at the moment of his death he found himself in the same kind of fix that Metzler experienced: sliding low on the track, seeming to over-correct, and catching the wall almost head-on. The track closed in his memory during his May 19 funeral, after which Speedway activity resumed with its customary high volume, full force.

On May 9, 1953, Metzler's comrade, Cliff Griffith (born Clifton Reign Griffith at Nineveh, Indiana, in 1916) who as an Indianapolis newspaper-delivering kid used to sneak into the Speedway, lost control of his No. 24 Ed Walsh–entered black Bardahl roadster, slapped the wall twice on the exit of turn one and exploded in flames that reached fifty feet. Having just posed for some publicity photographs, Griffith was wearing street clothing at the time. After workers loaded him into an ambulance, he was nearly dumped onto West Sixteenth Street when the driver turned left out of the Speedway and the back ambulance door swung open. Griffith spent weeks in Methodist lying mostly naked, his legs encased in what appeared to be loose cellophane wrappers. "I prayed to die," the decorated Indiana military flier, short track racer, and 1934 graduate of Indianapolis's Arsenal Technical High School remembered later. Griffith had been an employee at the P. R. Mallory Company in 1937, and after hours prepared a single cam Chevrolet-powered big car for co-worker George Metzler, whom he accompanied to the Salem, Indiana, fairgrounds. He borrowed Metzler's helmet and drove the car himself, thereafter becoming a midwestern "outlaw" driver of some repute.

Hefty Paul Russo, donning a helmet that looked for all the world like a mixing bowl, was leading the 1956 race in his red Novi when it blew a tire and plowed, full hammer, straight in to the southwest's wall, causing what appeared to be a large flash explosion on lap twenty-one. Russo then popped out and ran to the infield. Bobby Unser, incidentally, would do much the same thing on lap two of the 1963 race with another Novi. Russo, interviewed over the public address system, attributed his safety to a religious medal given him by a priest. In Russo's wake, Troy Ruttman spun into what has been described as "a Peony bed" on the inside of the southwest. Then on lap 160, Tony Bettenhausen slammed into the southwest wall, breaking his collarbone. The eighth of thirteen children, Paul Russo's brother Joe was a five-time starter at Indianapolis who died at the circular Langhorne, Pennsylvania, mile dirt track in 1934. Paul Russo, who had done most things in racing except win the Indianapolis 500, had ridden next to George Barringer at Roby, Indiana's oiled mile dirt track, and taken up racing on his own at the age of eighteen in 1932. He won the eastern AAA championship in 1939, and in 1940 raced at Indianapolis for the first of his fourteen runs. A Kenosha, Wisconsin, friend called on Russo one sweltering summer day, to discover that Russo had removed everything from his refrigerator backed himself inside, and lowered the temperature. Cool to the end, Russo died of heart failure on board a yacht off the coast of Clearwater, Florida, on February 13, 1976.

With only two minutes of practice time remaining on the eve of time trials in 1955 (the year after Tony Hulman assumed the presidency of the Indianapolis Motor Speedway following the death of Wilbur Shaw), four-time race veteran and post-war California track roadster and midget car standout Manuel Leaonedas "Manny" Ayulo, the mechanic and driver of Peter Schmidt's bright red No. 88 Kurtis 500C roadster, drove headlong into the wall in the southwest turn where witnesses reported that he appeared to be tugging at the wheel moments before the crash. The same Johnny Byrne who looked in on George Metzler on the evening prior to Metzler's fatal accident also had looked in on Ayulo. "I found Manny doing about the same things that I found George doing," he reported. "There were parts all over the garage floor. It was an unholy mess in there. Manny was getting ready to put his engine back together, and like George, he didn't seem to have anybody helping him. The next day, he was dead." An investigation of the wreckage revealed that a broken axle and a pin jarred lose from a steering arm. When help arrived, someone discovered Ayulo's pockets still bulging with wrenches. Nor was he wearing a seat belt at the time of the collision. Ayulo, the balding five-foot-eight-inch son of Don Manuel Ayulo, a wealthy and aristocratic Peruvian consul, had been raised with a governess, traveled much of the world in style as a child, graduated from Hollywood High School, and (with the customary racing driver's passion for airplanes) entered the Air Force Academy as well. An anonymous newspaper writer declared that "as the drivers line up before the pace car on Memorial Day, Manuel Ayulo will be with them, as he would have wanted to be. Now he is part of the imperishable tradition of the classic." Priests conducted Ayulo's second funeral (the first was in Speedway City) at the San Fernando Mission Cemetery with a representative of the Peruvian government in attendance. "Manny was such a quiet, retiring, unassuming sort of fellow off the track," wrote *Star* sports columnist Jep Cadou, Jr., "that he didn't get the wide publicity the more talkative and showmanlike drivers received." Within a month, Cadou married Ayulo's widow. The union lasted eleven years.

Norman Hall, a graduate of post-war midget cars on the Pacific Coast who drove at Indianapolis in 1961 (when he was roommate of winner A. J. Foyt) did not have an easy time of it at Indianapolis in 1962 when he wrecked two cars. The first of them was the Dean Autolite machine in the northeast turn; the second was the No. 41 Bill Forbes car that Hall managed to loop in the southwest on May 13, crunching the cement backwards and emerging with a broken left leg, a possible skull fracture, and other severe injuries. In 1965 at the Indianapolis Raceway Park road race, Hall overturned and required a foot to be amputated. Having driven no more since 1967, he died in 1992 of cancer. Another Indianapolis two-time runner, 145-pound Charles Rodeghier was an ex-Marine from Blue Island, Illinois, who moved his wife Janet (who playfully referred to her husband as "the Dago") and two sons aged five and six to a home with a small race shop in the rear, close to the old Speedway High School. He called himself "Chuck Rodee" after he began racing in 1948. Always on the fringes of big time racing, the contentious Rodee nevertheless became, indoors and out, one of the nation's leading midget car drivers who, incredibly, wheeled one of the small cars over the sands of Daytona Beach at 134 miles per hour. At Indianapolis in 1966, however, he misnegotiated his No. 92 Leader Card Special, spun and connected backwards with the whitewashed wall in the southwest turn, making him among other things, the first qualification fatality since Stubby Stubblefield who died in almost that precise spot in 1935. Rodee swallowed a denture that closed his windpipe. It was later decreed that no removable dental appliances could be worn by a driver at speed. In 1968 more drama unfolded in the southwest. On Tuesday, May 7, British driver Mike Spence, while testing a Colin Chapman-designed turbine car for his teammate Greg Weld, had difficulty with its behavior, lost control with forty-seven minutes of track time still available, and struck the wall with enough force to shear off two wheels and cause his helmet to come off. News of Spence's death came later that evening. Said a distraught Chapman in a press release, "I am filled with grief at the loss of my long-time friend and associate, Jimmy Clark [the 1965 Indianapolis winner who was killed at Hockenheim, Germany, on April 7 of that year] and the additional loss just a month later to the day, of Mike Spence. As an understandable result, I want nothing more to do with the 1968 Indianapolis race. I just do not have the heart for it."

Sunday, May 26, 1968, was to have been the final qualification session for that year's race, until May rains that persisted for twenty-three days interfered, necessitating a continuation the next morning, during which anyone with a car in line on Sunday was to receive one final attempt. Among those drivers eligible was Bob Hurt, the handsome Potomac, Maryland, driver who as a kid in Champaign, Illinois, was a high jumper and basketball player who at nineteen turned to driving stock cars. In 1962 Hurt had driven a Ferrari he owned to victory in the Puerto Rican Grand Prix. In 1963 he took to driving USAC stock cars. Hurt came to Indianapolis in 1967, passed his rookie test, but made no qualification attempt. On this day the track, that some witnesses claim was still damp, had been open nine minutes when Hurt slammed the southwest wall in the No. 14 Quaker State Special entered by the Caves Buick Company, that had originally listed husky Chuck Hulse as its driver. Hurt too had entered another car, the Jack Adams turbine, that he saw fit to abandon. Immediately upon impact the Quaker State car ignited for a few moments and then extinguished on its own. The next racing car on the scene was driven by another native Illinois driver named Arnie Knepper who spun his Bryant Heating and Cooling Special to avoid colliding with Hurt. By the time Hurt reached the infield care facility, it appeared that, like Wilbur Shaw who crashed at the same place in 1941, he was paralyzed from the neck down. Shaw had regained the use of his arms and legs. Hurt, whose neck was broken, never did. Instead, he remained at Methodist for two months and then transferred to New York's Rusk Center Institute of Rehabilitation, after which he passed the next thirty-two years doing what he could to stay alive by visiting experimental clinics in Russia and Sweden. Bob Hurt, who still revisited Indianapolis when he could, saw his weight plummet from 180 pounds to 140, living most of his last years at Daytona Beach where he needed constant attention for his needs, developed prostate cancer, and worked on a book. One visitor found him unattended there after a care worker abruptly disappeared. Hurt had not eaten in twelve hours. He died alone on Wednesday, September 23, 2000 in a Toronto hotel room while a hospital outpatient.

After Carl Williams bumped the wall on the second (southeast) turn on his 163rd lap of the 1968 race, his Sheratan Thompson Special rolled to a stop in a burst of flame. Williams was uninjured, but finally killed himself in a February 1973 motorcycle mishap. In the meantime, Joe Leonard (who initially created a reputation for himself by winning motorcycle races), at the wheel of another Colin Chapman screaming red four-wheel-drive STP turbine car, was in front and showed every indication of remaining so. Pat Vidan, the body builder and starter, then displayed the yellow caution flag while the wreckage of Williams's car was cleared from the course. As Leonard passed the starting line on his 190th of 200 circuits, Vidan reached for his green flag to resume competition on the next go-around, while STP public relations man David Blackmer located Leonard's wife Diana in the terrace tower grandstand and began to usher her toward Victory Lane in anticipation of her husband's winning the race. But as the green flew at the beginning of Leonard's 192nd tour, the turbine's fuel pump stopped pumping and the car lost power. Leonard raised his hand to signal drivers behind him that he was losing speed. He then stopped on the lawn in the southwest turn. "It's unbelievable!" wrote an unidentified newspaper man. "The stands go crazy, everyone goes wild as Leonard limps down to the infield in the first turn and off onto the grass just a few feet from Victory Lane. Blackmer and Mrs. Leonard stop at the pit gate, turn around, and walk slowly back. Leonard sits motionless in the car for several moments before climbing slowly out."

Michigan's Gordon Johncock, the 1973 winner, had the misfortune to repeat Leonard's act in the 1977 race. Leading in still another STP-sponsored car at 184 laps, Johncock also came to an unanticipated halt in the southwest when a faulty valve spring caused his George Bignotti–prepared Patrick DGS Wildcat to shrink from first to eleventh in the final race scoring. Exhausted from stress and intense heat, Johncock lifted himself gradually, sat on the car's sidepod momentarily, then teetered thirty feet toward Ditch Creek, otherwise known as Dry Run Creek, that flows into the Speedway beneath the entrance to turn one and back out again at its exit, where he anointed himself in the muddy waters of defeat as A. J. Foyt streaked past to a then-unprecedented fourth Indianapolis win. Johncock's 1973 triumph, however, was overshadowed by three deaths, wretched weather, and aborted starts and restarts. Late-blooming Art Pollard, the strapping forty-six-year-old Medford, Oregon, driver who did not begin racing until the age of twenty-eight and did not arrive with a suitcase at Indianapolis until he was forty, died there on Saturday, May 12, when he struck the cement upon exiting the southwest turn in his Cobre Eagle Offenhauser. According to Speedway records, Pollard's car clobbered the wall on its right side, executed a half spin into the grass in the south chute between turns one and two, and after a series of rollovers stopped upright in turn two after having slid an estimated 1,450 feet. The car's aerodynamic wings were torn off, as were two of its wheels. Pollard, whose previous lap had been in the 191 mile an hour range, was dead at the scene. Other drivers had their turn one problems that May, as well. Dick Simon faltered there on May 9 when he slid for 320 feet, connected with the wall, and continued for 100 more feet without injury. Joe Leonard also got out of control there on May 11, setting the car in a half spin without confronting anything solid.

Indianapolis 1973 was a thoroughgoing disaster for everyone with the possible exception of Johncock. Instead of being the toast of the town after winning the Indianapolis 500, he took his dinner, such as it was, at a 16th Street fast food drive-in. At the outset of what was to have been the race on Monday, May 28, an aborted start injured eleven spectators (nine of whom required hospitalization) on the outside of the main straightaway, severely burned driver David "Salt" Walther (whose car had taken to the air for about 120 feet), and damaged eleven of the twelve cars involved. The rains fell for the balance of the day. On Tuesday, with all cars except Walther's back on track and prepared to take the green flag, rain fell again. On Wednesday rain descended once more, but the race began shortly after two o'clock, then stopped for an hour and a quarter to deal with an ultimately fatal accident involving California's handsome David Earl "Swede" Savage in turn four. In the meantime, Armando Teran, an STP crewman, was fatally injured on the pit lane after being struck by a fire truck driving in the wrong (clockwise) direction. Johncock stopped his car near the Savage accident and was walking toward it when Foyt stopped him and advised him to go no further. Mercifully, rain fell again, and the race was declared over at 133 of a scheduled 200 laps. As a rule of thumb, races may be declared ended if they have exceeded 51 percent completion. By this time Indianapolis health authorities were threatening that unless three reeking days of accumulated spectator offal were removed, the race would be terminated.

Drivers Lee Brayton and Tom Bigelow tangled in a frightening incident in the southwest without injury during a pre-race testing session on

Tuesday, May 7, 1974. Brayton careened into the turn-one cement while airborne. Both cars suffered extensive damage. Leon Duray "Jigger" Sirois, named after eight time Indianapolis contestant Leon Duray (whose real name was George Stewart), and after John "Jigger" Johnson who rode with Indy winners Louie Schneider (1931) and Wilbur Shaw (1937), crashed there in 1975 when his car appeared to jump out from under him, causing him to execute a full spin and contact the outside wall with his right rear wheel. Duane "Pancho" Carter began to get wiggly in the southwest turn during the so called pre-race "Carburetion Day" (modern Indianapolis cars use no carburetors) tests, bopped the wall, slid off the track, struck a drainage pipe, and then a fire truck. This transpired on the Thursday before Sunday's race. His crew repaired the heavily damaged machine that Carter brought home fourth. Mike Hiss had difficulty in that same parcel of track while attempting a qualification run in 1976, sliding 400 feet backwards after problems in the southwest. Neither he nor the car participated that year in the race. More harrowing, however, was a particularly eventful ride taken by a person named Eddie Miller, a 1976 rookie whose Thermo-King Eagle appeared to have entered the southwest too high. It should be noted, however, that although there is always an orthodox running groove well delineated at Indianapolis by a streak of rubber on the asphalt surface. Even so, not all drivers customarily use the same entry and exit points. That said, Miller was not able to pull off having driven into the first turn on the high side during his driver's test, spun through the short south chute, plowed into a drainage ditch, hopped and rolled over two barriers, and up-ended not far from some spectator bleachers. Miller came out of this battering with a broken back, but the car was a write off.

Historians remember 1977 as a year of firsts. A. J. Foyt became the track's first four-time winner. Tom Sneva became the first man to turn a lap at over 200 miles per hour. Janet Guthrie became the first woman to compete in the Indianapolis 500. But on October 27, 1977, Anton Hulman died after thirty-two years of stewardship at the Speedway, leaving his widow Mary Fendrich Hulman as chairman of the board, and business associate Joseph Cloutier—who began working for the Hulman family in 1926 in its wholesale grocery business that manufactured Clabber Girl baking powder—as president. Said Cloutier later in an interview with *Indy Car Racing* magazine, "At 210 miles an hour out there on that track, and that thing starts sideways, you've got a problem. You've got a big problem, and what happens isn't in your hands. Somebody else up there is taking care of you from then on.'' Tom Bigelow, the generally low-key Wisconsinite who tangled with Lee Brayton in the first corner in 1974, became twitchy in that same place on May 14, 1977, a Saturday, fell into a 260-foot half-spin, veered toward the wall without actually contacting it, then slipped another 220 feet. Four hours later Steve Krisiloff did much the same thing, except that he hit the concrete with considerable right-side damage. Both drivers were examined and released from the infield infirmary. The following Tuesday, Dick Simon went out of control about 460 feet before he hit the southwest in mid turn, and continued along that wall another 1,180 feet until the car came to a stop in turn two. A medical exam revealed that Simon had received contusions to his chest and shoulder. Drivers by this time had learned that if they were going to hit a wall, they might at least make it less costly by hugging it, so to limit car damage to one, rather than both sides. They might also, for good measure, attempt to withdraw their feet from the pedals, hoping to avoid what was becoming a rash of broken legs, ankles, and feet. Witnessing Simon's accident from a suite in turn two, perennial car owner J. C. Agajanian shook his head in dismay, commenting that Simon and his car owner Rolla Vollstedt were on a limited budget, and therefore all the more unfortunate for the accident.

Minnesota's dirt tracking Roger Rager felt the southwest turn seem to disappear under him while running his rookie test in 1978. Rather than entering the turn too high, he appeared to have gone in too low. Although he slipped and slid 600 feet, he managed to hit nothing. Anything is possible at Indianapolis. Rager, to his eternal credit, was the endlessly resourceful guy who led two laps of the 1980 race with a car called the Advance Clean Sweep Special powered by a castoff school bus motor with 70,000 miles on it that Rager discovered while foraging through a junkyard. Had Eddie Rickenbacker been alive, he would have applauded Rager's amazing ingenuity. Rager reported years later that the car was to be found in Washington state where its owner had transformed it into a flower pot. None other than Bobby Unser, with sixteen 500s including two wins to his credit by 1978, misnegotiated the course through the southwest, caught the wall in the car's right rear corner, but kept on rolling. Wisconsin's Billy Engelhart crashed twice in 1979, the second mishap coming in the south chute where he had to be hauled away with a broken leg, the worst driver injury that year.

Others had miserable luck a year later in 1980. On Monday, May 14, Tom Sneva evidently ran over something that caused him to blow a front tire, fall into a 420-foot slide, and follow the southwest turn wall for some

230 feet in a car that had been qualified to participate in the race. The roller, however, was too mangled to repair, obliging Sneva to start thirty-third in a backup car. In one of the more remarkable drives in Speedway history, Sneva charged to second place behind winner Johnny Rutherford. During the race Dick Ferguson and Bill Whittington were involved in an accident out of the southwest turn that appeared nastier than it was, albeit Whittington broke a leg, Ferguson a toe. Eleven laps later Danny "Spike" Gehlhausen, in an effort to avoid some bunched traffic, found himself out of the groove and into the "gray" (mostly unused) parts of the track in turn one, where he clobbered the wall in a cloud of smoke and debris. But it wasn't over: on circuit 131 Jerry Sneva followed suit by spinning around and smacking the wall in the southwest with the right side of his Lola Cosworth.

Billy Engelhart lost his Beaudoin Racing McLaren Cosworth in the southwest on the 7th of May in 1980, socking the fence with both his right front and right rear, managing, at least, not to break another leg. On May 9, the same turn gathered up tennis pro John Mahler and Jim Buick the Berthoud, Colorado, airline pilot, when the latter spun to avoid spearing the former. Turn one claimed both playboy Tim Richmond and amply bearded Sicilian-American Phil Caliva on the 12th of May in 1981. Richmond and his Penske Cosworth made it through alive, and Caliva held on with white knuckles while his McLaren Chevy not only smashed the wall, but straddled it for an estimated 160 feet. Rescuers saw fit to filet the car to free the driver. Dirt tracker Steve Kinser was particularly spectacular, if not in an orthodox way, through the southwest on May 15 when he reportedly entered the corner on the low side, executed a half spin, slipped 600 feet, crunched the wall with the left side of his car, slid another 160 feet, banged the wall once more, then rolled to a stop in the turn two lawn. Just at that moment a person approached Kinser's disarmingly comical cousin Sheldon, another entered driver that year, and asked the whereabouts of his kinsman Steve. "At this moment," Sheldon replied with the straightest of faces, pointing toward turn two, "his office is over there." Two days later Gehlhausen and Rick Mears's brother Roger both lost it as they exited the southwest within half an hour of each other. Neither hit anything of consequence. Once the 1981 race was underway, certain notable dropouts (among them Mike Mosley, Tom Sneva, Tom Bigelow, and Scott Brayton) opted to parallel park their steeds on the first turn lawn before bailing out and heading to the showers.

Elder statesman Ken Hamilton who, though he never competed at

Indianapolis at least saw his son Davy do so a half dozen times, was bitten by the southwest in practice May 13, 1982 when he approached it on the low side, slipped and slid 300 feet, mowed the lawn (as they say), righted the car up, and motored on around the track looking for all the world as if nothing had happened. A more potentially serious interlude was Jim Hickman's mishap exiting the southwest on May 14 when he spun one and a half times, darted 820 feet across the track, careened into an inside steel retaining barrier, and stopped against the wall in turn two. A former Navy pilot, Hickman, both a rancher and owner of purportedly the largest Datsun (now Nissan) dealership in America, did manage to start the race and finished a creditable seventh, earning Rookie of the Year honors. He was killed at Milwaukee, also in the first turn, on the 1st of August that year, becoming the newly formed sanctioning body Championship Auto Racing Teams's first driver fatality.

It was not over quite yet in the southwest that year. Tom Bigelow, who had previously had difficulties there, managed to confront no obstacles when he exited turn one too high (according to observers) on May 16, cut a three-quarter spin, and came to a stop after 380 more feet. Female driver Desiré Wilson encountered some problems there three days hence when she lost it coming out of the southwest, looped one and a half times, stopped on the lawn, and found herself without a car to drive, inasmuch as for the race she was replaced by Johnny Parsons, son of the 1950 winner, who promptly spun the car close to the same place. On the 20th it was time for John Mahler's next turn one adventure. This time he slithered across the track 480 feet, spun around once, left his signature on the whitewash, traveled another 640, looped once more, and parked the car low in turn two.

Johnny Rutherford, a more than ordinarily determined Texan with nineteen Indianapolis races and three wins, suffered a bruised ankle and heel as well as a puncture wound to his right leg when in practice he slapped the wall in the southeast in 1983, causing him to miss the race except as a spectator. But wall hits at the Speedway have always, and always will, alter some of the more determined plans to conquer the track. Jerry Sneva, low-key younger brother of 1983 winner Tom Sneva, slammed the cement quite hard on May 10, 1983, reported to the infield care center where he was evaluated and released, after which he never again returned to drive after having competed there five times. Of greater seriousness was the John Paul, Jr. collision in the southwest three days later when the car became "loose" (i.e. its rear end slid around to meet its front end), and snockered the wall twice before coming to a stop on the grass between turns one and two. A medical report said that Paul had sustained "chin lacerations, leg injuries" including a "severe fracture of [his] left ankle" that would send him into surgery at Methodist Hospital, albeit the report listed the patient's over-all condition as "good." Still worse was the Pete Halsmer accident in turn one about an hour and a half later that entailed what the track report called a "nearly head-on" wall hit that left Halsmer with a "partial collapsed left lung" as well as a cut left leg. His condition, said medical authorities, was "satisfactory." The southwest's next victim was Douglas Wayne Heveron, a twenty-two-year-old bachelor from Liverpool, New York, who on May 20 found himself in a half loop that sent him into the wall, into the grass, and into Methodist for treatment of a broken left ankle. During the 1983 race Parsons, who had taken over Halsmer's car, began to get what racing people sometimes call "wormy" or "squirrelly" in the southwest, traded ends, and took circumspect Mario Andretti with him. Parsons struck the wall from the back, Andretti from the front. Parsons diplomatically assumed responsibility for the accident. Neither driver was injured.

Turn one, like Homer's Cyclops Polyphemus, ate a flock of cars in 1984, swallowed them like so many pretzels, and belched them up again. This grizzly process commenced with Halsmer who, on May 7, reportedly drove too high through that same snake-bitten piece of real estate that had bitten him a year earlier, knocked twice into the same concrete, and did not bring the car to book until he was in front of the suites located just past turn two. Then it was Jerry Sneva, another repeat wall smacker, this time costing him a two inch cut on his left shin and a badly damaged car. It was Steve Krisiloff who received more attention when he got out of shape entering the southwest, ramming the cement hard enough to be heard as a dull *thud* in the crowded cubicles of Gasoline Alley. One report claimed the force of the crash was nearly enough to push the engine into the cockpit. Pieces of shrapnel, nevertheless, hurled over the outside fencing. Krisiloff was coptered to Methodist with a broken left leg. A little over three hours later Michigan's Scott Brayton touched the wall upon exiting turn one, spun, and stopped on the track apron. Next into the wall was Steve Chassey, the Brockton, Massachusetts, native and Vietnam veteran, who on Saturday, May 19, engaged the wall with the left side of his car, and was also coptered off to Methodist like so many wounded before him. A little less than two hours later it was Jerry Karl's turn to spin and destroy his car, after which a man named Chuck Ciprich, in real life a Con-Rail electrician who had attended high school in Watkins Glen, New York, had his Indy problems. He, like untold others, seemed to lose control heading into the southwest and then propelled into the wall like a dart to a dartboard. Ciprich received treatment and went quietly on his way. Then on race day Gehlhausen lost it again in the southwest, this time on lap forty-five.

Danny Sullivan's famous 1985 "spin and win" 360-degree merry-go-round began when he came out of turn one on his 120th lap after which he tamed the car and drove straight as a hornet to Victory Lane eighty laps later. Other people spun moving into and out of turn one in 1985, but they did not win. Richard Vogler, destined to die while leading a 1990 sprint car race at Salem, Indiana, became quite sideways in the southwest on lap 119 directly in front of feisty Howard Samuel "Howdy" Holmes (who from his father Howard Sumner Holmes inherited control over Michigan's Chelsea Milling Company, renowned for its Jiffy muffin mixes, buttermilk pancakes, and waffles) and then banged the wall on the right side. On the scene arrived Tom Sneva who also spun and hit the wall hard enough to dislodge a wheel. Mario Andretti and Sullivan managed to pass the incident by driving low on the track and finished the day in the first two positions. It was all in a fun day's work.

Enigmatic former tire buster Danny Ongais had the honor of attempting to bust the turn one wall on May 6, 1986, managing to ding his car on all four corners. Robin Miller, the comical, much maligned Indianapolis newspaper journalist who was nearly pilloried for his editorial opinions, aptly wrote of Ongais, "For six years in the late 70s and early 80s nobody was faster or braver. His nicknames were 'On The Gas' and 'Flyin' Hawaiian.' His car was black and so was his mood on most days. He was as hard to quote as he was to pass. In ten years of driving Indy cars, he won six times, led 1,073 laps, and tied Tom Sneva for the most career concussions." True enough. Ongais advanced from motorcycles to drag racing and amateur road racing before he joined ranks with Goodyear's racing division with which he was assigned to the hard labor of mounting tires. On the same day as Ongais's wallwhack, Wisconsin driver Herm Johnson fractured his spine and both feet after parts of his new March Cosworth bodywork appeared to come undone near the same place Ongais hit. Authorities at Methodist estimated his condition initially as "stable, alert and awake." Johnny Parsons, all too well acquainted with Indy's walls, and they with him, hit again while exiting the southwest. Before the sun set, recent arrival Jim Crawford, emitting a huge trail of white tire smoke, whirled around twice in turn one, and consorted with the concrete with the car's right rear.

All these collisions were costly in the extreme, but never so much as in 1987 when Kevin Cogan, who said that he slipped in some unidentified fluid, went pellmell in the southwest's dreaded fence on May 6. Derek Daly slipped as well, heighho into the fencing hard enough to crack a right front wheel. Tom Sneva rapped the turn one cement on both May 8 and 10. On the first occasion he claimed that the car did not bother to so much as turn left when it should have, but instead went straight into oblivion, both outside wheels loose in mid-air, with the car emerging (to cite one observer) as "shredded wheat." That transpired on a Friday. Sneva prudently took a much deserved day's leisure, then returned to the race course on Sunday morning and proceeded, yes, to do it again: pop out of the orthodox running groove and move, as if pulled by some unseen but still inexorable magnet, into a savage wall crunch with sufficient brute force to rip and twist every body part on the racing car. It was anything but a pretty picture. Sneva reacted with puzzlement, a tempered dismay such as a laboratory researcher might display when an experiment goes awry. Nor was he the lone double hitter in the southwest. Phillip Eugene Krueger, who allowed that if he were not driving race cars his ambition was to pilot aircraft, followed suit. He was indeed a pilot, both in racing cars and in airplanes. A companion of his had thumbed a plane ride from Indianapolis to Milwaukee where there was a race scheduled, and was astonished that Krueger apparently filled his tank with precisely enough fuel to fly from point to point, without so much as a liter in reserve. After they touched down, the tank, if it was not dry, was perilously close to it. So it was on May 8 that Krueger veered a tad on the high side after exiting the southwest, ticking the wall with his right rear tire. That was enough encouragement to send him heading rapidly for the infield where he managed to exercise some control and sped on around the course. Nine days later he drove low but not slow through the southwest whereupon he (in the words of an IMS press release) "hit the outside wall, slid along the track to the infield grass and hit the wall with a half-spin (800 feet), then spun three and a half times and came to a stop," after which "Krueger was released after examination of abrasions on both knees."

Back on May 9 was Jim Crawford providing extreme excitement in the first corner during a qualification attempt when he entered the infamous left turn at a rate of speed that many felt to be excessive, pasted the outer wall, and suffered dislocations and breaks of both ankles as well as

Wisconsin native Phil Krueger caught the Indianapolis cement in this 1981 incident. Eight years later, in less than the best racing equipment, he finished eighth. *John Mahoney*

a broken right shin. He was operated upon later that Saturday afternoon. Having missed the race in 1987, Crawford participated in the next six Indianapolis 500s. On May 10, Gary Bettenhausen, oldest son of the famous Melvin "Tony" Bettenhausen who was killed on Indy's main straightaway in May 1961, lost control upon exiting the southwest and parked in the lawn without contacting anything substantial. Johnny Parsons, who had problems back on the 6th of May in the southwest, had another incident there on the 14th when he too pasted the wall and paid for it with breaks in his left heel and right ankle. Unable to walk and having no better place to recuperate, Parsons accepted the hospitality of Father Glen O'Connor, a perennial and rapid wheel-changing priest and pit man at Indianapolis. Father Glen, as he is known in Gasoline Alley, took his injured friend to St. Neri's Parish where for subsequent swelteringly hot weeks Parsons, his lower extremities ridden with surgical stitches and orthopedic pins, received guests in the parish house where he became another man who came to dinner and remained for quite some time. It was, of all unlikely people, A. J. Foyt who miscued in the southwest and hit the famous immutable wall followed by a quite rapid transit through the Speedway's south lawn in 1987. Barely had the race begun that year when Mexican heartthrob Josele Garza spun in turn one where all but Pancho Carter managed to drive around without incident. Sullivan spun through the south straightaway as he had in 1985, but this time he did not chasten himself and win the race. Victory belonged instead to New Mexico's Al Unser, taking his third of what would be four wins.

When the racers returned to Indianapolis in 1988, the same predictable problems prevailed in the old southwest. Roberto Guerrero, the good natured Colombian who in the first four of his seventeen Indianapolis starts had two seconds, a third, and a fourth, remarked once that "when a race car is working, it's the easiest thing in the world to drive. When it's not working, it's the hardest thing to drive. The differences are day and night. When the setup is right, my grandmother can drive the car." Guerrero, like most other jockeys, had his golden moments and profound discouragements at Indianapolis. Late in the 1987 season he survived head injuries sustained during an off-season testing accident there. His next four finishes were 32nd, 23rd, 30th, and 33rd. On May 10, 1988, he experienced a loose condition entering the southwest, whereupon the car touched the wall, parted with a wing, and spun through the south chute with minimal damage. Old soldier John Sherman Rutherford III felt his car push as it entered turn one, popped into the wall, and rebounded. The unpleasant encounter exacted from the fifty-year-old three-time Indianapolis winner some bruised ribs and a bruised ego. In the race he settled for a 22nd-place finish after colliding in that same southwest corner.

Indianapolis, heaven help us, has been known to bring together some strange bedfellows. One of the entering drivers in 1988 was forty-two-year-old Harry L. Sauce III, a native of Jackson, Mississippi, and a single father who had attended grade school in France and Germany, and high school in Japan. He later read law at Mississippi University and Indiana University, before calling Noblesville, Indiana, home and a Hamilton County Court judgeship his vocation. Sauce liked fast cars, and won SCCA (Sports Car Club of America) national championships in 1975, 1977, 1982, and 1983. He turned up in March 1988 entered in the Mergard Turbo Motorsports year-old March Cosworth, and after fifteen laps on the clock was running in the 195 mile per hour range. The fun ended on May 16 when he, a little short on practice time, hauled the Conseco Indy Special into the southwest with a little too much exuberance, spun in the grass, and stopped in turn two without having collided with anything of substance. In the meantime, Spike Gehlhausen was at it again two days hence when in the process of subjecting his mount to what the Speedway called "extremely heavy damage" did what numerous other seekers had done, walloped the wall, and teetered on down the track until he coasted to a stop in the middle of the chute.

As long as there is a southwest turn, it will continue to eat cars, careers, and sometimes lives. Scott Everts Brayton, born in Coldwater, Michigan, in 1959 and fated to die at Indianapolis, had driven there six times and returned for a seventh attempt in 1986 when on the 11th of the month he came high out of the southwest, slapped the wall, zoomed across the track, and came to a stop with his car backed against an inner guard rail. On the 14th, Phil Krueger was back for his third 500-miler when he executed a complete spin in the south chute, discovered himself pointed in the correct direction with his motor running, and soldiered on around to the pits. Also on the 14th, two rookie contestants tasted the wall at about the same time. One was Michael Greenfield, visiting from Manhasset, New York, and behind the controls of a 1987 car christened the Greenfield Industries Lola. The other was Belgian Didier Theys who, when he wasn't driving race cars was putting his life on the line with snow skis and motorcycles. At 11:14 on May 21 Greenfield entered the southwest on the low side, looped twice, and quite by accident ran into Theys. Their cars discovered an immediate attachment to each other that survived until they scraped to a halt in turn two.

One of the best and brightest of the rookies that year was Amarillo-born Steven Bruce Butler who, almost needless to say, was a pilot licensed with an instrument rating. Butler, always entertaining in his brief heyday, was somewhat more than usually wild and free in his driving, although he was also bright and conspicuously successful, having won the United States Auto Club's sprint car title in 1986, 1987, and 1988, as well as its championship dirt car series known as the Silver Crown in 1988. He was one of those young men who should have driven at Indianapolis, but did not. On a qualification warmup lap he reportedly executed the southwest too low and managed to pop the wall in turns one and two, shearing a wheel off in process. His accident was followed by another later that day when Parsons hit the same barrier he had struck often before. So it was with Jim Crawford in 1990, who seemed to lose downforce midway in the southwest and did considerable damage to his Glidden Paints Lola. Star-crossed Billy Vukovich III, the attractive twenty-seven-year-old amateur weather forecaster, was the grandson of the 1953 and 1954 winner (who had in 1955 died en route to what appeared to be his third consecutive win), and son of the second Bill Vukovich (who raced at Indianapolis a dozen times, finishing second in 1973. Vukovich III competed at the Speedway in 1988, 1989, and 1990). In this, the final year of his racing career, he too spun into the wall in turn one. He survived, but died that November 25th when his brakes locked while preparing for a short track race in Bakersfield, California. "Vukovich's death dramatized more than the dangerous world of auto racing," wrote Michael Martinez of the *New York Times*. "On a more personal level it focused attention on the intense, almost obsessive love and motivation that somehow drives sons to follow their fathers into a glamorous but potentially deadly pursuit of glory." Some two thousand mourners turned out for Vukovich III's Fresno, California, funeral.

Managing, without actually trying, to smote the outer southwest wall three times in a single accident in a 1990 pre-race shunt was thirty-three-year-old rookie Jeff Wood, the oil driller and former ski racer from Wichita. He was followed into the fence later in the day by Jim Crawford, who by this time well knew the immovability of Indy's adamant concrete, having confronted it five days earlier. Two weeks later the same wall attracted Bernard Jourdain who, though born in Brussels, considered himself a Mexican, having passed almost all his life there. Then it was time for Randy Lewis (aka John Ransom Lewis III) the Hillsborough, California president of a promotional firm, who was graduated from both San Jose State and Berkeley, to hurtle, full tilt, into the southwest. Pursuant to his fourth Indianapolis win, the amazing Rick Ravon Mears collided with the southwest in 1991 after something (a defective wheel nut pin) failed on his Penske Chevy V-8, causing him to crash the car's rear and right side and suffer a bruised foot. The 1991 race was a few seconds old when newcomer Buddy Lazier, later to win the 1996 race, and son of Bob Lazier who drove in the 1981 Indianapolis 500, spun into the southwest wall after Gary Bettenhausen looped in front of him. Shortly after, Kevin Cogan and Roberto Guerrero managed to get in touch as they screamed into turn one and into its wall. The former required hospitalization for right side injuries, while the latter walked away.

The 1992 racers' reunion at Indianapolis played out with an unprepared script reminiscent of many previous years. On the 3rd of the month it was Fabrizio Barbazza, the smallish (five-foot-six, 135 pound), smiling

Milanese import making his only run at Indianapolis a strong one with a third-place finish. Barbazza socked the southwest a good one, sliding a total of 1,160 feet, all of them out of control. Injuries: none. His fellow rookie Paul Tracy, the durable Canadian who at the advanced age of sixteen had won the Canadian Formula 2000, got the hang of the Indianapolis Motor Speedway by exiting the pits somewhat too rapidly on chilly tires, inadvertently slipping into the fescue, and zipping up the track and into the first turn wall, backwards. He came away with a bruised right arm and left knee. One of the uglier incidents ever to transpire at the exit of turn one was on May 6. It occurred when observers saw water spewing out of Rick Mears' Penske Chevy, the previous year's winning car, which then spun two and three quarters times, caught the wall with its left front, took to the air, overturned, and slid upside down across the track. Fortunate to be alive, Mears emerged from the wall-hammering with but a broken left foot and a sprained right wrist. He had, nonetheless, a charmed fifteen year safety record at the Speedway during which he never so much as spun out nor ran over a chipmunk. In 1992 he hit the wall twice. The second time was during the race when he got together with Crawford in that same south chute. Four times an Indianapolis winner, Mears was making a final appearance. "When the desire goes away, the fun goes away too," Mears told the Associated Press. "And when that goes away, you shouldn't be out there." Gary Bettenhausen, one of the most senior of wall smackers, did not disappoint, either, when his car began to smoke ominously as it made its way down the main straightaway, whirled around once, and kissed the southwest barrier. He was the fastest of the 1991 qualifiers, but did not start on the pole because he did not time in on the first of four days. Hapless Hiroyuki "Hiro" Matsushita, the agreeably polite Japanese visitor whose grandfather, said one press release, the Nipponese celebrate as "the father of Japanese electronics" for having founded Matsushita Electric Industrial Corporation of Japan, did other socially constructive things besides driving race cars, such as being the president of a real estate company. On the 9th of May in 1992 he apparently slipped in another car's juices, entered turn one on the low to medium side, and hightailed it into the wall. Car damage was such that Matsushita had to be extricated by first opening the car with a tool best described as a large can opener. In obvious pain, he emitted a brief yell (accountable to a broken right femur) when rescuers lifted him from the car that was itself totaled—and then some. Before the 1992 race ended there was more calamity in the southwest, beginning with Philippe Gache, the rookie from

Avignon, France, who ripped into the southwest turn barrier, spun across the track, and gathered up Wisconsin midget car driver Stan Fox. The second incident occurred when Jimmy Vasser plowed into the turn one wall.

In the spring of 1993 the Speedway unveiled certain innovative measures to improve spectator safety and viewing. Among the improvements: a higher steel reinforced concrete outer retaining wall around the entire course; new, almost twenty-foot-high, safety cabling and catch-fencing above the outer wall draped on twice the number of steel posts as before; two twenty-two-foot-wide warmup lanes separated from the race track by about a dozen feet of lawn that serve as pit exits and entrances; thirty-inch ribbons of asphalt rumble strips below the white lines in the turns to discourage cars from running too low on the track and causing sharper angles of impact with the outer walls; a four-acre lagoon and several new hills at the infield portion of the golf course; general admission spectator mounds along the inside of the backstretch, including an alcohol-free "Family Area" mound at the exit of turn two; a North Vista forty-row grandstand between turns three and four on the outside of the race course; a pit entry attenuator constructed from energy-absorbing foam material; and a rebuilding of Grandstands A and B along the outside of the main straightaway.

Duane "Davy" Jones, son of a sea captain and (for a time) son-in-law to John W. Mecom, Jr., who owned both Graham Hill's 1966 Indianapolis winning car as well as the New Orleans Saints, was first to plug the southwest wall in 1993, after which he was examined and medically cleared to drive on. The next casualty was Ross Bentley, the competition driving instructor who exited the southwest a bit high, cut two spins, and stuffed his AGFA Film car against the whitewash in turn two. Free spirited Robby Gordon, the Orange, California, owner of Gordon Feed Company whose business it was to nourish horses, misnegotiated turn one in an A. J. Foyt 1993 Lola Ford Cosworth XB, creamed the outer wall twice, and for good measure socked the inside guard railing without any apparent personal injury. Luckier still was Dominic Dobson, once a logger in the Washington rain forests, who whirled around twice in the southwest and still hit nothing.

The parade of problems attached in one way or another to the track's southwest turn continued inexorably in 1994 beginning with Mike (Michael Dennis) Groff who experienced some sort of engine malfunction as the turn loomed ahead of him on the 9th of May, cut a half spin, dinged the hard stuff in the south chute, and proceeded backwards into turn two. Groff, good-looking and again single, had expressed an interest in restoring both Porches and old homes, and confessed also that his life goal was to become a professional baseball player. Failing of that, Mike Groff eventually competed in five Indianapolis races, his brother Robbie in one. But no one named Smith has ever driven at Indianapolis, not even Mark Smith, the boyish twenty-seven-year-old University of Oregon graduate, Eagle Scout, and flier who had been twice bumped out of the 1993 race, and gave it his all in 1994, except that he brushed the side of his car on the southwest turn wall, slid through the south chute and hit on the car's other side. Once the 1994 race was underway, Mike Groff got out of shape in the southwest, and took Dominic Dobson with him. Then as the race neared its completion Stan Fox, whose racing career was to end in the southwest turn and short chute one year later, caught the wall there with seven laps remaining.

Michael Greenfield who had crossed swords with Didier Theys in the south chute in 1989, had continued problems there in 1995 when he drove another family sponsored car into the cement, ending, as most southwest mishaps do, in the southeast corner of the Speedway. Another repeat wall popper was Johnny Parsons, a frequent casualty of that section of the Indianapolis Motor Speedway. Both Greenfield and Parsons evaded significant injury. This good fortune, however, was not to be sustained. In the southwest turn on the race's initial lap there developed a multi-car pileup involving ill-fated Stan Fox, who leaned visibly forward in the cockpit as the starter's green flag flew; Eddie Cheever, the 1998 race winner; Davy Jones; Lyn St. James; Carlos Guerrero (not to be confused with Roberto); Eric Bachelart; and eventual (2003) winner Gil DeFerran, who limped around the track to his pit stall and retired for the day after one lap. Bachelart lasted six laps before dropping out. Fox, Cheever, St. James, and Guerrero did not advance as far as the second turn. Fox's car totally disintegrated, while the hapless driver's legs were fully exposed as he remained strapped in the back half of the liturgically purple No. 91 Hemelgarn Racing Reynard chassis fitted until the accident with a Ford-Cosworth XB engine that hurtled through the air, generously spewing shrapnel over the track.

Stan Fox (born Stanley Cole Fuchs on July 7, 1952) was widely regarded as one of the last holdouts from the old Indianapolis school of Speedway drivers who served long and arduous apprenticeships in midgets and ''big cars,'' later known as ''sprint'' cars. Indeed, since Fox's demise there have been fewer Indianapolis drivers whose careers advanced in that manner. Tony Stewart was one, as were Billy Boat, Jack Hewitt, Davy Hamilton, Steve Kinser, Mark Dismore, J. J. Yeley, Richard Vogler, Donnie Beechler, Jimmy Kite, Jason Leffler, and arguably three or four more. "I'm lucky," Fox once said, "because I'm one of the few guys who comes here with only a helmet bag, and works on a percentage." Their numbers are dwindling, and the number of such people in competition is ever on the wane. Unable to find rides at Indianapolis, some of them defected to NASCAR. Despite the Indy Racing League's implied, if not stated, preference for homegrown young American short track talent, the trend in driver orientation has gone quite the opposite way. There is no assurance, of course, that to drive open cockpit cars successfully on short, mostly dirt, tracks is the ideal preparation for a person to wrestle with Indianapolis. Evidence is more to the contrary. Recent Indianapolis winners such as Gil De Ferran, Helio Castroneves, Juan Montoya, and Kenny Brack have all been foreign guests of the Speedway who learned their skills driving rear engine cars on road racing courses outside American borders. There has been a feeling among such contestants (again: implied, if not stated) that racing on counter-clockwise, left-turn-only race tracks is a piece of cake. A few laps at Indianapolis, however, has convinced some drivers otherwise.

Stan Fox, conceding that driving front engine midgets and sprint cars around short circular tracks bore virtually no resemblance to driving at the Speedway, did at least argue that it taught a person how to race. Fox, who would chase the pants off anyone to win a $25 heat race, was born into wealth created by his late father (who perished in an automobile accident on an icy Wisconsin road) who created the LeMans Corporation, one of America's two largest purveyors of motorcycle and snowmobile aftermarket parts that in 1991, for instance, showed gross revenues of $100 million. Stanley's somewhat despairing parents decided when he was a teenager to pack him off to St. John's Military Academy in Delafield, Wisconsin. "I was a little wild," Fox confessed once, "and they thought it would slow me down." It did not. Fox packed himself off to Arizona State, from which he graduated with a marketing degree in 1974. At ASU he had the benefit of being in touch with western states racing circles during the winter. He once holed up in a shabby house trailer on the Phoenix ranch owned by retired Indianapolis 500 driver Wayne Weiler, and more or less refused to leave. Weiler got Fox off his property by bribing him with an airline ticket back to Wisconsin.

After Fox's Indianapolis turn one accident in 1995, Gasoline Alley was abuzz with the rumor that he had died. There was every reason to think so. Fox underwent surgery to relieve pressure from a subdural hematoma, but did not die just then, not physically at least. He remained in a coma for five days at Methodist Hospital, during which someone suggested that, were Fox to hear his favorite Janesville radio station, such familiar strains and voices might transport him back to consciousness. Someone furnished the necessary radio with access to Janesville, but the experiment bore no results. In late July, however, he left treatment both at Methodist and at an Indianapolis rehabilitation clinic. On the morning of the day he left Indianapolis for Janesville, an old friend asked whether he had reviewed photographs of his accident, "No," he replied. "Do you think anybody has any?" In time he climbed into a stock car and raced it, alone, around a half-mile track. Said one physician, "He thinks he's the same old Stan Fox." He was not. A year later when the Indianapolis Motor Speedway opened the track, Fox was back, looking for a car to drive, but he could not secure medical clearance to do so. He appealed the decision. A close racing friend took him to a go-kart track for a friendly two-car impromptu auto race. "I can beat you any time, any place," Fox teased. The friend, a driver of some note, good-naturedly took him on until Fox slowed suddenly, and wondered why. His right foot, as it turned out, had slipped off the accelerator. Back in Janesville folks spotted Fox motoring around town with his underage daughter at the wheel. His wife protested when he sawed down a perfectly attractive and healthy tree in their front yard. Their marriage deteriorated, and finally ended in divorce. In December 2000 he went to New Zealand, where in years past he had raced during the winter months, to see some of his old racing friends. On December 18 the van he was driving on the left hand side (as is proper in New Zealand) of a desert road roughly 200 miles from Auckland collided head on with another vehicle. Funeral services were conducted at the First Lutheran Church in Janesville, with burial at Oak Hill Cemetery.

Through some strange quirk of fate, Fox's 1995 accident cleared the way at Hemelgarn Racing for Buddy Lazier, who reacted by winning the 1996 Indianapolis 500 following three not particularly noteworthy performances and two other years when he raced there not at all for lack of speed. Others (although they were new faces), quite unnecessary to point out, persisted in getting themselves crossed up in the southwest turn. The first was hot footed Danny Drinan, the six-foot-two talented driver, builder, and mechanic born on the 4th of July in Streater, Illinois, who had spent a good deal of time on the carpet at the United States Auto Club for alleged infractions of good driving practices and the designs of his racing cars. Drinan was remarkable in certain ways. He had been the lead mechanic for Mario Andretti's 1984 championship season, been employed to build Klein racing engines, been a lead mechanic when Michael Andretti was with Kraco Racing, been lead mechanic with Hemelgarn Racing, and opened his own Drinan Racing Products in 1990, out of which came some conspicuously successful short track cars. In August 1992 he was given up for dead, literally, after a horrific spill in a midget car that flipped over fourteen times in turn three of the one-mile Illinois State Fairgrounds in Springfield. There were times when fellow drivers didn't care for his on-track manners, or lack thereof. There were also times when the competition was not pleased that cars of his design were winning races. On May 18, 1996, he did the commonplace thing, anent, taking his life in his hands through Indy's southwest turn that he may have approached a wee bit low. His car, a five-year-old Lola chassis fitted with a Buick V-6 sponsored by State Bail Bonding, and entered by an outfit called Loop Hole Racing in Black Forest, Colorado, touched the wall with its left side in the south chute, and eventually spun to a halt in the new warmup lane in turn two. Medically, Drinan was a difficult case: left hip and left foot fractures, a concussion, and a bruised lung. On May 20 he was reported in good condition with the prospect of his being released in "three to four days." Nor was he a damned bit happy. "I'm just exhausted," he told the *Indianapolis Star*. "My stomach's upset and the hip hurts the most." Small wonder.

Emerging uninjured in a first turn wall wallop on Sunday, May 19, 1996, was rookie Randy Tolsma, a six foot tall Boise, Idaho, driver who, following in the steps of his father who had raced super-modified cars in the northeast and Canada, began racing at the age of nine and committed to the racing life when he was twelve. He enjoyed considerable success with midget cars in the American northwest, partly with sponsorship support from a mortician named Bill Brewer who owned a funeral business called The Chapel of Chimes, and who hired Tolsma to usher, to deliver flowers, and, when necessary, to lug corpses around. Tolsma and his wife Tiffanie liquidated all their household possessions, gave away what no one cared to purchase, then hit the road to Indianapolis in 1994 with their truck and red Ford Escort. Tolsma later made the decision to leave open wheel cars in favor of racing NASCAR trucks, where he scored important career wins at Nashville and Bakersfield.

Three and a half hours after Tolsma's wall hit, Glendale, Arizona's no-nonsense William Leonard "Billy" Boat, another rookie and another second-generation racer (his father had been an Indianapolis mechanic with Arizona's car-owning Johnny McDaniel) had much the same misfortune that befell his racing colleague Tolsma, having slid 490 feet in the southwest turn, lapsed into a half-spin, struck the wall in the south chute, followed the wall for forty feet, then continued another 660 feet before stopping mid-track. He was held overnight at Methodist for observation. Like the late Stan Fox, Boat defended his background that began with open wheel cars on American short tracks. "The biggest thing that racing midgets has done for me," he explained, "is having taught me how to race, how to run close, how to run fast, how to be good in traffic." Through all his ups and downs, Boat started on the pole at Indianapolis and won an Indy car event at Fort Worth, Texas, both in 1998.

The southwest turn was comparatively easy on contestants in 1997. On May 16, Poughkeepsie, New York–born Johnny O'Connell, thirty-five, from Chandler, Arizona, experienced an engine problem with one of the Foyt cars that Scott Sharp had crashed twice the week before. The accidents had set Sharp down for the month, and now did the same to O'Connell. Spewed oil sent him skidding 660 feet in a three-quarter spin into the wall, finally coming to rest like so many others, in turn two. O'Connell required surgery to correct a dislocated arch in his left foot. On May 12, 1998, fate again put the finger on Dan Drinan, who had been bitten badly by the southwest turn in 1996. This time he fell into a half spin and hit the wall with the left rear and left front corners of the D. B. Mann Development Dallara. The Speedway reported that Drinan stopped at the edge of the infield lawn, reported for a medical evaluation, and was found to be without injury. "We had just changed the rear wicker tab before that lap," Drinan explained, "and it just caught me by surprise. I hope they can fix it." Added Drinan's mechanic-brother Jimmy, "Dan is a little sore right now." On Saturday, May 16, the first morning of time trials, it fell to Paul Durant (in private life general manager of a Reynolds Aluminum processing and distribution plant in Livermore, California) to cut a half spin in the southwest and pop the wall with the left side of his Cobb Racing entry, fortunately without injury. Remarked Durant, "I'm fine, although I banged my elbow a little. The car had a push, and we were trying to get rid of it. I just gave her a little extra, and around she went." A year before, he had taken over the Foyt entry that put both Scott Sharp and Johnny O'Connell out for the month, and started the Indianapolis 500 thirty-third, from where he worked up to twenty-first before he was put out of action on lap 111. Later in the day it was Jimmy Kite, in the midst of a distressing accident-prone period in his career, who not only crashed into the wall on the first lap of a qualification attempt, but slid into the infield guard railing and wacked it as well. Said three-time Indianapolis winner Bobby Unser, "some of these drivers that are crashing cars [make me] feel sorry for them. It's almost like they have too much pressure on them. They're almost driving blind. Like Jimmy Kite," he continued. "I was sitting in Al's [his brother Al Unser's] coach, and we just happened to be watching that. And he [Kite] realizes that it's lack of experience, but how long can a guy [be] doing that until he gets hurt or runs out of money?" Kite, a third degree blackbelt in karate, had attracted a great deal of favorable attention in racing circles by winning the 1997 Silver Crown 100-mile race on the final turn at Phoenix in his first ever start in such cars.

A half hour after smallish (five-foot-four, 125 pound) Kite's qualifying accident, the grief fell on Chilean engineer Eliseo Salazar (full name: Eliseo Salazar Valenzuela), a Toyota dealer whose penchant for superstition and symbolism prompted him to wear a left red shoe, a blue right shoe, a blue left driving glove and a red right driving glove. It was a scheme that displayed the Chilean flag, and also conveyed the imagery of the Cross. Be all that as it may, he careened into the southwest turn regardless, substantially destroying his car without destroying himself, except for a bruised left shoulder. Two hours later, into that same wall went Tyce Carlson, right side first. "It just wouldn't turn," he said. Sunday, May 17, 1998, was "bubble day" in racing language, meaning that any driver "on the bubble" (thirty-third fastest among thirty-three qualified cars) will be the first person eliminated from the race day starting field if someone turns in a faster four-lap qualification run and therefore forces the slowest person out of contention. At about 12:30 Scott Harrington's car commenced smoking on the main straightaway, spun, hit the wall, and spun again with no driver injury. The 1998 race had barely flagged away when rookie J. J. Yeley spun in the first turn, regained his composure, and ultimately brought his car home ninth.

The 1999 Indianapolis 500 marked the ninetieth anniversary of the track's original construction under the direction of chief engineer Park Taliaferro Andrews. Billy Boat, as circumstances developed, was the first man to smack the wall in turn one that year, and he did so on the second day that the Speedway afforded such a possibility. "I hadn't run this setup before," he commented on his Foyt entry, by then heavily damaged, "and it just jumped out on me and got away. It's too bad." Boat had still another accident with another of Foyt's cars later. "The worst thing about crashing A. J.'s car twice in two days," said Boat, "is you still have to go to dinner with him. And he makes you buy, and then eats your bowl of ice cream, too." Next to hit turn one on May 19 was Floridian David MacFarland Steele, a short track midget and sprint car specialist of some achievement, who felt the hit keenly. "Physically, I could hardly move because I was so sore," he said months later. It demolished the car. It happened so fast. To hit a wall like that is the most violent thing you could ever imagine. It's like stepping in front of a bus. It was painful even to breathe. I just took shallow breaths. The only thing I'm scared of is failure. I would be more afraid of going out there and have people say, 'I don't know if he can do this,' than try to hold it wide open going around a corner." On May 23 came an announcement that Steele, still suffering from a mild concussion and from back strain, was not cleared medically to drive at the Speedway in 1999. Fifty minutes after Steele's wall confrontation, the southwest bit Tyce Carlson whose car became squiggly and backed into the cement. Late in the afternoon it was Mark Dismore's turn to clap the wall, something he did twice, before climbing dejectedly out of his car without assistance. Dismore nearly lost his life at Indianapolis eight years before when he sustained fractures to his neck, right wrist, right kneecap, and both feet. On this day, however, he was somewhat mystified. "I don't know what happened," he told the press. "The car went up into the gray, and I just felt like a passenger. I feel bad for my crew."

On lap sixty-two of the 1999 race, thirty-five-year-old Sam Schmidt, like Billy Boat the son of former Arizona Indy car mechanic, cracked the wall in the first turn, and like most southwest turn accidents, came to a stop in the short chute, pounding the steering wheel in frustration. "I got into the grey stuff," he explained later. "I just lost it. It's too bad." This was to be the last Indianapolis 500 for Schmidt as driver, but not as car owner. In preparation for the 2000 racing season Schmidt struck the second turn wall at the Walt Disney World Speedway in Orlando, Florida, was airlifted to a hospital in critical condition, and was diagnosed, like Bob Hurt before him, a quadriplegic owing to a spinal cord injury at the C-3/C-4 levels. Schmidt remained on a respirator for months, but eventually recovered well enough to form a racing team of his own. Following the Schmidt incident, trouble befell Salem, Wisconsin, driver Steve Knapp in the same turn. "I went down into [turn] one," he reported, "and it went sideways on me. I had a lot of steering wheel cranked into it, and it straightened out in the south chute. Then it just got away from me."

It got away from quite a few drivers in 2000, as well, including Tyce Carlson who had smooched the wall before, bussed again at the exit of the southwest turn, slipped across the south chute and parked along the inside barrier. That was late in the Sunday afternoon the track officially opened for practice. Carlson showed up the next day on crutches, having, as it turned out, sustained a concussion and a bruised left foot. "It's part of the job," he told reporters. "I went through the corner, and the car came around on me. That's part of this track. That's why only the best come here." On the following day, it was likable Donnie Beechler, the Spring-field, Illinois, real estate entrepreneur and open wheel short track special-ist, who confronted the walls in both turn one and turn two. On the following Friday the daring dentist Jack Miller hit the same turn one wall he had hit before. The always exciting Jimmy Kite also reacquainted him-self with the southwest turn concrete, as did twenty-nine-year-old San Rafael, Californian and newcomer Memo Gidley (officially named Jose Guillermo Gidley) who had formerly worked as a mechanic at the Russell Racing School at Laguna Seca Raceway.

Observers recorded that Gidley "wiggled" in the first turn, planted a left front wheel on the lawn, and rammed the wall with the car's left rear corner. The action had not concluded though. Lyn St. James, the second of three women ever to drive in the 500-mile race, fell into a half spin after exiting the southwest and slammed the inside retaining fence with the right side of her car. She was examined, released, then spun on race day in the same corner, hitting the outer barrier this time. A day later Boat connected in the southwest again, as did Floridian Stan Wattles, another karate blackbelt who claimed to have overcome such handicaps as dys-lexia and dysgraphia, who lost control in the south chute and apparently did not run into anything until he reached turn two. "That was pilot error," he commented. The last person to lose it in the southwest before the running of the 2000 race was Canadian-born Doug Didero who men-tioned, quite incidentally, that one of life's simple pleasures was singing in the shower. On Sunday the 21st he lapsed into a half spin in the south-west, bashed the wall on his left side, and rolled to stop between turns one and two. During the 2000 race, Sam Hornish Jr. spun at the exit of turn one, without injury.

It was the Navajo-American driver Cory Witherill who ignited the turn one fireworks in 2001, by aiming straight at it, cutting a 180-degree spin at the exit of the turn, making incidental contact with the inside barrier, and stopping, faced the wrong direction, in turn two. He was followed later that Tuesday by Casey Mears, son of two-time Indianapolis runner Roger Mears, and nephew of the race's four-time winner Rick Mears. Casey, like Cory, did a 180 in turn one, scuffed the outside wall, and parked in the chute just in time for two-time Indianapolis winner Arie Luyendyk to happen on the scene and throw his car into a left half-spin and a right half-spin to avoid contact. Said Luyendyk, "I put my head back and waited for the hit that never happened." Other hits did indeed happen, however. All went fairly well until May 11, a Friday, when Helio Castroneves, who would win the 2001 and 2002 Indianapolis 500-mile races, occasioned what the Speedway said was "light right side damage" to his Marlboro Team Penske machine when he made "light contact" in the southwest. As an encore a day later, Castroneves hit it again, but not hard enough to keep him from proceeding most of the way around the track. Then Eliseo Salazar, after having entered the southwest with his left wheels below the white line at the bottom of the turn, crashed in the south chute, and kept on crashing, finally reaching a stasis with a small fire brewing. Salazar was next seen with an ice pack pressed to the right side of his face. Stan Wattles hit the same wall another time, with not more than usual results. "I hooked it," he commented, "and the car came around and slapped the left side." A bit later Shigeaki Hattori, known to some as "Shiggy," whirled around upon exiting the southwest, but mercifully managed not to collide with anything. On the first morning of time trials it was Salazar who struck the southwest yet another time, apparently because an engine failure blew oil under his tires. "It's unbelievable, that turn one," he remarked. Wattles did it again on May 13, followed by 1996 winner Buddy Lazier and Steve Knapp, both of whom eluded injury. Once the 2001 race was underway, pole sitter Scott Sharp lost his bearings on the opening lap, and spun in the same old place. Said car owner Tom Kelley, "It just looked to me like it was a matter of cold tires, and he got too low and just lost it. He got on the radio and said, 'I'm sorry, guys.'"

From time to time over the years, and particularly in recent Indianapolis 500 events, there has been an influx of drivers from the Formula 1 ranks who, amidst other customary racing procedures, have not been accustomed to hurtling into walls. Instead, the courses upon which they have previously raced have often been provided with some sort of runoff strip, the limits of which may be marked by passenger car tires designed to provide a kinder, gentler reception for wayward racing cars. Accordingly, on May Day 2000 the Speedway announced its acquisition of a so-called "soft wall" in all four of its turns, apparently acknowledging that, if the present walls will remain in place for the indefinite future, then they can at least be rendered less vicious. The result was an energy absorbing overlay known as the SAFER, an acronym signifying Steel And Foam Energy Reduction, under development since 1998 at the University of Nebraska–Lincoln's Midwest Roadside Safety Facility for use on highways. The IMS acquired some 4,240 feet of the new barrier for installations in its four corners. These "modules" were twenty feet long, thirty-eight and a half inches tall, and twenty and a half inches deep, constructed from rectangular steel tubes, behind which are bundles of two inch thick polystyrene. Said Dr. Dean Sicking of the University of Nebraska, "One of the prerequisites presented to us was to create a barrier robust enough to absorb an incredible impact and yet maintain its integrity so the event could continue with little or no delay for repair," adding that the "barrier system will remain parallel to the track and move back as a unit as it dissipates energy." The SAFER barrier was painted white, so as to be fairly indistinguishable from the track's customary wall non-color.

The next task was to test it out. In 2002 the track opened on May 5, two days after which Paul Tracy brushed the SAFER in the southwest and kept on going as if nothing happened. Rookie P. J. Jones, son of the 1963 winner Rufus "Parnelli" Jones, got into it a little more vigorously that same day, backing his car in, then rebounding to the inside of the track like a pinball, crossing the warmup lane and plowing into the inside barrier. Said he the day after, "Obviously the new walls really helped my impact and I probably wouldn't be in as good of shape as I am right now without them." It was not a scot-free mishap, however, since Jones came away with some cracks in his vertebrae. He said in conclusion, "I felt like we had the car to win the race." Commented University of Nebraska's John Rohde, a professor of engineering, "P. J.'s hit was kind of miraculous, really. He had a velocity change of one hundred feet per second, but it occurred in one hundred twenty milliseconds, which is a long time for that type of impact. It was a hit that had a tremendous amount of energy that was dissipated with moderate loads on the vehicle." Twelve-race veteran Raul Boesel from Curitiba, Brazil, stepped in for Jones, started third, and came in twenty-first. On May 9, a Thursday, it was Mark Dismore's turn to test the SAFER in turn one with the car spun this way and that before bringing the errant machine to a stop in the south chute. Like Jones, he did not escape injury, having sustained a concussion. Dismore finally received clearance to drive, started next to last, and finished last. "Mad Max" Papis and Alex Barron got into the soft wall in the southwest on May 10. Papis hit on his left side and slipped all the way into turn two without personal injury. Barron spun early in the same place, stopped in the grassy area, was treated, and let go from the infield hospital. "The SAFER wall absorbed the impact," he testified later in the day. It worked again for Jon Herb who caught the wall at the exit of turn one and eventually stopped on the backstretch. When the 500-mile race was thirty laps old, Greg Ray did a half spin, crunched the wall, and then dropped down on the warm-up lane. "The car just jumped out on me," he explained later. A large assembly of reporters took note.

At 12:37 on May 9, 2003, two time winner Arie Luyendyk felt his Morris "Mo" Nunn Panoz G Force Toyota slip out from under him on the exit of turn one, then slap the wall with the car's back, left, and right. Safety crews assisted Luyendyk out of the car and out of the track to Methodist where he was complaining of back pain. He commented later in the day that "I'm hurting between the shoulder blades pretty bad right now. But fortunately, nothing is broken; no fractures, cracks, nothing. My status is day-to-day. There is no telling when I'm going to be cleared to drive. The doctor says it's totally up to me. I was planning to go around one more time before really standing on the gas. But I didn't get that far, did I? I'll be back in the car sooner or later, though. This is too much fun." By the following Wednesday, Luyendyk was whistling a different tune. "Since the crash," he told the press corps, "obviously my back and neck had some pain. I also noticed that I wasn't as coherent as I should be. I got back in touch with Dr. [Henry] Bock and concluded it's not in my best interest to race because I don't think I can function the way I should in a race car." Asked whether his Indianapolis years had ended, he replied, "I don't know. I'm not really looking a year down the road."

It was Canadian attorney Marty Roth, a Speedway newcomer and Orange, California's feisty Robby Gordon who first provided the turn one fireworks in 2004. Both were driving cars they themselves entered. Roth began to spin on Monday afternoon, May 10 as he exited the turn, fell into a three quarter spin to the right, followed by a half spin to the left. When he finally halted, he was on the track's backstretch. Roth was as cavalier as any Speedway veteran, however, assuring reporters that "it got a little loose. I had to get that out of the way. That's the way you do it, where you can spin at Indy and not touch anything, throw four more tires on it and keep going." That little stunt happened at 4:56. He spun again the following day. Forty-five minutes after Roth's May 10 pirouette, Gordon came whistling through the same bend in the road, and executed much the same maneuver, cutting a half spin to the left, followed by a half spin to the right, except that he plowed in to the SAFER barrier in turn two, sustaining damage to the left side of his car. "As you can see, I'm fine," said Gordon. "No problems with me at all." Two days later on May 13, the North Yorkshire bachelor Darren Manning got close enough to the short chute between turns one and two to whitewall his tires and cause right side suspension damage. Fifty minutes after that incident, Scott Sharp fell into a quarter spin and made what the Speedway called "hard contact" with the SAFER buffer in the southwest. Sharp later referred to his experience as "a really productive day." Two days after that, Brian Herta had a really productive day when he made heavy contact with the turn one SAFER buffer. "I was scared," he admitted. "I've been in a few crashes before." Brazil's Felipe Giaffone and Alex Barron had productive days in the southwest when the former wiggled and spun, connecting the wall with his car's left side; and when the latter lost control entering turn one, hitting back first. "I wish I had given the crew a good qualifying run," he added. "We'll just have to get out there and try again tomorrow."

TURN TWO: THE SOUTHEAST

MOTHER: It's broccoli, dear.
CHILD: I say it's spinach, and I say the hell with it.
—E. B. White (cartoon caption) *The New Yorker*,
December 8, 1928

Like the foibled and fabled isle of Manhattan, the Motor Speedway is a microcosm divided into a good many segments, separate districts, different neighborhoods, multifarious aspects of mind and taste. During the Jim Crow thirties, it had even its own ghetto in the form of a designated place for black customers whose subsequent generations, by the way, were to take almost no interest in the track and its traditions. Over time there has been an on-site magistrate and jail, not to mention a reasonably adequate receiving hospital and some first aid stations, a bunch of public bathrooms, a wooded picnic ground, a day care, a gym, a variety of freelance clergy prepared to mend dislocations of the spirit, a lagoon, traffic cops, a restaurant or two, an aircraft landing strip, a muddy creek with toads and snakes, a helicopter pad, streets with names attached, parking lots, office buildings, stores, private suites, somebody's home, a museum, a tomato patch, a laundry, a golf course, and some flower gardens. Certain drivers have even discovered ways to take extended residence there, if only by slumbering atop work benches and in the cramped back seats of their cars and motorhomes.

Ticket buyers eagerly cue up the morning after each 500-mile race to repurchase the same locations they have known possibly for multiple decades. Indy is for them one of those once-a-year things like Independence Day and New Year's Day and Mother's Day and all those things combined with Christmas, Thanksgiving, saints days, and birthdays. On Memorial Day one comes to Indianapolis simply because it is *de rigueur*. On other days one goes other places and does other things. People who pass through the Speedway's gates and tunnels are familiar with sight lines; they know where the prevailing breezes, if any, originate; they understand where the sun will cast shadows; they know how many ham sandwiches to pack and where the restrooms are; they know how to keep from being trampled; they may extend a perfunctory annual greeting to others who hold the ticket rights to occupy certain places on race day; they know the basic Indianapolis script, the encomiums, the tin horn celebrities, the starting commands, the cliches, the hogwash; they know where to find refuge in a rain; they know the clever ways of track ingress and egress. They see some of the same faces grown a year older; they have some idea of what has transpired in their little territory of the track over the last ninety-six years and possibly beyond. It is apropos of Memorial Day, a retrospective and ambivalently sad and happy time when specters of the dead appear across the mind's broad proscenium. Mauri Rose Jr., son of the three time Indianapolis champion, said it in May 2003: "If there was a place in the world that has ghosts, this is it." They would not be anywhere else on this day of days.

Like wandering through a vanished battlefield with the clamor and commotion long folded into the ages, historic significations of certain sites at the IMS assume a mental discipline and devoted homework, without which every place is like every other. There is a huge panoramic grandstand that encompasses the southeast turn, also known as "turn two." From the top it is possible on a clear day to see every bit of track from turn one to turn three. It is not possible to observe anything else, except on huge electronic monitors, from the exit of turn three, through turn four to the entrance to turn one, the southwest. It is true with auto-racing tracks, particularly large ones, the way it is with football arenas, in that one wants always to be in some location other than where one is.

The southeast is there to greet any racing contestant who had come through the southwest without having collided with something or somebody. This, as the previous chapter has documented at length is, as people say, easier said than done. The 1911 500-mile race, the first such event at the Indianapolis Motor Speedway, was a mere thirteen of 200 laps in progress when the southeast claimed its first bounty. The Amplex team had two cars in the race entered by the Simplex Automobile Company, one driven by W. H. "Wild Bill" Turner (obviously not "Cactus" Jack Turner, best remembered for his automotive cartwheels down the main straightaway, who drove at Indianapolis between 1956 and 1962) who survived the day and the other thirty-nine cars to come home eighth in his red No. 12. His teammate Arthur Greiner in the Amplex No. 44, decked out in red and white, had the misfortune to lose a tire from a new kind of "demount-able" rim while exiting the southeast, and slammed a wall. One reporter noted matter-of-factly that the "mishap resulted in the only fatality of the day," as if one had a right to anticipate more, and that Greiner's riding mechanic Sam Dickson "was crushed to death under the car" that turned turtle and threw him against a fence. Dickson therefore became the India-napolis 500's first fatality. There would be at least sixty-six more by the beginning of the year 2003. Greiner himself, according to the same source, "suffered a broken shoulder and other contusions and bruises" but was trapped in the car.

A reporter for *The Horseless Age*, a New York magazine, indulged him-self prior to the 1912 race by joining celebrants at the Claypool Hotel, then in its ninth year as a hostelry with 450 guest rooms, each with a bath, then an uncommon amenity. He was impressed by the lavishness of the pre-race revelry. The Claypool, he mused, "resembled some of the hotels on Long Island. Almost everybody of prominence in the automotive industry could be found within a stone's throw. Gay parties were many the night before the race, and it is safe to say that there were a large number that did not see bed at all." Those still awake when the sun rose over the capital city on race day 1912 found themselves confronting traffic that congested the six miles between the Claypool and the Motor Speedway. An hour before the race's start the twenty-four contestants (sixteen fewer than the year previous) lined their cars on the track in rows of five, with a fifth row of four machines. Among those assigned to the third row was Bob Bur-man, adorned like his crew with an impeccably white starched shirt with "Wolverine Motor Club" printed across the back. Burman's No. 15 Cutting was an entry posted by the Clark Custer Auto Company of Jackson, Michi-gan. It was a twin seated car with barely sufficient space for Burman and his riding mechanic Harry Goetz. After the race was flagged off Burman worked his way methodically into first place, bedeviled every foot of the way by an unbalanced right rear wheel. He was riding third on his 156th lap, partly because he had stopped for service on seven occasions. Then as Burman rounded the southeast turn at ninety miles an hour the Cutting parted with both rear wheels. The man from *The Horseless Age* hastened to the scene to discover Burman and Goetz wrong side up. "It was thought that Burman and his mechanic had been killed," he wrote, "but when a rescuing party arrived on the scene of the accident they were both stand-ing beside their upturned car." Burman and Goetz were bloodied about the neck, shoulders, hands, thighs, and knees, but not so severely that they did not return later that same afternoon to the pits where they joined their friends and watched the conclusion of the second 500-mile race, won by Joe Dawson, a resident of the local YMCA. Years later, Wilbur Shaw voiced some strong opinions about riding mechanics who, he claimed, "were about as useful as cigar store Indians."

The 1912 race lasted six hours, twenty-one minutes, and six seconds, after which Burman gathered up his bloodied driving togs and caught a ride back downtown where he took to his bed at the Hotel English on Monument Circle to nurse his wounds, but not for long. Reporters knocked on his door, and Burman received them cordially at his bedside. "I never had anything happen to me so quickly in all my experience," he declared. "I thought that I surely would be killed and I was rather surprised that I was alive when it was over." Burman, who planned to set out shortly for an automobile race in Philadelphia, shrugged off the horrendous accident on the southeast only a few hours earlier. "It would take a worse spill than that to stop me," he assured reporters earnestly. According to his own account, he had tenaciously held to the Cutting's steering wheel as the car tipped over. Seatmate Goetz, Burman explained, catapulted some twenty-five feet away from the car while wearing Burman's stopwatch securely around his waist to calculate lap times while on board. When the dust of the mishap cleared, Goetz brushed himself off and ran back to Burman with assuring news: "Bob! I didn't break your stopwatch!"

Whereas no one named Smith has ever raced at Indianapolis, two men named Spence arrived there thirty-nine years apart. Both were killed. Brit Mike Spence died in the southwest turn while practicing for the 1968 race. The other, a twenty-four-year-old Los Angeles resident named Bill Spence who had been a regular contender at Legion Ascot in Los Angeles, ran into the southeast turn wall a short distance away in 1929 when his lavender and black supercharged Duesenberg slid upside down for a considerable stretch, leaving Spence behind on the track with a fractured skull, a cloth helmet having been his only head protection. He died en route to a hospital. This mishap occurred on lap ten of the 1929 race, staged on Thursday, May 30. "Outside of this regrettable incident," an account read, "there were no hospital cases." The Spence fatality was the first race-day death since 1919, when there were three. Although Joe Caccia and his mechanic Clarence Grover died during a practice run through the southeast in 1931, the Spence incident, as it turned out, was curiously prophetic of an occasionally discussed 1932 southeast turn adventure involving driver Milton Jones and his rider Harold L. Gray, who struck the southeast turn with sufficient determination to break a section of the concrete and then overturn. Jones received a crushed chest and lived only a few hours, while Gray acquired serious injuries but survived.

A similar mishap implicating another purple-hued Duesenberg and in virtually the same track location transpired in 1933. The driver this time was Mark "Bud" Billman, the twenty-seven-year-old son of an Indianapolis golf course groundskeeper who lived with his parents Nick and Anna Billman on Villa Avenue. Billman was an employee of the Ford Motor Company, had driven his first race at the now-vanished Hoosier Motor Speedway (a half-mile dirt track that was in operation for a little over two years between 1922 and 1924 on the northeast side of Indianapolis on Pendleton Pike), and had raced cars at tracks from Altoona to Oakland. Five years before coming to race at Indianapolis he crippled himself in a big car accident on Indiana's treacherous Jungle Park oiled dirt track. After going to confession and taking communion he made his way to the track on race day. Billman started as a rookie for the 1933 Indianapolis race with a Duesenberg christened the Kemp-Mannix Special, relegated to start in twenty-second position in an overflow field of forty-two cars. The Kemp-Mannix weighed a hefty but hardly unusual 2,100 pounds dry. After the race got underway it had persistent difficulty with the right front shock absorber that occasioned a pit stop after the race's first fifty laps. In the cockpit with Billman was Elmer Lombard, a daredevil in his own right, who had become increasingly uneasy about the track's growing oil slickness as the race wore on. The Speedway's solution to greasy conditions in the turns at that time was to station trackside what appeared to be holdover World War I doughboys with buckets of sand that they had license to hurl across the track's running groove with a mind to creating better tire traction. They were the same khaki-clad militia who disposed of any stalled or otherwise wrecked cars that came to a halt anywhere close.

One driving veteran of the middle thirties recalled track conditions in those days at Indianapolis with great vividness: "If there was an oil spill the state militia would have pails of sand behind the retaining walls on the turns. They'd pitch it right out in front of you. They didn't particularly care who was coming along the track at that moment. And if your car stalled, they didn't send a tow truck after you, or fool around with you at all. If you were on the outside of the track, the men picked your car up bodily and pitched it over the wall. If you were on the inside of the track, the same thing. About fifteen guys would slip two by fours under your car, and it was all over. Goodbye, Charlie."

The chief steward for the 1933 race was W. D. "Eddie" Edenburn who, after the contest had been run, advocated an immediate end to dumping sand on the Speedway. "Throwing sand on a dry track," he said, "produces a condition for the drivers similar to driving on ball bearings or marbles, and further, the sand pits the glass of the goggles and obscures the vision of the drivers." There was ample sand and oil in turn two on the seventy-eighth lap of the 1933 chase when Billman and Lombard had just overtaken future (1935) winner Kelly Petillo. As they rounded the southeast on the following lap the Kemp-Mannix began to slide out of control on the inner apron of the turn, then drift up the banking, tail first. AAA observer Tom Mulligan noted that something evidently went askew with the car's mechanical condition just prior to its accident. Billman's rear wheels apparently locked up while he attempted to brake and wrestle the steering wheel with a mind to bringing the Duesenberg back in harness. Instead, the machine continued its slip up the banking until it crunched a large v-shaped notch from the retaining wall. The car then bounced high in the air, eventually coming to rest with its hind quarters on the wall and its front still on the race track. Bouncing along the wall another forty feet, the race car pitched mechanic Lombard eastward over the wall, and well out of Mulligan's vision. Surprisingly, Lombard's injuries were comparatively slight. Forty years later from the living room of his Venice, Florida, retirement home, he seemed to relish the opportunity to relive the accident. "Neither Mark nor I wore seat belts," he began. "It was all a question of whether you wanted to stay with the car in an accident situation, or whether you wanted to part ways with it. There were no roll bars or anything like that, and most of us figured that it would be better to leave the car than to stay with it. I don't know what would have happened if we *had* been buckled in, of course. The newspapers had me listed as seriously injured, but there was no truth in the report. I went flying over the wall where the Southeast Vista now is, and landed in the middle of Pop Myers's tomato patch. Pop was vice president of the Speedway at that time. I was burned and cut a little, and I think the accident gave me a bad eye. Really, there wasn't anything much the matter with me. I let them take me to a hospital anyway." He remained there for three weeks.

Mark Billman was not so fortunate. As the No. 64 Kemp-Mannix straddled the wall in a flurry of sparks, he was plunged forward and caught beneath the car as it continued along the top of the retaining wall.

When it finally ground to a stop the right front wheel was resting on Billman's body like some beast that had conquered its master. After the passage of twenty minutes, when militiamen hoisted the car over the wall and allowed it to roll down the embankment outside turn two, Billman was more dead than alive. His left arm was all but severed, and his legs both fractured. His internal injuries were still undetermined. At the infield emergency hospital, doctors had no choice but to complete the amputation of his arm and make a determined effort to save his life with repeated blood transfusions, but their efforts failed. The Billman-Lombard accident had transpired at 1:59 P.M. on May 30, 1933. Seven minutes later the race was on again except at the south end of the Speedway where caution conditions prevailed until debris was cleared for the resumption of racing. Six decades later there appeared an article in the *Indianapolis Star* by writer Bonnie Britton, the late Mark Billman's niece, explaining that were he alive, he would be eighty-six, and that four of his five siblings survived. "Reporting has its privileges," Britton observed. "One of them for me was a yearly pit pass, a badge that brought me closer to the Bud Billman I never knew. He was there the last time I stood near the starting line as 33 cars shook the track. And I know I saw him in old Gasoline Alley, wiping the dirt from his face. He'll be there Sunday. If only in my dreams."

Fred Lecklider qualified to start in both the 1926 Indianapolis 500 when he came in twenty-fifth in the Nickle Plate Special, and in 1927 with the black and white No. 23 Elgin Piston Pin Special entered by Henry Kohlert, who called Lecklider pitside on lap sixteen, ordered him out of the car, and assumed the wheel himself. All went reasonably well until Kohlert involved himself with a bunch of cars at the south end of the race course, elected a high line, "tangled wheels" (as an eyewitness expressed it) with Hollywood stunt artist Cliff Bergere, then after clobbering a wall in the southeast turn, had the car not only turn bottom-up, but dump him on the race course in one swoop. Rescuers carted Kohlert off to the infirmary where he was deemed to have sustained "serious injuries," the exact nature and consequences of which history has found fit to ignore. It may suffice to say that Kohlert did not return for any subsequent Indianapolis races. As to Bergere, he maintained his composure as well as his momentum, stopped briefly to fix a radiator hose and a receive change of front wheels, then continued on to finish in ninth position, with a few laps of relief driving help.

When Floyd Roberts won the 1938 race in a Burd Piston Ring Special it was beneath threatening rain clouds. Far behind Roberts and beneath the same threatening sky was Chicagoan Emil Andres, who had dropped out after an accident and scored twenty-ninth among thirty-three starters that year in another Elgin Piston Pin Special, this one entered by Frank Brisco, a dozen-time Speedway contestant. Andres too had a long and eventful record at Indianapolis, having driven there first in 1936 and then in eight other Indianapolis races through in 1949, then lived another half century to tell about it. Andres, along with constant companion and racing competitor Jimmy Snyder, another Chicago figure, was the proprietor of a watering hole called the Jockey Club, later dropping the pari-mutuel name in favor of the more racy Speedway Cocktail Lounge that became one of the few Windy City racing hangouts in the 1930s. While Snyder (sometimes known as "the flying milkman") salvaged a fifteenth place in 1938, Andres did far less well after a curious turn two (southeast turn) incident that packed him off to a hospital and another man to a morgue. With one pit stop behind him, Andres was moving through the southeast when a wheel collapsed, sending the car into an uncontrollable 400-foot slide toward the inner safety apron and then through the inside guardrailing, shearing off several wooden posts at ground level as it did. Once through the railing, Andres dove into a wooden culvert where the car began a series of northbound barrelrolls. His left front wheel sheared off and went skyward while Andres was hurled from his car, that traveled another 200 feet before it ground to a stop. Gathered up unconscious by an ambulance crew, he was rushed to Methodist Hospital with a concussion (one report cited it as "a concussion of the brain"), a broken nose, and chest injuries.

Like Elmer Lombard, Emil Andres was alive and eager four decades later to retell his story. "1938?" he began. "I remember it all. I lived at the Riley Hotel, just across the street from Methodist Hospital. We all paid our own way. There was no such thing as a retainer fee for a driver in those days, and the money for room and board all came out of my own pocket. We could go to Indianapolis for the month of May before World War II for $250—and play the big wheel role. On the other hand, we weren't exactly what you would call flush in the middle thirties, either. [Duke] Nalon, [Paul] Russo, [Tony] Wilman, [Jimmy] Snyder, and I always had a buck in our pockets, though. We'd go out and buy a couple loaves of bread, a couple hocks of ham, a couple quarts of milk and a can of beans. We'd have lunch for three bucks. And it was fun! We called it 'bunching for lunch.' My 1938 car which was called the Elgin Piston Pin Special wasn't too much fun, though. It was a huge, six cylinder machine, and there was always something squirrelly about the chassis. I never knew what it

Three Indianapolis legends who, despite a combined thirty-seven attempts, never won the race. Left to right: Rex Mays, tough guy Joie Chitwood, and the possibly tougher Emil Andres. *Ed Hitze*

wanted to do, because it sort of had a mind of its own. On the forty-[fifth] lap my right front wheel folded under. We were using wire wheels in those days, and they had a certain lifespan to them. The ones I was using must have been pretty old at the time. When the wheel gave way, I took a long, looping spin into the infield. I went through the inside railing and was dumped out, remained unconscious for ten days at Methodist Hospital. On the eleventh day I woke up for the first time, and they wanted to keep me longer, but I was a pretty young bull, and I told the hospital people that I was leaving. About the time I was packing my clothes, Mauri Rose came to visit me and wanted to know what the hell I was doing out of bed. He finally drove me to Chicago in my own car. It [leaving the hospital prematurely] was a sorry thing to do, because by the time we got to Lebanon, Indiana, I started to bleed out of my nose and mouth, and I was about ready to turn back. But we drove on to Chicago, and by the time we got there I was feeling a little better. We were pretty brave in those days. You either had to drive a car and make a buck, or you had to get a job somewhere. So four weeks later I was back driving midgets again, turned upside down, and got a black eye out of the deal."

The worst consequences of the Andres accident in the southeast turn in 1938 escaped the immediate attention of most onlookers, whose eyes were fixed on Andres himself. Most of the turn two crowd apparently did not follow the trajectory of his errant wheel as it soared 125 feet through space, falling with all its malevolent force squarely upon the head of Terre Haute resident Everett Spence, a thirty-three-year-old Vigo County probation officer and father of three children. Spence (at least the thirty-fourth fatality, not counting lives lost at the track landing strip during World War I and the spectators who may have keeled over with coronaries and other socially acceptable means of dying) had been spectating the race from his perch atop the cab of a truck parked in the second row of vehicles lining the safety fencing inside turn two. Chaos reigned for several minutes before rescue teams realized that Andres was not the only casualty. By an extraordinarily bizarre coincidence, three unrelated people named Spence were killed within four decades at the south end of the Indianapolis Motor Speedway: driver Bill Spence in 1929, spectator Everett Spence in 1938, and driver Mike Spence in 1968. Twenty-two years would pass before any other spectators would suffer fatal injuries. It was in 1960 that a spectator-constructed thirty-foot scaffolding toppled in the direction of the backstretch during the pace lap, killing two and injuring as many as seventy others. Scaffolding was thereafter prohibited, although there was another spectator struck and killed by another wheel in 1987, and an interloper who drove his truck on the track without authorization three days after the 1991 race and managed to destroy himself.

Having taken home a sizable portion of the $91,075 Speedway payoff in 1938, and having established a new 500-mile race record of slightly over 117 miles per hour, popular Floyd Roberts, like a hard-bitten gambler unwilling to clear his chips off the table, was eager to stage a repeat performance in 1939. The jovial, slightly obese thirty-nine-year-old Californian derived what seemed a perverse pleasure from thwarting the generally superstitious tendencies of his driving companions at Indianapolis. Roberts adopted a large, ominous black cat as his Gasoline Alley mascot, and posed good-naturedly with the beast before the lenses of news photographers dispatched from across the nation. There were, indeed, certain prevailing racing superstitions of the time, as for example not having one's photograph taken before a race, not allowing peanut shells in the vicinity of a racing car, not allowing a car to be numbered thirteen (in 1914

The errant wheel, once attached to Tony Bettenhausen's right front (see lower left), was punted by Roberto Guerrero's car No. 4 into a grandstand at the north end of the track in 1987, killing a spectator. Bettenhausen, whose father died at the track in 1961, salvaged a tenth place, Guerrero second. *John Mahoney*

driver George Mason started thirteenth in car thirteen, dropped out at lap sixty-six, and was killed in France on September 13, 1918), not permitting the color green in the pits or on the track. Today there are green cars and green clothing everywhere at the Speedway, but the number thirteen didn't turn up again on a car until the 2004 race. It was driven to 27th by Greg Ray, who crashed.

Back at the Speedway in 1939, Roberts had as his companion the same austere ebony cat and the same car that had carried him to victory the year before: a 270 cubic inch Offenhauser mounted in a magnificent upright Wetteroth chassis, entered again by Lou Moore and sponsored by Burd. Although the car's red, black, and silver color scheme was unaltered, the car's number was changed from No. 23 to No. 1, emblematic of Roberts's having won the prestigious American Automobile Association national driving championship in 1938. During 1939 race qualifications Roberts ran the car more than three miles per hour faster than the previous year, but was nonetheless relegated to start the race far back in twenty-third position. Starting twenty-first was Emil Andres, back for another run on Indianapolis after his horrendous accident on the southeast turn the year before, driving this time for his friend and business partner Jimmy Snyder, whose destiny it was to die thirty days later at a midget car race in Cahokia, Illinois. As defending Indianapolis champion, Roberts was far more confident than Andres, however. On the night prior to the race he confided to his friend Henry McLemore, "I have the car that can do it. Tomorrow night I'll have twenty grand in my kick, and you won't hear any more about a driver not being able to win two in a row."

Whereas Roberts had triumphed the year before under threatening skies that dropped rain during his 192nd lap, race day in 1939 dawned bright and hot. When the contest flagged off at 10:00, Roberts could do no better than to dice with the back half of the thirty-three car field. The pace was terrific, with straightaway speeds exceeding 150 miles an hour. California midget ace Bob Swanson, who left the race after nineteen laps when his sixteen-cylinder cream and blue Sampson developed a rear axle problem, roamed pit lane offering his services as relief driver. After exhausted veteran Ralph Hepburn relinquished the seat of his steamy Hamilton-Harris Offenhauser on the 107th lap, Swanson donned his helmet for the second time that afternoon, climbed into the sweltering cockpit, and motored into competition in this car entered by Tony Gulotta (who was competing that day in another Burd-sponsored car) with which he was totally unfamiliar. Leaving the pit area in an inordinate rush, Swanson rapidly escalated to competition speed by the time he reached the south chute. As he approached the southeast turn, however, the car lapsed into a spin.

It was then 2:19. In the AAA observation stand at the outside of turn two, Tom Mulligan was back at the same post from where he had reported Emil Andres's accident the year before. At his side was another Detroiter, former driver Gene Haustein, a three-time Speedway aspirant in the early thirties. Swanson was sideways in the running groove when Floyd Roberts arrived and in a quick decision elected to slip between Swanson's car and the retaining wall. The attempt was unsuccessful, and Roberts crashed broadside into Swanson's automobile. Within seconds, both machines exploded, and Swanson's No. 25 reacted from the impact with three rapid rollovers, coming to rest on the outside of the track opposite old Gate Five. Swanson was thrown from the car and lay helpless in the middle of the track with his back and hands burned severely. Moments after Mulligan and Haustein flashed the yellow caution light, a third car entered the wild melee. It was the maroon No. 3 Boyle Products Special driven by Chet Miller who discovered Swanson sprawled on the track, his car in flames against the wall, and a huge hole in the outer guardrailing where Floyd Roberts had exited the Speedway for his final time. To avoid running Swanson over, Miller veered to the left, missing Swanson by inches, then slid across the track, through the safety apron and through the inner guardrailing, ripping out two lengthy board sections as he did. Miller flipped over in the grass some thirty feet from the track and was himself dumped from his car and into a hospital for a six month convalescence. In ceremonies a year later, Miller gratefully accepted a gold watch for selflessness and bravery.

Roberts was not nearly so lucky. After broadsiding Swanson, he plowed through some twenty feet of guardrailing beyond the point where the concrete wall ended at the exit of the southeast turn. Momentum carried him another 150 feet and propelled him through a section of Carl Fisher's original "tight board fence" downward toward the golf course where his car continued to burn. Rushed to Methodist, Roberts was nearly pulseless, and died forty-five minutes later from injuries at the base of his brain and the upper regions of his spinal cord. Because emergency crews chose not to deliver Swanson and Roberts to the emergency hospital in the Speedway infield, friends and associates of the injured did not immediately know what had become of them. Swanson lived only another year. At Toledo's quarter-mile dirt Fort Miami Speedway on June 13, 1940, the midget car he was attempting to qualify overturned three times. He was dead the next morning.

Eventual race victor Wilbur Shaw drove past the scene moments after it occurred. It was Shaw who had arranged a car for Roberts (whom he called "an honest, straightforward guy—the salt of the earth—with tremendous ability") to drive in 1935. "Actually, I didn't know Roberts was involved at the time," he said years later. "I could see the Swanson and Miller cars, but Floyd's car had rolled down an embankment and was out of my range of vision, although the smoke and flames from it were very much in evidence." Shaw, whose win that day was the second of his three at Indianapolis, did not react any less lightly than everyone else. "I guess every race has its gruesome side," he added. "I would just as soon not talk about it other than to say that Floyd Roberts, in going out, died the way he lived, thinking of somebody else. He was avoiding hitting Bob Swanson when he crashed to his death." Emil Andres underscored Shaw's reverence for a fallen comrade. "I was out of the 1939 race before Floyd had his accident, and I didn't see it," he recalled. "I remember Floyd as being just a big farm boy from South Dakota: a terrific, fantastic guy, and honest as the day is long. He really didn't have a chance to win the 1939 race, though, with that four-cylinder Offy he was driving, because the Maseratis that Wilbur Shaw and Jimmy Snyder [who finished second] were driving [Snyder's Thorne Engineering car was powered by six-cylinder Sparks engine] were just about unbeatable that year. There was no way to get around those two unless they quit running."

Roberts, Swanson, and Miller were not the only persons to suffer injury during the three car confrontation. For the second consecutive year, spectators were involved, as well. Mrs. Bruce Millikan of Thorntown, Indiana, received a broken leg after being assailed by a piece of flying debris probably originating from the outer wall. Martha Ponclite, visiting the track from Collinsville, Indiana, was struck about the head and shoulders with pieces of errant timber. Two men who were assisting rescue operations were also hurt. One of them, Glen Wills of Indianapolis, suffered burns on his head and neck. Another track attendant, William Allen of Brandenburg, Kentucky, paid a prolonged visit to the infield care facility for attention to a forearm laceration.

Harry Bennett, one of innumerable AAA observers stationed around the race course in 1939, rapidly jotted a series of notes during the Roberts mishap. When the yellow caution light flashed at 2:20 P.M., two-thirds of the track width in turn two was enveloped in flames from Bob Swanson's spilled Gulf gasoline. One minute from the accident's onset, Bennett wrote, "Three cars are in a mess, can't tell numbers. [Need] help on the job." The continuing sequence of his notes tells part of the story.

2:21   Fire Apparatus arrived O.K.
2:24   Fire is in general path of car on back stretch.
2:25   Fire not reduced any in last three minutes, another fire truck on apron . . . not much progress in reducing fire, seems same intensity on track and rail zone.
2:27   Car #3 [Chet Miller] on inside of guard rail, upside, #1 [Floyd Roberts] on outside of track, and #25 [Bob Swanson] is burning. Lots of water on straightaway from fire trucks.
2:30   Fire raging quite badly.
2:31   Fire broke out new on rail, really going again.
2:33   Fire is out, track flooded with water, very bad.
2:39   One driver [Swanson] dumped on track, then fire broke out.

In all, workers used thirty-one minutes to clear the track of debris, fire, and water. The green light flashed at 2:50, and the race was on again.

But havoc had not yet ended on the southeast turn in 1939. Three-time winner Louis Meyer, angling for his fourth Speedway coup, was riding discontentedly in second position behind Shaw (for whom he had driven relief back in 1927) with three laps remaining in the contest. Determined to find Shaw and pass for the lead, Meyer came within ten feet of Shaw's elusive maroon tailfin as the two swept through the track's dangerous south chute. Meyer elected a higher groove in an effort to move around Shaw's Boyle Maserati. It is probable that fire equipment washed rubber from what had been running the groove through the southeast, making it more difficult to grip the surface. Meyer lost traction there, rapped the wall, and commenced spinning up the backstretch, taking a long diagonal slide against the inside guardrailing. Miraculously, Meyer's Winfield-powered Myron Stevens chassis in red, black, and ivory Bowes Seal Fast colors spilled Meyer in the grassy safety area that insulated the backstretch spectators from the racing surface. Miraculously also, Meyer was uninjured, having been dumped on all fours and left to scamper across the lawn. It had been a more exciting day than usual for him, having spun earlier that same afternoon in the south chute in his quest to overtake Shaw, who accepted the checkered flag and received a prolonged kiss from sultry Hollywood actress Gene Tierney. *Fortuna favet Fortibus*: "fortune follows the brave." Meyer wisely interpreted two harrowing incidents in the same day as a sure and certain sign that he should hang up his gloves and helmet and embark upon a normal life. His illustrious career consequently reached its end, and when Meyer reached the infield hospital in stocking feet for a pro forma medical onceover, his wife asked what became of his shoes. He could not remember. Soon after, however, he remembered to sign a contract with the Ford Motor Company to recondition engines in his Los Angeles facility that employed 200 mechanics.

In 1940, Argentinean champion Raoul Riganti started his third 500 and ended the day dead last in a bright yellow and blue Maserati that he entered on his own behalf. The trouble started when he cut a nasty-looking tailspin while attempting to exit the southeast turn on his twenty-fourth go-round, crashed through thirty-five feet of low inside wooden guardrailing, executed two rollovers, remained on board as his car righted itself and, as happened to Louis Meyer in that seatbeltless era, felt himself be tossed—limp as a ragdoll—clear without serious injury. "Those spectators who attended the race for the thrills and spills," commented writer

Bob Hankinson, "had their money's worth." Indeed so. Some of the 1941 grief fell on lanky Sam Hanks, a likable twenty-six-year-old Columbus, Ohio–born resident of Alhambra, California, where he graduated from high school in 1933. He began racing midget cars in 1936, prevailed over a stellar field of drivers on a board track erected in the middle of Chicago's Soldier Field football palace, and won seven midget car races in succession at a track in Bedford, Ohio. Hanks eventually carved a distinguished Indianapolis record for himself with one first place, one second, and two thirds in a dozen attempts. On May 29, 1941, the eve of the last race prior to World War II, the track closed for a flurry of eleventh-hour housekeeping chores. In an early evening final practice period, cars that had qualified for the race pulled on the track for a final shakedown. Anticipating his second try at Indianapolis the following morning at ten, Hanks took one last run in his red No. 28 Tom Joyce 7-UP Special, a conventional but cumbersome 270 cubic inch Offenhauser mounted in a Kurtis chassis. Making his way through the southeast at 6:15, Hanks felt the engine seize (the consequence of a broken connecting rod) and the car drift into a slide. It careened through the inner railing as Riganti's had, and the impact threw Hanks halfway out of the cockpit, then the remainder of the way out when the racer turned on its top and cut through the railing a second time before cruising to a halt on the safety apron. Listed in serious condition with a concussion and a leg injury, Hanks was as battered as his car, although he insisted years later that he had been nothing more than bruised and shaken up. Cleanup crews found the right front wheel that had torn loose, stuffed it in the cockpit, and towed the wreckage off. Returning to Indianapolis after the war, Hanks was forced out of the 1946 race after eighteen laps in Gordon Schroeder's sixteen-cylinder (two ninety-one cubic inch Miller eights) Sampson once driven by Leon Duray and sponsored by pistol-packing musical madcap Spike Jones (aka variously Lindley Armstrong Murray Jones), who was born the year of the first Indianapolis 500 and died in 1965 at the age of fifty-three. The vehicle left the race early, but Hanks drove relief for auto stuntsman Joie Chitwood, the ersatz Cherokee Indian, bringing the Noc-Out Hose Clamp car (the one that Mauri Rose and Floyd Davis won with in 1941) to fifth place. Hanks won the 500-mile race in 1957, announced his retirement from Victory Lane, then went racing again the following Sunday. He died on June 27, 1994, his ashes distributed over the Pacific. His widow Alice survives.

There was more unforeseen excitement in the southeast turn during the 1946 practice runs, when Swiss driver Rudolf "Rudi" Caracciola whom

Stunt driver Joie Chitwood poses in Fred Peters's Wetteroth chassis in 1946. Chitwood started twelfth and finished fifth that year. *Ed Hitze*

automotive historian Floyd Clymer called "a fearless driver of great ability," lost touch with his Thorne Engineering car and was heaved out on his head, sustaining injuries from which he managed to recover. Only five minutes prior to the accident wealthy car owner and sometime-driver Joel Thorne engaged in a verbal altercation with AAA Chief Observer Ike Welch over whether Caracciola might be permitted on the track with a silk "helmet" instead of the usual fortified racing headgear. Welch held his ground, and the use of a more conventional helmet may well have saved the European driving champion's life. Reports from the accident indicated that Caracciola had been struck in the goggles by a low-flying bird that blinded him temporarily and set the mishap in motion.

The 1949 race was only two laps down when the powerfully built thirty-year-old Detroiter George Lynch in the orange and black Automobile Shippers Special, an Offenhauser-powered Snowberger chassis, got himself out of shape in the southeast and descended from eighth to thirty-second quite quickly. The car was wadded up from collision damage, and so was Lynch, who endured a broken ankle from the encounter. Lynch, born in Miles City, Montana, in 1918, hitched rides on freight trains early in life and arrived in Detroit when he was fourteen. At the age of twenty he had never driven an automobile, and when he accepted an offer to drive a racing car, so he reported, it was the first time he sat behind a steering wheel. During World War II, he served with the 11th Airborne Paratroopers for twenty-one months in the Pacific, twelve of them in occupied Japan. At Indianapolis in 1949 he, his car owner Lou Rassey, and associated mechanics, contemplated a nonstop run to the checkered flag, thanks to what they called a "secretly installed" supplementary fuel tank. It did not happen and Lynch, though he returned to the Speedway in 1950, never raced there again.

Revisionist rerunning of the rain-abbreviated 1950 race has it that when the heavens cut loose, so in the southeast (not the northeast as first reported) did South Pasadena, California's affable John James "Jack" McGrath, a gangly six-foot, 150-pound star of the southern California track roadster circuit, of which he was season champion in 1946 and 1947. McGrath had begun the day on the outside of the second row in the last 500 when there was a second row (instead of an undisciplined rush to the starting line), and for most of the race that ended at 345 miles, raced with the leaders, being sixth at ten laps, eighth at twenty laps, seventh at thirty laps, fifth at forty laps, third at fifty laps, and second to traveling companion and eventual winner Johnnie Parsons at laps seventy, eighty, ninety, and 100 before stopping on lap 102 for fuel and outside tires. By lap 130 he worked his way back up to thirteenth, and then spun in the rain-soaked southeast turn on lap 131 to end the day in fourteenth. McGrath spent most of his adult life (he died at thirty-six) a disappointment to his wealthy father, a Los Angeles meatpacker, whose expectation was to usher his son into the family business and who for long intervals did not speak to him, nor witness his races aside from Indianapolis. Jack's only other sibling was his sister Betty, whose life was as much absorbed in pursuit of golfing championships as Jack's was focused upon things automotive. By dutifully threading his way through grammar school, high school, and junior college in Pasadena, he did to some degree comply with family expectations. But McGrath went irretrievably astray in 1933 when for fifteen dollars he purchased a junkyard Model T that he restored to life, but that his father would permit him to drive only over the access roads to the packing plant. By 1935 he had a 1929 Ford roadster he prepared for a ninety-six-mile-an-hour run at Muroc dry lake, and by 1942 he opened an engine shop, mostly for the benefit of his dry-laking friends. After three years of this, he confessed, "I was just making ends meet." McGrath finished second in the California Roadster Association's 1948 standings, and then turned up at Indianapolis to drive for his friend Bill Sheffler who, along with Rex Mays, died a season later. In the meantime, McGrath was on a qualifying roll at Indianapolis where he competed in every race between 1948 and 1955, the year of his death between turns three and four on the mile dirt track at Phoenix. McGrath attracted the attention of Bill Vukovich, the two-time winner who was also killed on the Speedway's backstretch in 1955. Vukovich, according to various sources, offered to tow McGrath and his race car around the Indianapolis Speedway with a chain, and release him after he found some serious speed. At Indianapolis McGrath started first once, third four times, and sixth once. On the day that McGrath died, master racing mechanic George Bignotti had made a deal to purchase McGrath's car, although it finally ended up in the hands of one R. D. Whittington, father of the controversial Whittington brothers Bill, Dale, and Don who turned up at Indianapolis between 1980 and 1985. McGrath's death on November 6 occurred six years to the day after Rex Mays (about whom McGrath once remarked, "[I] wish I could be like him") also paid with his life.

Mauri Rose drove in fifteen Indianapolis races, the last of them in 1951 when he was rounding the southeast turn in his low-slung black and red Howard Keck front drive supercharged Pennzoil Special on his 127th lap when a wire wheel collapsed. The car turned over and dug into the lawn off the second turn, but Rose emerged essentially unharmed by slipping down in the cockpit and pressing up on the steering wheel for stability until the worst was over. This was the end of his racing that had begun in 1927, although he considered himself more of an engineer (without portfolio) than a driver. In 1951 he became a Studebaker employee in South Bend, Indiana. Along the way, he invented a device that permitted physically handicapped persons to drive automobiles. By 1951 Rose, who had been divorced at least twice, had two children who contracted polio, and for whom he designed an exercise device for their therapy. He had a cocky, outspoken disposition that rankled people. Wilbur Shaw, for one, wrote of having driven with Rose to California in 1930, saying, "Mauri spent almost all of the time telling me what a wonderful driver he was. According to him, no one knew half as much about racing as he did and this was particularly irritating to me because I was equally certain I was the best in the business." Both won Indianapolis three times.

Indiana's popular Patrick Aloysius "Pat" O'Connor, who spun through the southeast turn and parked in the lawn without injury on lap 181 of the 1954 race, was driving a Kurtis 500c roadster. O'Connor was born on October 9, 1928 in a somnolent, archaic crossroads town halfway between Cincinnati and Louisville called North Vernon where he had a sister also named Pat, and a succession of two wives and two sons. He was a Jennings County local hero who worked as a mechanic at the local Chrysler dealership and turned later to selling Chevrolets. O'Connor began racing a 1927 six-cylinder truck engine in a Model T at Indiana venues like Franklin, Scottsburg, and Columbus. Although he later dabbled in midget cars with some success, his metier was with the extravagantly dangerous Midwest sprint car circuit during the AAA–USAC transition period, when in a tenacious performance curve he ranked third (1952), first (1953 and 1954), third (1955), and then first again (in 1956). He captured the pole position at Indianapolis in 1957, won two championship races (Darlington in 1956, Trenton in 1957), and may well have driven more laps at Indianapolis than any other active driver of his time, owing mostly to a rigorous and ongoing program of Firestone tire testing with which he assisted. O'Connor established unofficial records at Monza, Italy, in 1957 and later tried sports car racing at Sebring and Willow Springs. Back home, he invested in a coin laundry and undertook a partnership in a hotel and restaurant. O'Connor was a clean-shaven, handsome young man cut down at the age of twenty-nine in Chapman S. Root's Sumar Kurtis roadster in an often-discussed multicar pileup on the first lap of the 1958 Indianapolis 500. He is buried in Vernon (south of North Vernon) near the graves of Wilbur Shaw and his second wife, and the resting place of driver Jim Hemmings.

The catastrophic 1955 multiple car accident set in motion at the southeast turn was every bit as destructive as, and similar to, the 1939 Floyd Roberts affair. On-track circumstances often defy description and lend themselves to different explanation and different interpretation, as does this mishap that took the life of Fresno, California's enigmatic Bill Vukovich, who had won in 1953 and 1954 and had every intention of dominating Indianapolis for an unprecedented third consecutive year, this time in the car that Pat O'Connor had driven in 1954 and spun in the southeast. The simplest accident account has it that Rodger Ward, a subsequent two-time Indianapolis winner, spun and dumped over in turn two when an axle snapped on his car, called the Aristo Blue Special (under the sponsorship of a company that marketed women's furs), entered by E. R. "Ernie" Casale and Lyle Greenman. The car had won for Troy Ruttman at Indianapolis in 1952 when painted in red and cream Agajanian colors, after the same Bill Vukovich fell out with steering problems that put him into the wall at the north end of the track. In 1955, however, Vukovich, with a seventeen-second lead, poured through the southeast at about the time Ward spun out in the southeast. Driver Al Keller (who was a member of Ward's pit crew in 1960) then arrived on the scene, and to avoid Ward cut to the left and headed toward the pedestrian bridge that then stood at the exit of turn two. In doing so he made contact with Johnny Boyd, a Fresno comrade of Vukovich, and sent Boyd into Vukovich's path. Vukovich's left front wheel climbed Boyd's right rear, causing Boyd to begin barrel rolling and Vukovich to launch over the outside wall, apparently without touching it, and into the air where it rolled once, hit on its front, went aloft about fifteen feet, bounced again and exploded in flames, then landed upside down with Vukovich still strapped inside. A popular magazine soon published a photograph of the wreckage of the car with what was purported to be the driver's gloved hand exposed, as if to be reaching for assistance. Vukovich was the second Indianapolis winner, after Floyd Roberts, to die at the track. In the meantime, Boyd, who also landed upside down, and Ward were both injured, along with two safety patrolmen in a Jeep parked outside of the track.

Vukovich (closer ethnic spelling *Vucurovich*), a taciturn Yugoslavian, was born on December 13, 1918, in Alameda, California, one of eight children. He was thirteen when his father died, and sixteen when his mother (who called him "Vaso") died also. The Vukoviches toiled in the truck gardens of Fresno where Bill dropped out of Fowler Union High School after three years and began racing a Chevrolet at the age of nineteen in 1938. He married the former Esther Schmidt in 1941, stayed out of service in World War II, and instead worked as a civilian in California military camps. After the war he returned to racing, this time in midget cars. Danny Oakes, who raced with him at the time, remarked that "He was always banging into somebody when it wasn't necessary. We never got along." Added Johnny Boyd, "He told me that if he could psych out seventy percent of the drivers, then there's seventy percent he won't have to beat on the race track." Like him or not, Vukovich kept on winning. When Vukovich died at Indianapolis he was driving for wealthy Atlanta and Miami entrepreneur Lindsey Hopkins, every inch the quintessential Southern gentleman, whose cars never saw Victory Lane at Indianapolis.

The Vukovich fatality was a painful turning point in the career of eventual two-time winner Rodger Ward. "When the axle broke and took Bill Vukovich's life," he reflected many years later, "it damned near destroyed my life. I suddenly realized that maybe I was in the wrong business. Billy and I were close friends, the fact that I could have contributed to his demise, I felt very difficult to live with. It made me decide to change my way of life. In 1955 I drove for Lyle Greenman. Ernie Casale was the chief mechanic. We didn't understand the car [an Eddie Kuzma chassis with a 270 cubic inch Offenhauser engine], and it didn't perform. It won here [Indianapolis] in 1952, but Casale had a philosophy of not running any weight in [the right rear of] the car, so it didn't go around this race track very fast. The front axle had a crack in it that showed up on Magnaflux [a metallurgical x-ray system intended to identify structural defects], so they welded it. But the truth of the matter was an internal crack with the plate that welded to the spool.

"Because of the accident here in 1955 I really took a look at my life and realized that if I was really ever to become a good race driver, or achieve any of the goals I had set for myself, I was going to need better race cars. To get better race cars I had to be a team player, not a loner. New Year's Eve in 1955 I made my mind up. I said to myself, 'This is it.' I poured out the drink I had in my hand, I threw the cigarettes over the balcony, and I said, 'Until I either win Indianapolis or retire from racing, I will not smoke a cigarette or drink a drink.' In those days the attitude toward those who chased broads was that they were bums. If a guy was married he could go to the local saloon, wind up in some motel, and be a 'sport.' But if you were single and you did these things, you were a 'bum.' A lot of car owners were saying, 'Hey Rodger! We know you can drive fast, but we don't know if you can run 500 miles. You're out there with the booze, and you're out there with the girls.' I was going with a lady, we moved in together, got married, and [I] made this commitment to become a successful race car driver."

Vukovich's death was at least as painful an encounter for Johnny Boyd who endured track abrasions and chemical burns from spilled fuel while he was pinned in his overturned car on the backstretch near the southeast turn. In Boyd's eyewitness opinion, Ward had nothing to do with the Vukovich fatality. Keller, he said, lost control of his car after he caught sight of Ward's accident. As Boyd and Keller approached Ward's car stalled diagonally on the track, Boyd claimed that there was room to pass him on both sides. Boyd slowed and prepared to pass Ward on the inside, whereupon Keller lost control and began spinning toward the pedestrian bridge at the exit of turn two, then hit Boyd. "He hit me like a freight train," Boyd recalled. "My car got upside down, dragged me on the race track and took the skin off my back. When I started over his [Keller's] wheel, Vuky ran into the back side of me because he had nowhere to go. I missed Vuky's funeral because I was still in a hospital under treatment for back injury. The accident hurt me, and I still think about it.''

Al Keller, a deputy sheriff in Greenacres City, Florida, was born beside the St. Lawrence River at Alexandria Bay, New York, on April 11, 1920, and began his auto racing career in a stock car at Leroy, New York, in 1938. After World War II he returned to driving stock cars, and supported his wife and daughter as an automobile mechanic. Keller had driven only one championship car race, on the mile dirt track at Syracuse, before he arrived at Indianapolis in 1955. "He had a hand brake," Boyd said of Keller, "and locked it up and got sideways. I was going straight. Keller was out of control and hit me dead center. Vuke hit me in the right rear. We both took off like rocket ships." Keller's Indianapolis car owner remembered him as a man with a fierce temper who, after the Vukovich affair, seized a photographer's camera and punted it skyward like a football. Keller's moment of racing fame eluded him at Atlanta in 1956 when, while holding the lead at ninety-nine of 100 laps, he waved Eddie Sachs (whom he presumed to be a lap down) on to victory. Keller was killed during the championship season finale on the mile dirt track at Phoenix on November 19, 1961, when he exited turn four and slid into an infield chain link fence.

As long as there are walls, there will be people to slam into them. On May 8, 1956, it was Buddy Cagle's turn in the southeast in Pete Salemi's Central Excavating Special with which he had just completed his Speedway driver's test. Cagle, a divorced, twenty-six-year-old Tulsa, Oklahoma, plumber on a forty-five day leave from the Navy, received bruises and facial cuts as a result. No stranger to on-track accidents, Cagle had previously sustained a broken back, arm, and some ribs in a midget car spill in Toledo, Ohio, that occasioned a two-month hospital incarceration. On race day, Jimmy Daywalt popped the same wall on lap 134 in a Sumar Special and came away with a head injury that kept him in a hospital and out of racing until late August. Daywalt, who died of cancer on April 4, 1966, at the age of forty-one, was a World War II veteran who returned to his home town of Wabash, Indiana, out of which he began driving big cars on the rickety wire-fenced Logansport, Indiana, half mile dirt track in 1947. In the 1940s he drove delivery vans for the Brown Trucking Company, and in the 1950s he was employed by the Teamsters union as a business agent. Daywalt presented himself at Indianapolis in 1949 with a car called the Bill and Bud Motor Sales Special owned by sometime driver Steve Truchan, at whose Gary, Indiana shop Daywalt arrived unannounced one day in 1948 with a load of cargo en route to Chicago, and proposed that Truchan enter his championship car (the former Floyd Dreyer–Joe Silnes Mark's Special that Duke Nalon drove at Indianapolis in 1940) at Indianapolis in 1949. Truchan remembered Daywalt as an erratic person who "drove like a jitterbug," and was at the time feeling the stress of a divorce from his first wife. He then married a dark-haired religiously-inclined Indianapolis night club organist and local television personality named Carmelita Dodd, whom he may have met at Indiana's Lake Shafer. At least until then, he was a veritable magnet for unattached women who found his wiry five-foot-nine, 155-pound frame and his tight, curly hair of more than casual interest. Some championship car mechanics, however, found Daywalt mercurial, given to sudden temperament changes and to occasional impatience with chassis setups and support personnel. Daywalt drove eight times at Indianapolis, the first of which, 1953, was his best finish, a sixth place that won him "rookie of the year" accolades.

Quotable John Woodrow "Johnnie" Parsons (1918–1984) possibly most representative of the post-war generation of western American drivers who started in midget cars and made it big at Indianapolis, had ten tries there, and hit paydirt on the second. That was in 1950, in the so-called "Kurtus Kraft Special" (sponsored by Wynn oil additive) that started Indianapolis five times, with a ninth, a second, a first, a second, and a tenth. Parsons was a showman who came by his talents honestly, having been born into a vaudeville family whose act he joined at the age of four, attired with top hat and cane, his theatrical gestures down pat. His father was Kentuckian Harmon Parsons, a song-and-dance man, and his mother, the former Ruth Bridges, was an attractive woman to whom his father did not long remain married. From them Parsons inherited good cosmetic features and a theatrical flair, evidenced in part by his escapist passion for Hollywood films. When the Parsons divorced, Johnnie found himself shuttled from one foster home to another, but came of age in the Los Angeles suburb of Lincoln Park, near Legion Ascot, where as a kid he fraternized with big league race drivers such as Chet Miller. Like Freddy Agabashian and Duke Nalon, Parsons was one of the few championship car luminaries who knew how to play a crowd and to comprehend the value of smart, heads-up public relations. Unusually articulate, good-looking, and available to press, radio, and television, all three men added a little elan into a colorful yet necessarily mundane era. As a child Parsons heard lore about the exploits of Frank Lockhart, the 1926 Speedway winner to whom his uncle had leased a garage. Lockhart, in turn, lavished enough racing lore on Parsons to seal the latter's fate as a driver. Parsons began driving in 1940 for Bill Rice in the United Midget Association in California, then later for Ernie Casale, and ran some big cars at Southern Ascot for black driver and owner Mel Leighton. After the war, during which he worked in a defense plant, Parsons began driving for Willie Utzman, former riding mechanic Danny Hogan and Fred Gerhardt, then came east to team up with car owners like Rudy Nichols and Curt Gosma. In 1948 he passed his driving test at Indianapolis in a front drive Ford provided by Andy Granatelli. Parsons marketed himself superbly, and not only won races, but won people. He brought showmanship to Indianapolis. "It's all public relations," he told Judith and David Lyon, "and it's like the peak. If you're gonna get there you've gotta hustle. If you're gonna stay there, you got to hustle more and watch 'em coming."

During a prerace run on May 12, 1958, Parsons had cut several laps in the 142 mile an hour range (Pat O'Connor's four laps at 143.948 won him the pole that year) before he crunched the cement wall in the southeast turn, doing substantial damage to J. C. Agajanian's car that was repaired but subsequently bumped from the field. Interviewed on the public address system race morning, Agajanian reminded everyone that eleven of his cars had faced the starting line in years past, and that he would be back in 1958. Parsons, in the meantime, picked up a ride in Dick Rathmann's Sumar roadster after Rathmann was injured in some whispered-about but never quite clarified off-track altercation. Parsons also returned in 1958 for one last go at the 500-mile race when he placed twelfth, and thereafter retired from driving after turning up at the track in 1959. "The spirit just left me," he told writer Tom Madigan, "and when I had problems qualifying for the fifty-nine race, I decided to quit running down the back straightaway. I had gotten everything I wanted out of racing. I was a champion." He did, however, enter one final midget racing event at the Saugus Speedway in California, finishing second. Parsons thereafter turned the driving over to his son John Wayne (after the actor of the same name) "Johnny" Parsons who took Indianapolis on a dozen times, with two fifth-place runs his best.

The late Bill Vukovich had been known in Gasoline Alley as a tough customer on and off the track, but no more than Melvin Eugene "Tony" Bettenhausen (1916–1961) who in 1959 was entered in an Epperly roadster owned by Bill Anstead, only to wreck it spectacularly in practice while exiting the southeast turn by clunking the wall twice, then slipping

Five Indianapolis champions pose with Dodge president Bill Newberg in 1954. Left to right: 1952 winner Troy Ruttman, 1953 and 1954 winner Bill Vukovich, 1951 winner Lee Wallard, 1950 winner Johnnie Parsons, and 1949 winner Bill Holland. *Ed Hitze*

through a wooden infield guard railing, rutting in the grass, and overturning. Bettenhausen received a light sentence in the form of a nose cut and a leg bruise. The car was a total washout, although what remained of it went to Milwaukee driver and car builder Harry Turner who rushed home with the wreckage, attempted a rapid rebuild, and then returned to the track where the car, painted maroon and now assigned to driver Eddie Russo, who missed qualifying for the race. Bettenhausen was a tenacious man of German extraction, albeit he was known as "The Flying Dutchman" and sometimes "The Tinley Park Express," in acknowledgement of his suburban Chicago address. He traced his involvement in racing to his childhood when, at the age of eight, he pedaled his bicycle on a thirty-four-mile round trip from Tinley Park to watch a big car race at the Roby Speedway, a mile long oiled dirt track in Hammond, Indiana, where 1930 Indianapolis winner Billy Arnold began his driving career. During the war Buick hired him as an inspector in its huge, newly built Melrose Park aircraft plant. Twice married to Valerie Rice who bore him four children (Gary in 1941, Merle in 1943, Susan in 1945, and Tony Lee in 1951), Bettenhausen followed in the wake of other Chicago drivers such as Duke Nalon and Emil Andres by purchasing his first midget car from another Chicago tough guy named Wally Zale, a barnstormer from midget racing's early days in the 1930s. Tony Bettenhausen was fatally attracted to automobile racing for the balance of his life, although his two supposed retirements and his becoming a Tinley Park Kaiser-Frazer dealer evidenced as much as anything a rational desire to live a safer, more conservative existence. It was not to be. He embarked instead upon a sometimes frenetic sequence of race meets, most of them in midgets, some of them in big cars and championship Indianapolis cars. In his last years he took an occasional fling at stock car racing, as well. As a consequence, Bettenhausen (one eye blue, the other gray) suffered some hard physical knocks over the years, such as severe head injuries at Chicago's Soldier Field in 1954, and a 1956 wall crash at Indianapolis that left him with a broken shoulder blade. His death at the age of forty-four, that occurred near the finish line at Indianapolis on May 12, 1961, while on a good-will mission to test a car assigned to his old cohort Paul Russo, left a wound in the fabric of American motorsports that has never altogether healed. After 400 mourners witnessed Bettenhausen's Masonic funeral rites in Chicago Heights, his funeral cortege, estimated at 200 automobiles and extended symbolically for two and a half miles, led to the Tinley Park Memorial Cemetery. Among the pallbearers were Andres and Indianapolis-winning car owners Murrell Belanger and J. C. Agajanian. Flower arrangements, so the *Tinley Park Times* reported, filled five station wagons. Depending upon one's point of view, automobile racing was not good to the Bettenhausens, whose heart's desire was to win at Indianapolis. Tony Bettenhausen qualified for the race fourteen times, with his best finishes a second (1955) and two fourths (1958 and 1959). Son Gary, who attempted Indianapolis on twenty-one occasions, recorded a third (1980) and two fifths (1973, 1987), although a 1974 dirt track accident at Syracuse rendered his left arm severely compromised. Brother Merle lost his right arm and sustained serious facial burns at the Michigan International Speedway in 1974. A third brother, Tony Lee, his wife Shirley (daughter of Indianapolis driver Jim McElreath whose son died in a racing accident), and two business associates were all killed on Valentine's Day 2000 when Tony Lee's Beechcraft Barron airplane dove 11,200 feet in icy weather near Leesburg, Kentucky.

They were en route back to Indianapolis after attending an auto racing "spring training" session at Homestead, Florida. Tony Lee, a driver turned car owner, had been participating.

During the 1960 Indianapolis 500 two more drivers hauled into the turn two concrete. On lap eighty-four it was Eddie Russo who in a cloud of smoke seemed to catch the wall almost head-on in a car entered by Arcadia, California's Ollie Prather, and who lost an eye after his seatbelts failed and he was dragged between the car and the wall. Having one eye placed him in the company of other Indianapolis drivers such as Bill Schindler, the first of two Al Millers, Cal Niday who had but one leg to stand on, Allen Heath who drove with the only hand after he lost the other at an Indiana racing accident, and pugalistically inclined Pennsylvania-born Andy Linden who seemed to function tolerably well with one lung. Eddie Russo was the son of Joe Russo, the Duesenberg project engineer who raced at Indianapolis four times during the Depression and died in a 1934 racing accident at Langhorne, Pennsylvania. He was also the nephew of fourteen-time Indianapolis aspirant "Pudgy Paul" Russo. Eddie, in another sense, was anything but singular, having as he did a twin brother named Donald. The twins entered elementary school in Grosse Pointe, Michigan, and were nine years old when their father died. Eddie joined the Marines in 1941, and for seventeen years remained in the Marine reserves. His life was full of surprises, among them six marriages and winning the pole position for the 100-miler at DuQuoin, Illinois, on Labor Day in 1955. People with long memories will recall that Russo was hit from behind by Speedway owner Tony Hulman's son-in-law Elmer George during the pace lap pursuant to the 1957 Indianapolis 500. Instead of accepting the green flag on that occasion, Russo limped back to the pits with a badly punctured fuel tank. In later years he shrugged the incident off, calling it merely another of racing's manifold disappointments. "Those things happen," he said.

After Russo hit the southeast wall on lap eighty-four of the 1960 500, Arizona's Wayne Weiler slammed it twice eighteen laps later in Bill Anstead's cream and black Epperly roadster, supposedly because a right rear sway bar anchorage came undone, punctured Weiler's right rear tire, and sent him into a spin. This, as luck would have it, was the first of Weiler's only two Indianapolis appearances. Although he returned to Indianapolis a year later with Coca Cola magnate Lindsey Hopkins and finished fifteenth, Weiler's racing days at Indianapolis ended after a nearly fatal sprint car spill at Terre Haute's half mile Vigo County Fairgrounds on Sunday, June 11 when he ramped off of Jim Hurtubise's right rear wheel and took to the skies, lapsed into a series of end-over-end maneuvers, then crash landed on the clay track with enough force to tear off the helmet that Weiler claimed he had borrowed from A. J. Foyt. Weiler passed sixteen days unconscious in Terre Haute's St. Anthony Hospital where a physician pledged to release him at such time that he could walk under his own power from his bed to his door and back again. He returned home to Phoenix on June 21 where he received physical therapy, and where he returned to area racing wars in 1966, winning against some of the younger local talent until 1974. He then retired with the same wife he married in 1953 to a fifty-acre farm to grow alfalfa, cotton, and sugar beets. "I'm ready for Medicare," Weiler said at the age of sixty-five. "I'm a has-been."

Other drivers such as Leonard "Gig" Stephens and William "Red" Riegel, who happened to bump into each other in the southeast turn at 12:47 P.M. on Thursday, May 19, 1966, became Indianapolis never-beens. Riegel, who was at the helm of the No. 87 California Speed and Sport Shop Special entered by resourceful Joe Barzda, spun into Stephens, who had recently departed the pit area in the No. 71 Fairchild-Hiller Special entered by Karl Hall of Orleans, Indiana. The United States Auto Club, which in those days supervised racing at Indianapolis, sent Riegel packing for this gaffe, while Stephens never qualified for that or any other Indianapolis 500. Riegel died shortly after on June 10 in a crash at Reading, Pennsylvania, that also took the life of two-time Indianapolis runner Jud Larson the dirt tracker.

In the race that year, the Stephens-Riegel incident found its parallel on lap twenty-two when northern (Bakersfield) California's George Snider (riding fourth in an Anstead-Thompson Lotus-Kuzma Ford) and southern (Downey) California's Chuck Hulse (riding sixth in a Leader Card Watson Ford) collided in the southeast with no injuries. Snider, by temperament a pure and absorbed racer, qualified for the Indianapolis 500 twenty-three times with two eighth-place finishes his best. He was more accomplished on the championship open wheel (mostly) dirt track series, winning seven times. Snider's worst day in racing happened at the Winchester, Indiana, sprint car track in late June 1975 when, to avoid a spinning car during a heat race, he flew over the track's thirty-eight-degree banking at about 100 miles an hour and then crashed down on its forty-five-foot outer edge. Both of Snider's arms were fractured, necessitating treatment at a nearby Muncie, Indiana, hospital, then further treatment in Indianapolis. At the behest of his long time friend A. J. Foyt, Snider boarded a commercial airliner to Houston for additional treatment and recuperation. Chuck Hulse, like Snider, came up in racing through the short open wheel tracks. Foregoing what he believed to be a promising naval career in favor of automobile racing, he was the 1959 California Racing Association champion and drove at Indianapolis four times. Hulse's worst day occurred at New Bremen, Ohio, on May 3, 1964, when he launched over the wheel of another car and executed a series of end-over-end cartwheels that affected his vision severely enough to keep him off the speedways for the balance of that year and 1965.

Graham Hill, forty-six, the two-time Formula 1 champion, died with five passengers in an aircraft accident on Saturday night, November 29, 1975, when their American-registered Piper Aztec that had departed from Marseilles, France, came down through heavy fog and crashed on a golf course near Barnet, England, a little north of London and about ten miles from Elstree toward which it apparently was making an instrument approach. Police could not immediately confirm that Hill, who as a rookie driver won the 1966 Indianapolis 500, was aboard, since the bodies of all six victims, believed to be men, were burned beyond immediate recognition. After Hill won at Indianapolis, a victory that, owing to some scoring irregularities, could not be definitively certified until hours after the race, he returned twice more but did not finish and could not score better than nineteenth in 1968 with his fluorescent red four-wheel drive Lotus turbine car that ended its day in the southeast turn when a wheel came off, sending it backwards into the concrete. Such are racing's vicissitudes. In 1969, Michigan driver Alan "Sam" (his dog's name) Sessions experienced a problem in the southeast and crashed, breaking a knee cap, something that did not prevent his putting a Finley chassis into the race, and working his way from twenty-third to twelfth at the finish line. Sessions, a sprint car specialist who won twenty-two such races under the United States Auto Club banner, died in a snowmobiling accident in December 1977. He had participated in seven Indianapolis 500-mile races with a fourth, in 1972, his best.

There has long been a consensus that the man in recent Speedway history who should have won its May race was Wichita Falls, Texas's Lloyd Ruby who, in eighteen starts, could not improve upon the third-place money he collected back in 1964. Over the years, Ruby turned a little short of 6,100 competitive miles on the Indianapolis track in those eighteen attempts, and led the race in five of them. His fellow driver Johnny Boyd has opined that of the hundreds of men who attempted Indianapolis in that era, Ruby showed the greatest near-mastery of the race course in his ability to make on-track moves that no one else could apparently duplicate. In 1974, however, the southeast got the better of him when he lost control of his Offenhauser-powered Eagle chassis on exit, slid roughly 400 feet, nipped the wall, and continued sliding 280 more. Ruby was not injured, but his car was warped enough to warrant repairs. Crew chief Mike Devin and his long-locked seventies men had both car and driver back in motion the next day. In the race Ruby moved his brown and white car from eighteenth starting position to ninth at the end, although, with all too typical Ruby luck, he ran dry of fuel, then returned in 1977 to hit the same wall once more, except with more verve. He was again uninjured.

Mike Hiss, freshman Chuck Gurney, and sophomore Tom Sneva all tasted the cement there in 1975. Hiss, motoring around the track in a car christened the Midwest Sunflower Sue Special whammed the inside barrier shortly before the cocktail hour on May 5 after the machine slipped out from under him causing the car's nose cone to detach. Gurney, driving a V-4 engine entered by California camshaft developer Bruce Crower, hit the southeast cement at almost the point where Hiss had the day before. One of the better dirt track specialists to come out of northern California, Gurney nonetheless never raced at Indianapolis. Sneva had monumental problems there on lap 126 of the race while holding down fifth place and attempting to move around free-spirited Canadian driver and car fabricator Eldon Rasmussen. The two touched wheels, sending Sneva's Norton Spirit bicycling on both left wheels, slamming into the concrete, then flying end-over-end in smoke and debris toward the center of the track while his engine was dumped elsewhere. Rasmussen made another lap of the track, then stopped at the accident scene to inquire about Sneva who, fortunate to have survived at all, had acquired burns on his face, hands, and legs. Relieved, Rasmussen (so it was reported) was reduced to tears. Thoroughly undaunted by a major accident, however, Sneva drove his eighteenth and final Indianapolis 500 in 1992, having placed second there in 1977 and 1978, and won there in 1983. In 1987, however, he crashed again in turn two, this time on lap 144 and without further injury while holding down ninth place. Larry Rice, the mild mannered, circumspect driver, television commentator, elementary school teacher, national USAC midget car champion in 1973, national championship dirt car champion in 1978, Indianapolis co-rookie of the year (with Rick Mears) in 1978, made only one additional Indianapolis appearance, that in 1979, when he crashed his

S & M Special in the southeast turn and parked on the track awaiting a service truck that was quite nearly struck by another racing car.

Six-foot-three-inch John Paul, Jr. had neither an easy time of it in life nor at the Speedway. Back in 1983 he broke a leg in an effort to qualify for the Indianapolis 500, and later that summer made a breathtaking last lap pass on Rick Mears to win the CART-sanctioned Michigan 500. In 1984 he sustained more leg injuries at Indianapolis. In 1985 after parting with a wheel he seemed to drive straight into the wall at the southeast turn on lap 165, spewing shrapnel in all directions, but emerged more or less unhurt. In 1989 he was bumped out of Indianapolis altogether during qualifying. In 1993 he missed the Speedway again. In 1997 it was another broken leg at Indianapolis. In 1998 he led thirty-nine laps of the 500, then fell back to finish seventh. He then won his first Indy-style race since the 1983 Michigan triumph by beating Robby Unser to the line at the Texas Motor Speedway. Starting in 1985, however, he did three prison years in Florida for some sort of involvement with his father's drug smuggling, attempted murder, and kidnapping. Through it all, John Paul, Jr. started seven times at the Speedway. By 2003, he accepted an appointment as driver/coach for the IRL's Infinity Pro farm circuit designed to bring younger drivers up to speed for the Speedway.

Death came to twenty-seven-year-old Philippine driver Jovy Marcelo on May 15, 1992, five days before his birthday, in the approach to turn two when his No. 50 Euromotorsport Fendi AGIP Marcelo Midas Taumarin 91 Lola Cosworth DFS appeared to exit turn one on the low side, fell into a half spin, clipped the wall with both ends and came finally to a stop at the entrance to the southeast turn. This occurred at 4:07 on a Friday afternoon. He was pronounced dead at Methodist hospital twenty-eight minutes later. An autopsy revealed the cause of death as a "blunt force head injury." Marcelo's speed on the previous lap was in the 172 miles per hour range, easily enough to kill someone, but still far away from the 221–224 speed range that more experienced drivers were turning at that time. He had won the North American Toyota Atlantic championship the year before. Someone shipped Marcelo's body back to the Philippines, accompanied by his pregnant wife and their five-year-old son.

Nor has Scott Donald Pruett (who has competed at various times with IMSA, NASCAR, SCCA, IROC, Trans-Am, GTO, and CART) had an easy road in racing, especially in 1990 when he passed a full season on the bench after body blows incurred at a West Palm Beach Indy car testing accident that included, but were not limited to, a broken back, broken knees, heels, and at least one broken ankle. As undaunted as Tom Sneva and John Paul, Jr., Pruett was at Indianapolis in 1995 (the last of his five appearances there) when in the closing laps his Patrick racing entry careened into the southeast wall, rebounded backwards across the track and connected on the inside as well. The car parted with its rear assembly and then erupted in flames. Along the way, Pruett did almost 10,000 miles of Firestone Tire testing. "Truth be known," said Firestone's Al Speyer to the *Indianapolis Star*, "testing is a long, hard, dirty job. There [are] no fans there cheering you on, no autograph sessions. There's no races, no victory lane kisses."

The 1996 Indianapolis race will be remembered as much for its determined Colorado winner Buddy Lazier, the kid who finished last in his initial race there in 1991, as for the death of Coldwater, Michigan's Scott Everts Brayton, son of Lee Brayton who had entered Indianapolis three times in the early seventies without ever having raced there. In 1996, Scott Brayton was in search of his fifteenth Speedway 500 start and his first win. Having driven there fourteen times before, Brayton was therefore the most experienced driver on track at that time. Even so, he was long overdue and on the hunt for any win anywhere he could find it, having never bested the third-place finish he earned at Milwaukee in 1992. Scott, who began racing at the age of fourteen, always appeared to be on the verge of some marvelous breakthrough at Indianapolis, only to have it elude him. That said, at the time of his death he had won his second consecutive Indianapolis pole, although his best Indianapolis run was a sixth in 1993. Notwithstanding, Scott Brayton may well have been sublimely happier at Indianapolis than any of the hundreds of grateful drivers who preceded him there. His breathless, enthusiastic, witty, and voluble pressroom recitals after fast runs on the race track always produced quotable copy in abundance. "I figured I needed to smoke it in there as hard as it would go," Brayton said one afternoon about his car and the track. "The most ironic thing," said his widow Becky, "is that he was so passionate about Indy, [that] it meant so much to him. He could never get enough of that place, and sometimes I would have to drag him out of there because he didn't want to quit talking to people."

Scott Brayton died from a basal skull fracture (so said Robert L. Ward, chief deputy coroner of Marion County) after plunging into the wall in the Speedway's southeast turn at 12:17 P.M. on May 17, 1996, at precisely the moment that IMS President and CEO Anton Hulman "Tony" George was in pitside conversation with aspiring Speedway driver Robby Flock from

Murrieta, California. The cause of the accident was apparently a deflating right rear tire on the backup car that Brayton was then driving. Reports filtered through the Speedway that debris has caused the tire to puncture, and that prior to impacting the wall, the bottom of his Menard Glidden Quaker State Special, a 1995 Lola Menard V-6, bottomed out twice, went into a half spin at the approach of the southeast turn, slid an estimated 420 feet and connected on the car's left side. The car then rode against the wall for 360 more feet, bounced off the wall and slid 600 more feet before stopping on the backstretch. Later that day a memo from Firestone racing spokesman Tony Troiano stated, "Our preliminary analysis tends to indicate [that] the right rear tire on Scott's car did lose air[,] but the manner in which it occurred leads us to believe [that] the tire was cut. We are continuing to analyze what we have left of the tire[,] and that analysis does not indicate any internal structural damage. Our prayers are with Scott's family at this time."

Then came instructions from some unknown source on how and where to find Brayton's funeral on May 22: "Interstate 69 to Michigan exit 13 (U.S. 12; Coldwater/Quincy). West on U.S. 12 to the third traffic light (Marshall Street). North on Marshall Street. Church is on the east side." Bill Benner of the *Indianapolis Star/News* covered the funeral. "With quiet dignity, warm recollections and appropriate humor," he wrote, "this southern Michigan town said its final goodbye to its fastest favorite son Wednesday." Before roughly 1,000 mourners, Benner continued, Brayton "was laid to rest on a forested hillside of Oak Grove Cemetery, by the calm blue waters of Lake Coldwater." Accompanying the article was an Associated Press photograph of the Braytons' daughter Carly, with the title "Goodbye, Daddy," followed by a caption that read, "Carley [sic] Brayton, two-year-old daughter of Scott Brayton, holds a flower as she walks behind the hearse carrying the body of her father. Behind Carly are Brayton's parents Jean and Lee Brayton; Lee is holding his son's racing helmet." Among those present was Greg Brayton, one of Scott's two brothers who, despite blindness since childhood managed in off moments to play basketball, ride a motorcycle, and manage the family sand and gravel business. Greg, whose voice sounded eerily like his deceased brother's, had studied at the Michigan School for the Blind where he first met aspiring teenaged entertainer Stevie Wonder. It meanwhile later developed that although Scott Brayton carried life insurance, it did not apply in the event that he died in auto racing. "Being killed racing," Becky Brayton said, "wasn't a concern of Scott's." The daughter of Fred Rhue, a vice president of PPG Industries (a series sponsor of CART in the eighties), Becky liked show horses and, apparently, adored automobile racing. In days to come, she married another Michigan race driver in the person of Grosse Pointe's Robbie Buhl. Lee Brayton remained in the racing business as an engine developer. Driver Danny Ongais pinch-hit for Scott Brayton in 1996, and finished seventh.

In short, things were getting back to abnormal. When May 1997 rolled around, it was business as usual in the southeast turn. Arie Luyendyk, warming up for his second Indianapolis win, got loose as Scott Brayton had in the south chute, executed two full spins over a distance of 580 feet, crashed into the wall at about the point where other notables had in decades past, and rolled another sixty feet without injury. That was on May 8 at 3:17 P.M. Thirty-two minutes later there came on the same scene Stephan Gregoire, the wiry (five-foot-eleven, 140 pounds) long distance running Frenchman from Neufchateau who claimed he got his racing days off to a flying start by munching on a brown sugar cinnamon Pop Tart. Gregoire cut one complete spin in the southeast and came to a halt at the inner guardrail that slightly bent the nose of his car. Gregoire, as it turned out, would join four others in an accident before the race flagged off, and did not run a single competitive lap. His colleague Claude Bourbonnais got into hot water several days later when he drove too high, brushed that same fearsome wall with his right rear tire, and continued around the course. Like Gregoire, he went nowhere in the race, either, falling out after but nine circuits. The next day, Sunday, May 18, Scott Harrington inflicted extensive left side and front damage to his Johansson Immke Motorsports/ A. J. Foyt Racing car by doing the usual thing: losing control low in the southeast corner, sliding 600 feet, falling into a half spin, hitting the outside wall with the car's left side, crunching along the wall about 270 feet, sliding off of it backwards, and creeping to a halt in the middle of the race course. Harrington, believed injured, was sent to Methodist where physicians concluded differently, released him, and sent him home.

Like Gregoire and Bourbonnais, Harrington had a terrible month. On the final Sunday of race qualifications he turned in a respectable first lap (of four) in the 214 range, and then in that same turn two he lost control, hammered the concrete, and was packed off to Methodist again where physicians deemed him uninjured again. It came to pass that because of a sudden suspension of the so-called "twenty-five and eight" quota system, wherein twenty-five starting positions were protected for those cars pursuing points in IRL (the IMS-organized Indy Racing League) competition, and the remaining eight were open to CART (Championship Auto Racing Teams) entries, the starting field for the 1997 Indianapolis 500 would be expanded from thirty-three to thirty-five cars. All one needed to do to make the field was exceed the arbitrary 203 mile per hour minimum speed. Johnny Unser and Lyn St. James easily exceeded that mark. Apparently unaware of the change, Scott Harrington had taken to the track for a banzai run that stuffed him again into the southeast turn wall. Had he known better, he need only have cruised over the track at a more moderate pace and then participated in the race. He was out of luck.

Born on Christmas Eve 1963 in Louisville, Kentucky, Harrington tried the University of Louisville for a while, raced motorcycles, attended a bunch of professional high-performance driving schools, raced with SCCA for a few years, moved on to Formula Atlantic, ran a Porsche in the Twelve Hours of Sebring, tried the Shelby Can Am Pro Series, and arrived at Indianapolis in 1996 where he started thirty-second, tangled with Lyn St. James in the southeast turn, and came in fifteenth. It was his only run there. Then Robin Miller of the *Indianapolis Star* revealed in an August 9, 2000, article that since 1984 Harrington had "been arrested six times for DUI," and that in August 1999 he had been "arrested by the Marion County Sheriff's Department for confinement and battery of his wife." Responded Harrington, "I'm embarrassed for the bad press I've brought on and for the people who have supported me. I hope it's not the end of my career, but racing is secondary right now. I've got to get myself together."

Getting together, however, was what Harrington and a number of other drivers who continued to be buffaloed by Indy's second turn, the southeast, did. When Harrington and St. James tangled there in 1996, St. James broke her hand in the melee. Harrington banged it again in 1997. Ohio's forty-seven-year-old dirt tracking rookie Jack Hewitt spun there in 1998 without hitting anything. Eliseo Salazar and Steve Knapp whacked it in 1999. Drivers' repeated attempts to knock down the southeast turn's wall in the year 2000 failed decidedly. Donnie Beechler did one and a half spins in the south chute, clipped the southeast wall, and spun up the back straightaway. Rookie Ronnie Johncox fell into a half spin, then brushed the southeast and thereby clipped off the front wing of his Byrd-McCormack Motorsports car. Indianapolis dentist Jack Miller did much the same thing on the same day. Then it came time for "Indiana" Andy Hillenburg (there were at the time two unrelated Andy Hillenburgs in racing) to pay his disrespect to the turn-two barrier. Saturday, May 20, at 9:56 in the morning he found his Sumar Special wiggling at the apex of the south warmup lane, inadvertently slid across the grass, onto the track, and into the wall. Hillenburg unbuckled and climbed out of his dented Sumar Special without assistance. He did, not too incidentally, qualify for the 2000 race, lasting ninety-one laps, at which time a wheel bearing failed.

Rookie drivers at Indianapolis are inordinately fond of relying upon the cliche "dream come true," when asked how it feels to race at this, the supreme speed summit of the world. Sooner or later, they all discover that one golden moment to utter those infamous words. For Hillenburg it was, by George, indeed a dream come true, however. An Indianapolis kid born in 1963, that *annus mirabilis* when Parnelli Jones crossed the finish line ahead of racing greats Jim Clark, A. J. Foyt, and Rodger Ward, and when hurricane Flora ravaged the Caribbean. He was six when his father took him to the Indianapolis Motor Speedway for the first time, and it is safe to say that he never got over it. Andy Hillenburg's first race was gliding hell-for-leather down Wilbur Shaw Memorial Hill at the 1974 Soap Box Derby. At fifteen he volunteered as an unpaid pit helper on a sprint car owned by Rufus Gray and driven by Gray's son Gary. Later, Hillenburg was graduated from Indianapolis's Perry Meridian High School, and identified Johnny Rutherford, Gary Bettenhausen, Mark Donahue, and Foyt as his high watermark heros. Then he built himself a sprint car. After that, he did it all, except the incomparable Indianapolis 500 that was impossibly beyond his grasp: midget cars, sprint cars, championship dirt cars on the mile state fairgrounds tracks, and NASCAR Winston Cup and Busch series races. In time, he appointed himself president of the Fast Track High Performance School, located in Charlotte, North Carolina, around which all serious stock car drivers seemed to camp out. After having once established the fourth-fastest practice lap prior to a Daytona 500, NASCAR invited him back a week later to undergo some testing. En route back to the track his truck broke down, and he thumbed a ride back to Daytona with a vacationing couple. Asked his favorite vacation destination, he responded, "anywhere with a race track." At Indianapolis in 2000, Hillenburg remarked, "Oh, yeah. It's really, really great to be at the Indianapolis Motor Speedway." Asked about growing up near the old storied track, he responded, "If my mind gets to swaying too much on pit road, I about come to tears." After television commentator Bob Jenkins "told me he was really proud of me, I about lost it. And I did, too. It's been tough to get out of the car [without emoting]."

Such is the inexorable lure of Indianapolis. If the likes of Floyd Roberts, Johnnie Parsons, Tony Bettenhausen, Rodger Ward, Graham Hill, and Tom Sneva could not help but be drawn into the southeast turn's maw, then in 2001, so too could Jeret Schroeder, rookie Brandon Erwin, Davey Hamilton, Steve Knapp, and Stan Wattles, all without injury. By 2002, the SAFER (Steel And Form Energy Reduction) barriers were in place on the turn walls of Indianapolis. When in the 1960s overhead "cage" protection became mandatory for short track open wheel racing cars, there evolved a theory that, in the knowledge that one could in all likelihood avoid serious accident injury, cages would give license to drivers to proceed with still more abandon. This may well have been borne out. With so-called "soft" walls at Indianapolis, it also remained to be seen whether drivers might find pretext for still higher speeds through Indy's corners, imagining that the consequences of their mishaps would be minimized by driving, as it were, into a huge pillow. It is a bit soon to form any conclusions, however Canadian Paul Tracy (who claimed to have won the disputed 2002 Indianapolis 500 when his last lap pass was or was not executed under yellow flag conditions) smashed into the turn two SAFER with the rear of his car on May 11, and after treatment for knee and heel abrasions was freed from medical scrutiny and given permission to reenter the racing wars. Inglewood, California's George Mack, the second (to Willy T. Ribbs) African-American racer to compete at the Speedway, challenged the SAFER barrier on May 15 with what was apparently a little lighter force than Tracy had, and still came through the contact without consequences. In Mack's wake on Sunday, May 19, stormed feisty Arizonan Billy Boat who also escaped personal injury. All three drivers, determined to stay off of Indy's man-eating walls, were still in the chase at the end of the 2002 contest, with Tracy scoring second, and Mack and Boat each two laps back in seventeenth and eighteenth, respectively.

In 2004 two famous names in racing tasted the SAFER coating in the southeast turn during the race that ended twenty laps early under extremely threatening weather conditions. Rookie Larry Foyt, youngest son of four-time winner A. J. Foyt, ran high into turn two on lap 56 and put himself out of competition. "It's always been my childhood dream to come here to Indy," he said pre-race. Another first year man, P. J. Jones, older son of 1963 winner Parnelli Jones ran high on the track on lap 94 of the race, and did much the same thing. It had not been an outstanding year for second generation contestants.

TURN THREE: THE NORTHEAST

"Watch the wall, my darling,
while the Gentlemen go by!"
—Rudyard Kipling, *Puck of Pook's Hill* (1906)

Turn Three (the northeast) is the most remote of the Speedway's four treacherous corners, if only because it is the farthest from the main gate near the southwest turn and the farthest from any public access road. It is the Speedway's answer to Nova Scotia. The north side of the track is supposedly a foot or so higher than the south side. To the east is the golf course, to the north some open acreage. To look northward in 1925, in fact, was to view an expanse of farmland. Nevertheless it has been possible for quite some time to drive an automobile around the track without driving *on* the track, inasmuch as there is an outer utility access road that encircles the inner Speedway, although it is difficult to impossible to use when there are pedestrians milling around in any number. The third corner is also arguably the least noticed and followed, except of course by those sturdy souls who people the huge Northeast Vista, and the sturdier souls who race in front of it.

Nevertheless, folks have died in the northeast, races won and lost there. Norwegian-born marine engineer Gilbert "Gil" Anderson, for example, started on the pole and scored sixteenth out of twenty-four when his gray and white Stutz chassis with a four-cylinder Wisconsin engine was running at almost an eighty-one mile an hour average when he and mechanic Frank Agan discovered themselves upside down in the northeast. "Fortunately," one commentator wrote, "the few accidents that did occur did not result in the serious injury of anyone, and the race goes down in motoring history [this was only the second running of what was then called the 500-mile International Sweepstakes Race] as one of the best ever held." Anderson was to drive the first six Indianapolis 500-milers, with a third (his best) in 1915.

Exiting the northeast (originally believed in earlier accounts to be the "south turn") on lap sixty-one of the 1916 race was Jack LeCain, driving relief for Jules DeVigne in a yellow and black Harry Harkness Delage. LeCain lost control (as so many others would in the subsequent eighty-nine years), ran into a wall, and overturned, occasioning internal injuries, a fractured skull, a broken jaw, and a broken back (deemed "very serious" by medical personnel) for himself, while mechanic Bob Moore seemed to escape without so much as a hangnail. There is nothing to suggest that DeVigne, LeCain, or Moore ever again took to the Indianapolis's bricks. There was no such happy ending in the 1919 race, however, beginning on lap forty-four when Art Thurman from Washington, D.C., driving his own gray Duesenberg, was killed when he too upended in the northeast. Shortly before the accident he had visited the pits for water and a change of plugs. Thurman's riding mechanic Robert Bandini fractured his skull.

Pete DePaolo, three years away from his only Indianapolis win, cracked the northeast wall but good, on lap 111 in 1922 while chasing leader and eventual winner Jimmy Murphy. DePaolo and his mechanic Jimmy Brett restarted, limped back to their pit with a bent axle, retired the car, and reentered the race in Joe Thomas's ill-handling Duesenberg that ended the day in tenth position. Far more serious was the 1927 race when Jules Ellingboe, piloting a front-drive Miller for Earl Cooper, contacted the wall in the northeast. Said a news item, "The driver was so seriously injured that he was taken to the hospital as quickly as possible." This was Ellingboe's sixth and final try at Indianapolis, where he never managed to break into the top ten finishers. Ellingboe, not too incidentally, died on April 26, 1948.

There was an abundance of activity at the northeast in 1930, beginning on lap twenty-three when a driver named Red Roberts, driving relief for Peter DePaolo who said that his car was too difficult to steer, slipped in turn three, whereupon he collected Elbert "Babe" Stapp, also mistakenly known as "Egbert" Stapp. Deacon Litz then collided with Marion Trexler while Lou Moore deliberately spun his car and then trailed the retaining wall. Johnny Seymore and Jimmy Gleason then got together, after which Gleason's car broke timing gears, but continued around the course to his pit box. There were cars scattered over the whole northeast turn and beyond. Litz's riding mechanic "Shorty" Barnes suffered a head laceration, while others escaped the multicar crash without too much bodily harm. Litz left the Speedway that night with his right wrist in a splint, which prevented him from competing in the next AAA championship race on the mile dirt at the Michigan State Fairgrounds in Detroit on June 6. Stapp's mechanic Johnny Apple required treatment for a leg contusion, as did Ted Everrode, Johnny Seymore's mechanic. Stapp remembered the accident with faint amusement in the late 1970s: "I got my left hand scratched a little bit," he said. "I didn't know it at the time, but one of my knuckles must have jammed against something. But no one had any serious injury at all. We all got out and walked away from it, you see. But that's an awful mess, to be sitting there looking the wrong way down the race track and seeing everybody spinning and coming right at you. It's just like the Hollywood Freeway." Wilbur Shaw, who participated in the 1930 race but dropped to the sidelines when he developed an oil leak, referred to the turn three pileup as "one of the most spectacular accidents in Speedway history."

Shortly after there occurred more turn three problems, some of them deadly. The corner's next ward was unheralded Charles Moran, a rookie from Long Meadow, Massachusetts, sharing the cockpit of his cream colored DuPont Motors Special with mechanic Gene Reed. When the boxy machine "kissed the wall," as one reporter expressed it, the occupants of the racer were injured only slightly. The worst was yet to come in the northeast that day. At the age of twenty-eight, Cy Marshall was the proprietor of a garage on Indianapolis's Fort Wayne Avenue. Twice married and the father of two children, Marshall had driven relief for Earl Devore in the 1928 race and finished eighteenth after a skirmish on the southwest turn. He skipped the race in 1929 but returned in 1930 at the tiller of a green eight-cylinder Duesenberg entered by George E. Henry, then a member of the Indianapolis City Council. This, after all, was the Depression, when any money was good money. As a local driver entered in a local car by a local politician, Marshall found special favor with the local press. One paper approvingly referred to him as "an Indianapolis boy, especially well-liked, and considered a good driver."

Qualifying tenth at a speed of 100.846 miles per hour, Marshall had given in somewhat reluctantly to his brother, thirty-four-year-old James Paul Marshall, Jr., who wanted to become his riding mechanic. James, a widower of three months, supported his four children by working as a carpenter and house painter in Detroit. Although Cy Marshall had acquired a middling reputation on Indiana dirt tracks, his brother had never so much as sat in a racing car, much less at Indianapolis. It was soon after the start of the 1930 race that, having somehow avoided Chet Gardner's first turn, first lap spin, the brothers experienced clutch trouble that necessitated a prolonged, sixteen-minute pit visit. At the time of the accident involving Red Roberts, Babe Stapp and others such as the Marshalls were several laps off the pace set by winner-to-be Billy Arnold. Returned to the track with their clutch problem tentatively corrected, the two approached the northeast turn on their twenty-ninth lap. Looming in front of them was a missing six-foot section of guard railing, a result of the earlier mishap. Cy Marshall may have been applying as much throttle as he had when his clutch was slipping, or the clutch may have ceased functioning altogether. Whatever the explanation, the brothers felt their car begin to slide out of control and point toward the inside wall. Having wrenched the steering wheel to the right to correct this slide, Cy Marshall succeeded only in pointing the Duesenberg toward the outer wall, loosening it for more than thirty feet. The Duesey then veloplaned over the cement fence, fell about fifteen feet, nose-first, and then tumbled for another 165 feet before stopping. Cy Marshall, whose headgear offered little protection, lost his left ear, fractured his skull and jaw, and sustained numerous other cuts and scrapes. Attendants rushed both men to the infield hospital where physicians worked diligently to save both lives. Only Cy, rescued from beneath the wreckage of his car, survived. Unaware of his brother's death, he pleaded with the medical staff to "fix up Paul first." At City Hospital on the day after the 1930 race, Cy had recovered sufficiently to ask his brother's condition and to request a newspaper. The question went unanswered and the request went unfulfilled. Writer Harold Blanchard accorded the accident ho-hum treatment, passing it off lightly as if to suggest that fatalities and injuries were an everyday nuisance at Indianapolis. "Cy Marshall took a spin in the north turn," he reported, "and broke through the outer retaining wall. His brother died almost instantly, but Cy is on the road to recovery." Marshall eventually did recover, and after a hiatus of seventeen years (like his driving colleague Roland Free) returned from his Jacksonville, Florida, home at the age of forty-five to the Speedway for one final time, logging 197 laps in the Tattersfield Special, a supercharged Alfa-Romeo entered by Bill White, finishing eighth. That same car, incidentally, had competed in the 1946 event with Jimmy Wilburn at the helm. Cy Marshall died on December 20, 1974.

Stapp recollected, at the age of seventy-four, about the specter of death on American speedways. As racing people, he began, "we are associated with death. We know it, we accept it, and there's not much that we can do about it. Losing friends in racing hurts a lot, especially if they have been real close. I quit racing for a time when Bill Spence got killed in 1929. He and I were very close. You hate to lose a friend, regardless of whether it's in racing or not, but when the friend is in racing, he seems a bit closer to you. Some sports writers and editors condemn automobile racing because someone gets killed. But if a steelworker falls from a building, they don't make any big story about it because he's been doing something that's constructive. Everyone can be a part of it, and use it, and appreciate it. There's a different attitude in sports, though. In horse racing, jockeys now and then get killed. A race driver is out there racing because he wants to, or he wouldn't be driving in the first place. There's not much that can be done about it.'' There were plenty of things that could have been done about it, had anyone cared to address them. For the nonce, no one did.

In 1931 there were those who crashed their way into the track, and others who crashed their way out of it. Among the former was the celebrated but rather eccentric professional gate-crasher known simply as One-Eyed Connelly who made his annual appearance and was up to his old tricks again at the Speedway's means of ingress where he feigned a fit and was chauffeured to the infield for medical attention. Left alone for a few minutes, Connelly devoured a bowl of apples designated for the race day medical staff. After treatment, they advised him to recline on a cot, from which he covertly disappeared in time to see the race flag off. Al Bloemker recalled that once Connelly was securely inside the track, his first act was to pull off his raincoat, thereby revealing a green flannel shirt with fancy stitching that read, ''All gates I've crashed, I'm here to tell./ I'll crash St. Pete and then crash H. . . .''

If Connelly's skill at breaking in was flawless, his timing was not. The skies over the Speedway were ashen gray and rain-laden. Weather delayed the race, and the National Broadcasting System moved its air time from 2:15 to 4:15 P.M. Pre-race activities commenced as scheduled, however, as the Speedway's long-anticipated 1,500-piece marching band proudly strutted up the home stretch to the tune of ''Betty Coed.'' When the event began, it was rife with excitement. On lap sixty Wilbur Shaw, driving relief for Phil Pardee in a Duesenberg, got out of shape in the northeast turn and disappeared over the wall. By pre-race arrangement, Shaw had agreed to take Pardee's place beside mechanic Walter ''Otto'' Hannowsky who, as a smallish chap, was all but hidden as a stowaway in the cockpit. Having had no practice time in the car, Shaw never so much as peeped through the windshield before the team manager ordered him into battle after early race traffic thinned. There being no restrictions governing oil consumption in 1931, the track was impossibly greasy. To complicate matters, the big Duesenberg was an unruly, ill-handling missile. "Weighing 2,400 pounds," Shaw said in his autobiography, it "rode like a baby buggy." That is principally why Shaw and Hannowsky launched out of the track, taking to the airways for about twenty-five feet, and tearing out a considerable footage of telephone wire anchored on utility poles outside the third turn. Landing on its wheels, the car rested momentarily in a billow of smoke before the two crawled out. Shaw was unhurt. Hannowsky's forehead was cut.

At the time of that mishap, Freddy Winnai in a Bowes Seal Fast Miller swerved to keep from hitting Shaw, but drove through ten feet of outer wall a short distance from Shaw's point of sudden departure, and developed slight injuries to his back and leg. All three men visited the infield medical facility for scrutiny. Ambulance drivers "darn near killed us as they tried to set a new record for a trip to the emergency hospital over some of the roughest terrain ever navigated by a four wheel vehicle," said Shaw, who had his superficial cuts and scrapes dressed with iodine before setting out once again for the pit area in search of another car to drive. Once there, he donned his helmet and goggles, then took over Jimmy Gleason's car, another Duesenberg, this one painted orange and white like the first one. Shaw proceeded to finish the day in sixth. The drivers who had witnessed his launch out of the Speedway in an orange and white Duesey on lap sixty could not reconcile seeing him back on track with what appeared to be the same car later in the day.

The northeast furnished more undesirable race day excitement in 1932, as 1930 winner Billy Arnold ramped the wall on his fifty-ninth lap, rolled his gray and blue Miller-Hartz, and broke his shoulder blade. Mechanic William "Spider" Matlock suffered a fractured pelvis. This not-insignificant incident was a curious reversal of the previous year when, in the northwest turn, it was Matlock who broke his shoulder and Arnold his pelvis. In 1933, however, a May 28 time trial incident in the northeast had infinitely more serious aspects. The Brady and Nardi Special with thirty-two-year-old "Bill Denver," aka William Orem of Audubon, Pennsylvania, at the pedals, spun out at about 110 miles per hour in the northeast, darted to the top of the track, and catapulted down the embankment on the outside of the race course. One observer remarked that the car "spent its force against a tree." Denver and his mechanic Hugh "Bob" Hurst were thrown clear as the car ruptured its tank and exploded in flame. Neither man survived. It had been on the Monday previous that driver Al Aspen and rider Mitz Davis both failed to survive a wreck in the same car when it struck the retaining wall in the southwest turn. Crews had worked uninterruptedly to restore the car for Sunday qualification runs when Denver and Hurst were to have placed the machine in the field for the twenty-first running of the 500-mile classic.

On the occasion of the twenty-second running of the race in 1934, atmosphere at the Speedway seemed ironically felicitous in contrast with the desperately serious economic depression that cast its pall over virtually every aspect of American life. "Sex Adds to Speedway Color," was the headline attached to one reporter's impressions of the 1934 mob scene that assembled at West Sixteenth and Georgetown Road. "Gay little ginghams and seersuckers, pique and bastes went to the race today and won out in a big way in the fashion sweepstakes." Elsewhere in the news, Clyde Barrow, the FBI's foremost public enemy in the American Southwest, died after a Louisiana police ambush, along with his cigar-puffing gun moll, the celebrated (if indelicate) Miss Bonnie Parker.

Closer to home, Indianapolis police mistakenly believed that another fugitive roamed the area. He was thirty-year-old Hoosier anti-hero John Herbert Dillinger, bank robber *nonpareil* and sixteen-time murderer who at the time of the 1934 Indianapolis 500 was actually not anywhere near Indianapolis, but was instead with his dear friend Jimmy Probasco (as in *probocis*) at 2909 Crawford Avenue in Chicago undergoing plastic surgery and fingerprint removal at the hands of the good doctors Wilhelm Loeser and Harold Cassidy. They removed his bandages the day after the 500, whereupon Dillinger repaired to the Barrel of Fun nightclub for some much deserved frivolity before an FBI agent, believed to be Charlie Winstead, gunned him down in front of Chicago's Biograph movie house on July 22. Afterword, Dillinger's corpse went to the Maywood, Indiana, home of his sister Audrey Hancock who placed it in her front room for public viewing until it was lowered to an eternal rest on July 25 beneath the sod of Indianapolis's Crown Hill Cemetery on West Thirty-eighth Street, twenty-two blocks north of the Speedway.

On race day, 1934, however, it was Willard "Big Boy" Rader, twice a relief driver at the Speedway, stuffed behind the wheel of a La Salle who for the third time paced the Indianapolis 500. People with a sense of track history may have noticed that Bill Denver's 1933 spill at the northeast was similar to the unpleasant 1934 mishap of George Bailey, thirty-two, of

Detroit. Bailey drove a beautiful tan, black, and white Studebaker-powered Scott Special (Snowberger chassis) that cleared the wall on the northeast turn, and incurred head gashes, a broken rib, injuries to his left wrist, as well as numerous body bruises. His airborne companion Jim Johnson sustained head injuries, occasioning a bloody nose and the loss of four teeth. Swathed in bandages, he was permitted to leave the Speedway hospital not long after having been seen. Oily track conditions constituted a major problem since, as Shaw commented, racing cars were burning fifty to sixty gallons of oil, 80 percent of which ended up on the track surface. Partly as a consequence, Gene Haustein's eight-cylinder Hudson spun around three times in the northeast while he and his traveling wrench Ed Beaudine were trying to survive their fourteenth lap. The Martz Special with which they were entrusted finally lost its momentum and ended against the outer wall, the car's nose pointed toward the inside of the track. Opinion had it that a good bit of the slippery stuff had been deposited by the crankcase of Shaw's Red Lion Miller. "Here again," proclaimed a local reporter, "is demonstrated the courage and sportsmanship of the drivers, in their desire to prevent further accidents, when Haustein and his mechanic braced themselves against the car and kept it from rolling down the track, thus preventing further accidents. For this courageous deed, Haustein [but not Beaudine] received the Julius Wark annual trophy, consisting of a Swiss timer."

Well and good, but the day was not yet over. Eager to rejoin the race, driver and mechanic eased the car to the track apron where they attempted to restart the engine by pushing the bulky 2,100-pound speedster back to life. When the car gathered momentum, Haustein tripped the ignition switch and dropped the racer into gear. As the Hudson began to sputter and belch, Beaudine leapt on the car's tail and prepared to retake the passenger seat. Then along came George "Doc" MacKenzie (killed on the mile dirt at the Wisconsin State Fairgrounds in Milwaukee on August 23, 1936) in a tubby 2,559-pound orange Studebaker, and plowed into them, tearing the tail out of Haustein's car and dumping Beaudine on the track. Albeit not the easiest of days, at least there were no serious injuries recorded from the fracas. Coverage in *Motor* magazine said nothing about Haustein and Beaudine, but did remark that MacKenzie, "by the way, is the only driver to sport a beard since the Vanderbilt Cup racing days of Heath and Jenatzy—thirty years ago." Before the 1934 race only a few drivers sported helmets worthy of the name. The rest donned jaunty, tight-fitting aviation-inspired cloth caps that fastened about the chin and were, in an accident, the next best thing to worthless. This time, however, helmets became a requirement, although the AAA mandate was hampered by an insufficient inventory of approved headgear. Some of the helmets, like those worn by Bob Sall and Jimmy Snyder, caused the driver's head to resemble a twenty-five pound jellybean that afforded little if any protection around the temples or at the base of the skull.

AAA eastern dirt track champion Johnny Hannon, a twenty-five-year-old Norristown, Pennsylvania, rookie at Indianapolis in 1935, needed every bit of protection he could find. On May 19, while establishing a new one-lap record of 40.61 seconds at Milwaukee, Hannon crashed through the inside fence and rolled his car twice in an immense cloud of dust without injury to himself or anyone else. Undaunted, his next stop was Indianapolis where he had been offered his first Speedway ride in one of Leon Duray's red, white, and black Bowes Seal Fast cars. Hannon arrived in town with his long-suffering mechanic Oscar "Shorty" Reeves, an Indianapolis native who had ridden with Hannon for five years on the dirt tracks, and had the scars to prove it. Both Duray and fellow racer Tony Gulotta insisted, however, that they each take practice runs with Hannon to familiarize him with the track before they set him free on the bricks with Reeves as passenger. Hannon agreed. Duray and Gulotta cautioned Hannon not to take much liberty with the turns at Indianapolis nor to underestimate their potential peril.

Weather was clear on Tuesday morning, May 21, when Gulotta eased behind the wheel of the car for his final practice session, turning a lap at 117 miles per hour. Gulotta returned to the pits where Hannon and Reeves prepared to practice on their own. Reeves, an employee of Indianapolis's Sugar Creek Creamery by day and a dance-band drummer at the local Alpine Inn by night, gamely joined Hannon in the Bowes cockpit. Whereas even experienced Indianapolis drivers work up to speed incrementally, methodically getting accustomed to car and track, Hannon took no such precaution when he set out with his right foot down hard on the throttle as he roared through the first turn, the second turn, and up the backstretch while his engine sounded like it was at full rhapsodic song. But as he approached turn three the car began to zigzag and skidded toward the inside wall without making contact. It then made an abrupt turnabout and headed toward the outside wall, where it removed a yard of concrete as it quit the track entirely. Inertia threw Hannon an estimated fifty feet, after which he sustained head and chest injuries that took his life. Reeves, at least, survived. Before the month was over, Clay Weatherly would die in the same car.

Although treachery in turn three during the running of the 1935 race was less serious, there was excitement nonetheless. The protagonist this time was a citizen named Junior Oldham, aged thirty-six, from Louisville. According to reports, Oldham, in somewhat the manner of the famous One-Eyed Connolly, entered the infield unnoticed and climbed an exceedingly tall tree near the northeast turn. He was supposedly up the same tree during the race's running, but fainted when the contest was about half completed and became wedged between two large branches sixty feet above the ground. A crowd below summoned constable Plez Oliver of the Indianapolis Police Department who summarily borrowed a hundred-foot length of rope and enlisted the services of volunteer Renciel Williams, described by newspaper reporter Robert Early as a "Negro tree climber, 1850 Peck Street," who assured constable Oliver that he could "shinny up a tree like a cat." After Williams had indeed scaled the tree, secured the rope around Oldham's chest and given an all clear signal to the resourceful Oliver, Oldham felt himself lowered gingerly to earth. "When Williams had scrambled to the ground," Early wrote, "spectators praised him, slapped him on the back, and showered him with coins," after which Williams "gathered them in his hat and ambled away."

The race was five laps down after the garage-fire-delayed 1941 race when in the northeast turn Emil Andres in a yellow and red Kennedy Tank Special fitted up with a six-cylinder Lenki engine spun as he prepared to execute the turn. Twenty-six-year-old Joel Thorne, the somewhat controversial Burbank, California, millionaire driving his own car, plugged Andres on the latter's left side causing him to spin a second time, after which he dinged the wall and rolled to the center of the track. Then out of turn three there appeared Louis Tomei in a black, front-drive Offenhauser, making his eighth Indianapolis bid. Tomei collided with Thorne, and survived the mix-up with his right front inner tube unaccountably wrapped around his axle. Continuing on his way he stopped in his pit, replaced his right front wheel, and charged back on track where he finished all 500 miles in eleventh position. Thorne and Andres were unhurt and their cars towed off the course. Starter Seth Klein displayed the yellow for the next seventy-five laps, while workers in their own good time cleared the track of incidental debris. It was not until 1954 that Klein, who had been flagging at the Speedway twenty years, yielded the assignment to Holland, Michigan's deep-tanned Bill Vanderwater, a regular flagman on the AAA midget car circuit with a reputation as a natty dresser and an accomplished tippler who ably handled the Indianapolis flags between 1954 and 1961.

The unorganized movement of race day motor traffic for the 1946 Indianapolis 500 may have caught the new Hulman ownership team off guard. "As the thirtieth renewal of the 500-mile race started here today," wrote Bill Fox, Jr. after the race ended, "thousands of persons were milling outside the gates, victims of the worst traffic jam in the city's history. Several squads of police fought traffic at Union Station," he continued, "as race-goers waited in line for the railway facilities to the Speedway. Along the route which I followed in reaching here in exactly three hours time, people were leaving their cars, running ahead to houses, and grabbing buckets of water to pour into overheated motors." With a significant proportion of spectators stranded outside track gates, the race got underway at 11:00 A.M. as scheduled. At sixteen laps, Paul Russo crunched his 2,510-pound Fageol Twin Coach Special, powered by twin 91 cubic inch supercharged Offenhauser midget car engines (one fore, one aft) with equal weight distribution on all four corners of the car, against the northeast wall. The portly Russo fell out of the car, thereby breaking a leg. Reports indicated that he had dipped below the inner white line in turn three, slid into some soft infield dirt, and then struck the outer barrier that had not, because of the World War II auto racing suspension, been struck by anything stronger than gale winds in at least five years. A loud explosion sounded as Russo's front tire burst on impact. While this was happening, car No. 31, an orange and black Automobile Shippers Special driven by mild mannered Henry Banks, slid deeply through the track's inner grassy area opposite Russo's car, coming to rest with the rear wheels of the car mired in dirt. Eased out by a wrecker, it continued around the track, tooled around for eleven more laps, and stalled.

Exactly thirty minutes after the Russo affair Mauri Rose, in the No. 8 Blue Crown, banked his car against the wall in the northeast amid a cloud of debris. It was Rose's fortieth lap, during which he slid through turn three just as a rescue truck was preparing to remove Russo's rumpled Fageol from the course. Rose proceeded to pile into Russo's wreckage, whereupon he too found himself dumped on the track. Having crawled to the outer wall, he was assisted over it by track attendants and made to lie down on the wall itself. This accident compounded by a second wreck was not something that northeast turn AAA observers (Vanderwater, and two Chicagoans named Jimmy Thompson and Harry Lynch) were anything but surprised to see, having noticed Rose slip-sliding through the turn on two earlier laps. In twelve minutes the track was clear and the race resumed.

In 1947, observers in the northeast were reminded of Banks's spin through that stretch of track the year before, when they spotted 200-pound Frank Wearne, a Pasadena, California, driver do much the same thing in another orange No. 31 car (this one called the Superior Industries Special) entered, like the first one, by Detroit's Lou Rassey. But it was not the same car. Wearne's short wheelbase Offenhauser had once dominated competition in its class at the annual Pikes Peak hill climb, but its stubby upright Miller chassis seemed far more suited to a dirt track than realisticly threatening for the Indianapolis 500, even in 1947 when cars were mostly prewar holdovers. Wearne looped the car on his 138th lap without running into anything. In this, his seventh consecutive race at Indianapolis, he called for relief. Veteran Louis Tomei assumed the driving chores, finishing fourteenth. Wearne, meanwhile, who had finished in the top ten on five occasions, had made his final Brickyard appearance.

Ralph Hepburn had fifteen Indianapolis starts behind him in 1948, having made his Speedway debut in a Miller Special in 1925. Out of competition since 1946 when he piloted a Novi to fourteenth place, Hepburn was fifty-two when he replaced Cliff Bergere behind the wheel in one of Lew Welsh's two Novis, howling supercharged front-drive 180 cubic inch methanol burning V-8s, consisting of two four-cylinder blocks joined at a forty-five degree angle, with two valves per cylinder. Bergere spun in what writer Norman Werking called "the North trouble patch" during a practice session, felt understandably spooked, and declared that the Novi to which he was assigned (and had driven the previous year) was indeed unsafe to drive. He was probably right. Hepburn, in the meantime, arrived at the track with one of Don Lee's supercharged Mercedes-Benz racers. After Welsh offered him the seat of Bergere's vacated Novi, he changed cars immediately. Referring to the Novi, Hepburn told his friend Charles Lytle, "That's my baby." One of the most admired competitors at Indianapolis, Hepburn had raced motorcycles as far back as 1915. His goal, like everyone else's in Gasoline Alley, was to win the Indianapolis 500. With a third-place finish in 1931, a fifth in 1935, and a fourth in 1941, Hepburn had repeatedly come within striking distance.

After Bergere's Novi was repaired and deemed trackworthy, Hepburn posed for photographers before he took to the track for a shakedown run on May 17. It proved to be his last. Having turned one lap at 133 miles an hour, the car slid sideways as Hepburn attempted the northeast turn on the following lap. Pointed toward the bottom of the track, the car dipped below the white line and into the grassy infield. Hepburn apparently applied the throttle to regain control, but instead the car swung 180 degrees, headed back on the track, and connected with the wall at an angle of about forty-five degrees. The impact caused his helmet and goggles to fly loose, while Hepburn himself went momentarily out of the cockpit and back again. "Death had been instantaneous," Shaw wrote, "I walked to where my car was parked in the garage area and climbed into the front seat. Sitting there, alone, I recalled our many experiences together—as well as our strained relations during the ASPAR episode [the American Society of Professional Automobile Racing driver consortium that threatened to strike in 1947]—and cried for at least five minutes." Writer and motor book publisher Floyd Clymer joined the huge funeral entourage that descended on Glendale, California's Forest Lawn Cemetery. It was a double funeral service, Hepburn's eighty-three-year-old father having succumbed four days after his son's death. The elder Hepburn, so said reports, had never been notified of his son's passing.

The experiences that Bergere and Hepburn had with the Novi prompted Chet Miller to withdraw from his assignment in the twin car. He was superseded by perennial Speedway favorite Dennis Clayton "Duke" Nalon who clocked fastest in the field (although because of the lateness of the run he did not start on the pole) and ably guided the car to third place in the 1948 race, the best ever finish for both Nalon and the Novi. The articulate Nalon, also known as the "Iron Duke," who died four days before his eighty-eighth birthday in late February 2001, had put the Novis on the pole at Indianapolis in 1949 and 1951, commenting much later that it "was quite an accomplishment. I thought that was pretty good for a kid from Chicago." He was one of nine children born into a working class family that he claimed had descended from aristocratic French origins. Be that as it may, the peripatetic Nalon was associated, in his Depression Era racing days at Hammond, Indiana's Roby Speedway, with what was romantically but accurately known as the "Chicago Gang," composed of stout hearts like Emil Andres, Harry McQuinn, Paul Russo, and later Tony Bettenhausen. Nalon worked in a steel mill until he was twenty-one, at which time he became a mechanic for area midget car ace Wally Zale, and commenced driving racing cars himself, traveling the country and winning races excluding any AAA national championship (Indianapolis car) events. Although he conveyed a crowd-pleasing charisma in public, he

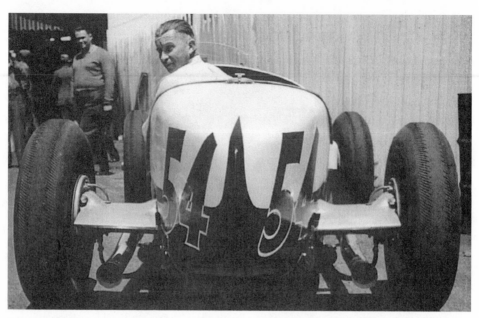

Former motorcycle racer Ralph Hepburn in the black, white, and red Bowes Seal Fast supercharged, four-cylinder Offenhauser, prepared by William C. "Bud" Winfield. The 1946 race marked the thirteenth of Hepburn's fifteen Indy appearances that ended with his death in Indianapolis's northeast turn in 1948 in a Winfield eight-cylinder Novi. He was buried at Forest Lawn Memorial Park in Glendale, California. *Ed Hitze*

also conveyed a certain invincible egotism in private. Through it all, there is no gainsaying that Duke Nalon was one of the imposing personalities who helped build the Speedway's immense, even mythic prestige.

Race day in 1949 was to be the most memorable few hours in Nalon's life, not only for what happened on the track, but what transpired off it, as well. Minutes before the race Lew Welsh ordered the Novi garage in Gasoline Alley cleared of all persons except himself and his drivers Nalon and Rex Mays. Once the door closed securely, Welsh's message was as direct as it was surprising: so long as both cars were running competitively, one car was forbidden to overtake the other for the lead. Furthermore, said Welsh, whichever car was ahead at the end of the first lap was to remain ahead; the other driver was not to overtake him. On the remote chance that the Novis were to finish the race in the first two positions, prize money was to be divided equally. Welsh, in Nalon's words, "did not want Rex and me to be running through our rubber [tires] trying to pass each other." Both drivers, nevertheless, were aghast. Any departure from this pre-race understanding, said Welsh, would result in the offending driver's being black flagged (disqualified) and fired from the Novi racing team.

By 1949 the twin Novis were not the twins they were alleged to be. Both machines were equipped with three forward speeds, but the gear ratios in Mays's car were all in a lower range from those in Nalon's. Side by side on the backstretch during the pace lap, Nalon (having magnanimously thrown kisses to the crowd) heard Mays, from the middle of the front row, rev his engine and slip into second gear. Nalon assumed that Mays would race him to the starting line (although by rule and tradition the pole position car must cross the starting line first) in this intermediate gear, and then make a determined effort to remain ahead at the conclusion of the first lap. Nalon then pulled somewhat ahead of Mays and made an obvious gesture of slipping into his own second gear. It was nothing more than a gesture, however, since Nalon intentionally held his car in low.

Chicago driver Dennis "Duke" Nalon poses in the maroon Marks Special in 1940, his sophomore year at the track. Over the years, Nalon developed a sanctimoniously aloof theatrical flair for attracting public attention. In ten Indy starts, his best was a third in 1948. *Ed Hitze*

Mays, assuming that his second gear would out-drag Nalon's, felt confident that he would intersect the starting line first, and that he could thereafter assume the lead and hold it for the crucial first lap. For Nalon, the ruse worked. Pressing down hard on the throttle, he wound the engine near the limit, floating its valves and reaching the starting line ahead of anyone else. At least four cars crossed the line ahead of Wilbur Shaw's Oldsmobile pace car, now on the pit lane. Shifting into second gear and then third, Nalon held the lead over Mays on the backstretch. It was then that volatile George Lynch spun his Automobile Shippers car in the first corner, rapped the wall and ended parked in the infield. After Seth Klein displayed the green again, Nalon turned a record race lap of 126.564, and then established another record for the first twenty-five miles. At the fifty-mile mark he continued to lead, with Mays trailing as per instructions.

Nalon's racing luck, however, was brief. Moving up the backstretch, Nalon claimed, his left rear axle snapped, and the Novi's weight loaded on the right side of the chassis. Riding behind Nalon was Rose, who recognized Nalon's problem before Nalon did. On this, Nalon's twenty-third lap, the ensuing accident was regrettably reminiscent of Hepburn's the previous year. Nalon began to spin toward the base of the northeast turn while a detached left rear wheel rolled to the outer edge of the track and rebounded off the wall as Nalon himself would do momentarily. As the Novi backed to the top of the track its fuel tank ruptured, igniting almost 100 gallons of a witch's brew that was 90 percent methanol and 10 percent benzol. A fiery trail followed in the car's wake as it skirted the contour of the retaining wall backwards. When the car rolled to a stop, still backwards, next to the wall, both left-side wheels were missing, and the car deposited an eight-foot-high wall of flame down the track through which some oncoming cars were obliged to drive. The force of the explosion had blown the seams out of Nalon's driving uniform and burned him extensively. His fate was to spend the next four months in Methodist Hospital where physicians performed painful skin grafts. So tightly were the grafts applied to the backs of his hands and fingers that Nalon's ability to achieve a tight grip on a steering wheel thereafter was compromised. Back in Gasoline Alley Lew Welch, who had gone through three drivers and would four years later lose a fourth when Chet Miller crashed in the first turn, denied that the accident had been triggered by axle failure. Film footage of the 1949 Nalon accident became standard Hollywood crash-and-burn fare in films like *The Big Wheel*. After his dismissal from Methodist the following September, Nalon recovered sufficient strength to make a courageous return to the Speedway to qualify a Novi, but failed to bring it off. In 1951 he was on the pole again with the Novi, but the car stalled three quarters of the way through the race. He tried the car again in 1952 but left the race at eighty-four laps when a supercharger failed. In 1953 he started at the back of the field, but spun out. The man who tamed the Novi, as some journalists claimed, had in reality been tamed by it. He attempted four different championship races with four different cars that year, missed qualifying each time, and thereafter retired after having surprised everyone by timing fastest and winning the (then) high profile 200-lap AAA midget race at Terre Haute, Indiana, in October 1954. That not insignificant feat became his last hurrah.

In the rain-abbreviated 1950 classic Troy Ruttman and Jim Rathmann, later Speedway winners, spun in the northeast as rainwater flooded the track almost instantly. A year later, the northeast lured Sam Hanks and his red Peter Schmidt Special, an off the shelf Kurtis Kraft 3000 chassis that almost did not start the race, out of competition on lap 135. Hanks climbed out, uninjured. In 1952 when the 245-pound Ruttman won the race at the age of twenty-two, the victory had initially seemed securely in the hands of hard-charging Billy Vukovich I, then in his second Indianapolis appearance. His car was a mouse-gray Fuel Injection Kurtis 500-A entered by Californian Howard Keck and prepared by Jim Travers and Frank Coon that developed steering problems on Vukovich's 192nd lap, parked against the northeast wall, and lost the race, relegating him to seventeenth position at the finish. Vukovich, in the meantime, had been hampered by the steering wheel's tendency to twist rightward as he approached the northeast in the middle of the track, rather than in the running groove. This time the car veered to the right, scraped the retaining wall, bounced off, and scraped it a second time before it ceased running. A profoundly disgusted Vukovich stayed with his stalled car at the northeast turn, like a rider might his fallen steed, for the remaining eight laps of the race until the somewhat overweight Ruttman crossed the finish line waving his bare right arm in triumph. Esther Vukovich, the driver's wife, waited in near hysterics at the track's infield hospital, believing that her husband had suffered injuries. Vukovich was indeed injured, but not physically so. "What a dirty lousy break!" he exclaimed back in Gasoline Alley, and returned to win the next two Indianapolis 500s. "That Ruttman never won an easier one!" Ruttman, in turn, said that he had energy enough to race another 500 miles. It was his greatest day in racing, and most of what became of him after that (his inability to deal with the demands to which an Indianapolis winner is subjected, his alcohol addiction, his racing injuries, his abusive domestic behavior, his broken marriages, his near-poverty) clouded his last years. His death came at the age of sixty-seven in 1997, and his Moorland, Oklahoma, funeral began just as that year's Indianapolis 500 flagged off. Ruttman, through good times and bad, was arguably America's greatest automobile racing talent.

It is commonplace to refer to the 1953 race as "the hottest 500," which it probably was, with track temperatures reaching 130 degrees Fahrenheit. Relief driving, gone well out of fashion in recent years, suddenly came back, as drivers found themselves physically incapable of tolerating the suffocating heat of the day, in addition to the noxious fumes that wafted from the engines back into the cockpits. Tony Bettenhausen patted himself on the helmet, a signal that he wanted to retire from the race and allow someone else to take charge. His replacement was 1952 AAA national champion Chuck Stevenson, who in turned surrendered the wheel to youthful Gene Hartley, a boyish-appearing second-generation midget car performer from Roanoke, Indiana. Hartley had spun in the northeast earlier that day in a yellow and blue Federal Engineering Special dirt track car, and now was about to do it again, this time in Bettenhausen's Agajanian Kuzma chassis, another dirt car. The second mixup occurred when the car was on its 196th trip through the northeast where Hartley, affected by the day's intolerable heat, guided the machine in serpentine fashion, finally smacking the wall in the north chute. Then as now, any driver involved in an accident at the Speedway makes a mandatory appearance at the infield hospital whether it be necessary or not. When Hartley presented himself the first time, his wife Carolyn was there to receive him. When he called the second time, she remained in a grandstand seat, disinclined to make more than one hospital visit a day, unwilling to fight the race-day crowds and reluctant to brave the high temperatures. Even track physician C. B. Bohner thought it strange that one driver would make two race-day hospital visits. "Gene Hartley's back again," he wrote in his notebook. "Twice he hit the north wall, twice he was brought into the hospital, and twice he had only minor injuries. What a two-timing record that is." Nalon, by the way, spun his Novi on the grass through turn three in an effort to stay out of Hartley's path. Neither driver was injured as the yellow caution light flashed for fifty seconds before Seth Klein's red and checkered flags brought all the commotion to a much-needed halt, partly because unruly spectators had stormed through a section of fencing at the north end of the track and were converging on the area of the Hartley-Nalon shunt.

Bill Vukovich, accustomed to the sun that fell with scorching intensity over the vineyards of Fresno, California, was the winner. The loser was Illinois-born Carl Scarborough of Clarkston, Michigan, who had made what is even today an obscure reputation for himself in so-called "outlaw" (non-AAA) race meets on rutty dirt tracks around Michigan, Indiana, and Ohio, and who gave his age as thirty-eight. Scarborough, who was quite capable of going extremely fast at Indianapolis with extremely ordinary racing equipment, had planned a two stop race in 1953. After the first one, he was sickly from the heat and fumes, climbed out of the car, returned to it for the purpose of tightening a hood strap just as a small fire broke out on the car's left rear side, the result of a fuel spill. He then climbed over the pit wall and collapsed on a portable garden chair with a wet towel over his head while Californian Bob Scott, whose former Spider Webb car had quit on him after fourteen laps, got behind the wheel of Scarborough's mahogany and copper hued McNamara Kurtis Kraft dirt car, motored away, and finished the afternoon in twelfth position. Before the afternoon ended, Scarborough was dead in the infield hospital despite the heroic efforts of several physicians. When the race mercifully ended, the once liberal supply of eligible relief drivers was exhausted, and more than one racing car capable of continuing the 500-mile race sat abandoned along pit lane, driverless.

The intense heat had taken its toll in the northeast earlier that day when drivers doggedly continued to give their best in the world's most prestigious automobile race under circumstances that would have destroyed men of lesser stamina. With three laps down, former prize-fighter Andy Linden, a contentious Pennsylvania coalfield-born resident of Manhattan Beach, California, spun twice. Gerald Frederick "Jerry" Hoyt then spun his turquoise No. 55 five dirt track car entered on his behalf. The ill-fated Hoyt, who had recently been discharged after eighteen months of military service in Germany between 1951 and 1952, was a hometown Indianapolis kid, graduated from Arsenal Technical High School, although he was born in Chicago on January 29, 1929, to Art and Betty Hoyt, he with a serious stutter, she with a simple Hazard, Kentucky, hill country upbringing. As a kid, the young Hoyt became the mascot for the Lucky Teeter traveling auto stunt show. His life ended in an Oklahoma City sprint car accident in 1955, the year that he had started on the pole at Indianapolis. An hour and eighteen minutes after Hoyt spun at Indianapolis in 1953, however, Pat Flaherty, a red-headed Chicago bartender who had signaled his pit crew frantically on the previous lap, spun through the northeast and struck the outer wall, continuing for another 270 feet. Not seriously injured, Flaherty (who won the 1956 Speedway classic) found himself trapped temporarily in the red Peter Schmidt Kurtis 3000 chassis while crews struggled to free him, which they did expeditiously in less than seven minutes.

It was in 1958 that the most complicated, most photographed, and most discussed of all Speedway mishaps in the northeast turn occurred. Instead of the customary practice of lining cars on the track prior to the start, the 1957 and 1958 protocol had all thirty-three cars positioned at an angle along the pit wall, with each driver buckled in and supposedly prepared to form up and go racing. On both occasions, drivers seemed incapable of departing the pits and positioning themselves three abreast in eleven rows. In 1958 their incapability developed into a monumental fiasco as it had threatened to do the previous year. Pole sitter Dick Rathmann, flanked by similarly pugilistic and emotionally troubled Ed Elisian, the controversial Oakland, Californian, and Oklahoma's Jimmy Reece, were to fall in behind the Pontiac Bonneville pace car driven by 1957 Speedway winner Sam Hanks, but instead left the pit area in front of it for reasons never satisfactorily clarified. The result was that the front three cars were at one end of the track while the other thirty contestants were at the other. Receiving contradictory signals from United States Auto Club officialdom on one hand, and from pit crews on the other, the front three drivers knew not whether to speed up and join the pack, or slow down and allow the pack to join them. Three laps later Hanks pulled the pace car off the course while the field, in relatively orthodox formation, began the day under starter Bill Vanderwater's green banner.

During the month of preparations that led to this most climactic of moments (since from a psychological point of view the beginning, rather than the end, is the more climactic) Rathmann and Elisian had been locked in a battle for speed supremacy that escalated into an intense, somewhat adolescent warfare of nerves. Pre-race speeds have little or nothing to do with race-day performance. Nonetheless, after one driver posted a rapid practice lap, the other found it incumbent to turn a still faster one. Rathmann had won the pole with an average of 145.974 miles per hour on the electric eye, while Elisian, who had developed an unnerving way of dirt tracking his car through Indianapolis's four corners, was only a tick of the stopwatch behind with a four-lap sequence of 145.946, partly because their cars were nearly identical A. J. Watson chassis powered by Drake Offen-hausers. Johnny Boyd of Fresno, California, who had qualified in 1958 almost two miles per hour slower, started in eighth position. He remem-bers ninth-place starter Tony Bettenhausen paying him a garage visit the day prior to the race. "Tony warned me," Boyd recalled, "that there was going to be trouble up front at the start of the race, and that I had better hang back in the pack with him until things got sorted out up there. That's pretty much what I did, except that when we got the green flag I found myself leading one pack of cars on the backstretch, while Tony was further back leading another group. I kept my eye on the third turn all the while, wondering if and when something was going to happen. Sure enough it did, and I headed for the grass, pretty much as I had planned."

Bettenhausen's troubled prediction was unfortunately borne out. Eli-sian and Rathmann charged into the northeast turn at full tilt, each seem-ingly daring the other to back off the throttle last. As Rathmann pulled behind Elisian, the latter began to slide out of control in front of Rathmann and thirty-one other cars. The two cars backed into the number three turn side by side. The ensuing chain of events defies sequential description. Reece was the next to whirl around, only to be struck from the rear by Boyd's traveling companion Bob Vieth, and shoved into the path of Pat O'Connor, the popular southern Indiana driver, who in turn rode over Reece's wheel. For an instant the front of O'Connor's dark blue Sumar roadster hung ominously over Reece's head. It then rolled over, landed wrong side up, then righted itself. For several seconds there were two cars off the track for every one car on it. Jerry Unser's McKay Special ramped over former motorcycle racer Paul Goldsmith's City of Daytona car and sailed over the wall. Unser, who sustained only a broken shoulder, became the last man ever to clear the walls at Indianapolis. Meanwhile, drivers Len Sutton and Art Bisch found their cars too bent to continue. O'Connor was dead, his car demolished along with seven other vehicles. Veith, a hulking Oakland, California, driver, limped his Bowes Seal Fast car around the track to the pits with a leaking fuel tank, thereby logging one full lap that finished him ahead of seven other hapless contestants. Twelve of the thirty-three starters (more than one in three) who competed in the 1958 Indianapolis 500 eventually died from racing-related injuries. A thir-teenth driver, Billy Garrett, survived his racing injuries in a wheelchair, and died in February 1999.

Cigar-chomping, free-spirited Arizona cowboy Jimmy Bryan, whose exploits primarily on dirt tracks accounted for the better part of his remarkable reputation, managed to avoid the eight-car pileup and win the race in the same yellow car that had won it with Sam Hanks the year before: the George Salih experimental Epperly chassis with its "lay-down" sidewinder 250 cubic inch Offenhauser engine. In second place was a car of virtually the same description driven by Wisconsin's George Amick, a hard driving, high flying competitor who was decapitated the following April at Daytona Beach. Boyd was third, Bettenhausen fourth. After the race Bettenhausen called on Boyd again. "In a way," said Bettenhausen philosophically, "it was a good thing that there was trouble over in turn three." Boyd asked why. "Because," Bettenhausen continued, "you would have been the laughing stock of the Speedway, driving all over the grass that way, while the rest of us were on the track where we were supposed to be." Boyd looked up. "What about you, Bettenhausen? You were down there with me!" Bettenhausen shook his head. "I stayed on the track where I belonged." Boyd remembered the exchange with amusement. "I looked at the films of the wreck later," he recalled, "and Tony was mowing the grass down there with the rest of us."

No amount of death and dismemberment was to keep aspiring driv-

As part of a crusade to abolish automobile racing at Indianapolis, and everywhere else, this 1958 magazine image purported to show the location of every driver, mechanic, and spectator fatality at Indianapolis. *Steve Zautke*

To be sure, there are some who presumed to profit from calamity. This Indianapolis skull and bones image appeared in *Life* magazine, circa 1959. "Every year on Memorial Day the huge crowd comes to the track to see a contest—but keeps in mind the exciting possibility that it will see violence, smashed cars and death itself." *Steve Zautke*

ers away from Indianapolis in the decades that followed. Among the entries for the 1959 race was driver Bob Cortner, thirty-two, from Redlands, California, who captured the Bay Cities Racing Association midget car championship in 1957. He came to the Speedway with no experience on the "championship trail," the national Indy car circuit, then run half the time on dirt tracks. Cortner's Cornis Engineering car began leaking oil badly enough on Friday, May 15 to postpone the final stages of his driver's test until the Monday following the first weekend of time trials. Once the test was behind him, driver-turned-car-builder Don Edmunds, from Anaheim, California, offered him the seat of the Braund Plywood Special. Cortner asked for a day to consider but, in the meantime, the car went to another Anaheim driver named Dale Van Johnson. The following day was extremely gusty, and therefore especially hazardous for drivers looking for speed at Indianapolis. Called back to the pits to correct a faulty brake, Cortner set out afterward for another round of practice laps in the Cornis car. In the northeast turn that day was 1950 winner Johnnie Parsons, who reported that a wind gust had apparently caught Cortner by surprise, causing him to spin through the infield, then travel 138 feet into the wall. Unconscious, Cortner lived until 6:50 that evening at Methodist Hospital.

All told, it was a bad year in the northeast. During the forty-fifth lap of the 1959 race the McKay Special, with Illinois midget driver Chuck Weyant on board, went out of control and spun near the outside wall, where it was nailed by New Jersey's Charles Edward "Mike" Magill, who managed to wedge himself between the wall and Weyant. Magill's roadster stood on end for a moment before sliding upside-down over the upper regions of the track for about 250 feet. There he slammed the wall again and slid to the infield with serious injuries. During the war Magill was with the Army Air Corps, and returned stateside in 1944 after seeing action in Guadalcanal and Bougainville. He lived virtually his entire life in the same house on Mount Vernon Avenue in Haddonfield, New Jersey, with his wife Jean who, he said, was the first woman he saw after his years in the military who did not have (as in the Pacific) a bone through her nose. Weyant, meanwhile, parked in the middle of the track. Comical Texas dirt tracker Jud Larson came together with California native Richard "Red" Amick (more closely identified with the Indiana short track roadster racing scene, however) as they struggled to avoid Weyant's black and yellow car, joining Magill in the infield. Never in World War II had Mike Magill been as imperiled as he was at this moment with a back injury that required a period of convalescence at the home of his car owner George Walther in Dayton, Ohio. Magill returned to the Speedway (his wife having packed his bags) for another two years, failing to qualify for the race both times.

At 115 laps in the 1959 race, wealthy Ray Crawford, who owned not only his Edgar Elder chassis but a syndicate of California supermarkets, crashed in the same northeast turn. The former P-38 pilot sustained back injuries and three broken ribs. Son of a Roswell, New Mexico, beekeeper and grocery store owner, Crawford passed part of his life testing aircraft, then became a Sam Hanks protege in midget cars. "They called me the Millionaire Playboy," he said. "I got in a race car, sat down and put a helmet and goggles on. I looked like a racer driver, anyway." A gentlemen hobbyist driver, Crawford enjoyed forays into hill climbs (Pikes Peak), sports cars (Sebring), and hydroplanes (Lake Mead). He even won the 1954 Mexican Road Race by rehearsing it, and joined other American drivers on two visits to the "Race of Two Worlds" at Monza. The once modest grocery store that his father opened had long since mushroomed into a chain of supermarkets on both sides of the Mexican border, although Crawford's Mexican partners seized their store and never returned him a peso. The flagship store in El Monte, allegedly the biggest of its genre in the world, was allegedly also grossing $22 million in sales, raising a few bucks for Crawford to go racing while putting sufficient food on the table for his wife Marian and their two sons.

In more recent years, the saga of the Speedway's northeast turn evolved through a series of incidents, some of them with less serious overtones. Having spun on his previous lap, the loquacious racing comedian Eddie (Edward Julius) Sachs of Center Valley, Pennsylvania, slid his Bryant Heating and Cooling Special, a Watson roadster, through the northeast at 181 laps in the 1963 contest after having parted ways with his left rear wheel. With characteristic theatrical flair Sachs set out in search of the errant wheel that he recovered and rolled back to the pit area, waving to an appreciative throng the whole way. Then, at the same location, Tucson's Roger Frank McCluskey spun through accumulated oil on his 198th circuit, with little more than two laps remaining. McCluskey made a clockwise half loop, pinballed off the wall, and came to a stop in the middle of the north chute. On the day following the race, Sachs and McCluskey took verbal aim at race winner Parnelli Jones and at the reigning chief steward, arrogant Harlan Fengler (who, having driven in the 1923 race, became known as "The Boy Wonder") who had refused to wave Jones off the track in the final laps when he appeared to be losing oil. "Give Harlan the Fengler," was then a popular mantra among hippies at the track's turn one Snake Pit. "One thing about him," Sachs said of Jones, "he sprays oil all over the track. I can't begin to tell you how many lives were in jeopardy because of it." He continued, "I went up the back straightaway, the whole straightaway, and to this day I don't know how I kept control." McCluskey (who years later became executive vice president and CEO of the United States Auto Club until his death from cancer in 1993) agreed, saying, that his spin cost him between thirty and forty thousand dollars in potential prize money. The confrontation reached its resolution when Jones decked Sachs. "The enemy had the oil," concluded Milt Dunnell of the *Toronto Star*. "The losers lacked experience."

McCluskey drove relief for Mel Kenyon in the 1970 race in a brilliant green car painted in the colors of its sponsor, Sprite soft drink, and spun again in the northeast (he would do it again in 1976), taking sports car driver Ronnie Bucknam with him. Although Alan "Sam" Sessions, Bobby Unser, and Jerry Grant were involved in the mixup, there were no casual-

Four famous faces at Indy in 1961. Left to right: Tucson's Roger McCluskey started eighteen 500s but never placed higher than third; A.J. Foyt started thirty-five times and won on four occasions; Foyt's fellow Texan Lloyd Ruby seemed to a near-certain winner in several of his eighteen starts, but like McCluskey, he never finished higher than third; Californian Bob "Traction" Veith tried Indianapolis eleven times. All survived a particularly dangerous era in racing. *Ed Hitze*

ties. Race day spectator casualties, however, prevailed. At 5:00 that morning when the gates opened, three men injured themselves when they attempted to scream through a track underpass on two Harley-Davidsons. The result was a twisted mess of wadded up motorcycles, two men were flown by copter to Methodist, while a third was operated upon then and there for a ferocious hematoma by a team of Speedway physicians. Later that day a man with severely sunburned legs arrived at the track hospital requesting a pair of pants.

A curious replay of the 1970 third-turn incident unfolded in 1971 when Mel Kenyon, a born-again Christian, was back once more in a No. 23 Sprite Special, equipped this time with a Ford V-8 instead of a Meyer and Drake. Only ten laps were down when Steve Krisiloff of Parsippany,

New Jersey, in a new florescent red STP Gas Treatment car, "lunched" his Ford engine that in turn dumped water and oil through the northeast. Pursuing Krisiloff hotly, Kenyon inherited a slippery track that set him into a spin, causing him to trail the wall for a hundred feet and stop with the car's rear quarters mashed against the cement. With firemen to his left and right, and another en route, Kenyon extricated himself at his leisure until he happened to notice the orange No. 7 Norris Industries car with Gordon Johncock on board driving at a healthy rate of speed, straight at him. Kenyon, half way out of his car, slid all the way back in, and then some. Johncock arrived, and went up and over Kenyon's head, while the firemen pressed themselves against the wall as soon and as tightly possible. It was all in a day's work, albeit Kenyon averred that it had been "the hairiest thing that ever happened" to him. After removing his helmet, he discovered Johncock's tiremarks across it. Cut slightly about the shinbone, Kenyon reported to the usual place, where he was told to be seated and wait his turn while victims of the pace car's having plowed into the portable photographer's viewing stand were being treated for their various injuries. "Gordie came over to the hospital while I was getting sewed up, and apologized all over the place," said Kenyon. "I told him to forget it. He certainly didn't mean to do it."

Denver's Jim Malloy, thirty-six, was killed while testing for what would have been his third Indianapolis 500 when he lost control of his Thermo King Eagle chassis (vacated by Gary Bettenhausen when he accepted an offer tendered by Roger Penske) on Sunday morning, May 14, 1972, when he failed to negotiate the corner after timing an unofficial lap in the 186 range. Evidence indicated that he drove nearly straight into the wall and that there was accident debris over a 150-yard radius. The force of impact apparently accordianed the car from the front on back. A rescuing party required ten minutes to remove Malloy, who never regained consciousness. He had sustained head injuries, fractures of both legs and hips, a broken right arm, and various second degree burns on his feet and hands. Malloy, born in Columbus, Nebraska, in 1925, had gone to school in Englewood, Colorado, where he lettered in football and baseball, had attended Colorado State for two years, and then gone racing, especially in the American northwest and Canada where he won the CAMRA (Canadian American Modified Racing Association) championship in 1964 and 1965. His parents and his wife Mary were with him at his death. Jim Malloy left two sons and a daughter.

Gerald Edward "Jerry" Karl of Manchester, Pennsylvania, in his second of six Indianapolis races, held on for 115 laps in the 1974 mayhem before losing his grip in turn three in Lindsey Hopkins's 1973 Eagle Offenhauser that spun backwards in a billow of tire smoke, slipped to the outer edge of the track, and banged the wall with enough force to disengage the left front wheel that sailed over Karl's left shoulder and sat atop the back of the car. Prevented from bailing out of the machine because one of his feet was wedged in the wreckage, Karl received assistance and seemed to be limping, but apparently was otherwise uninjured. Car owner Hopkins, a thoroughly pleasant southern gentleman who inherited money that his family invested in Carl Fisher's Miami, was a major Coca-Cola stockholder who involved Speedway owner Tony Hulman in Coca-Cola bottling, and developed a holding company of his own before dying in 1986. Hopkins made a valiant effort to capture the flag at Indianapolis with drivers like Henry Banks (who managed to win the 1950 national championship for him), Pat O'Connor, Bill Vukovich (who died in Hopkins's roadster at the Speedway in 1955), Jim Rathmann (who brought Hopkins two Indianapolis second places), Wayne Weiler, Don Branson, Bobby Marshman, Roger McCluskey, Chuck Hulse, Wally Dallenbach, Mel Kenyon, Bob Harkey, Gary Bettenhausen, and Jerry Karl, but the chemistry never produced an Indianapolis champion. Hopkins's racing car often carried his signature image of a white rabbit and a top hat, emblematic of its owner's penchant for amateur magicianship, but his magic had its limitations in racing. Miami's Lindsey Hopkins Technical Education Center that fosters careers in fields such as business and health, carries its benefactor's spirit forward today.

In a fiery wall contact at least as devastating as the Duke Nalon 1949 Novi catastrophe, Danny Ongais (having briefly assumed the lead) powered his Teddy Field (of Chicago's Marshall Field department store family) black Interscope Cosworth straight into the northeast turn outer barrier where it exploded and disintegrated on lap sixty-four of the 1981 race, paced by Nalon himself. Ongais was as exposed to the fury of the fire and destruction as was Stan Fox after his 1995 wall collision at the south end of the track. To have witnessed the Nalon, Ongais, and Fox accidents was to have allowed no possibility that the victims survived. All three did, however. Ongais was out of action for the balance of the season but raced at Indianapolis six more times. The following year, he hit another wall.

So did upbeat Gordon Eugene Smiley, thirty-three, a Nebraska native from Grapevine, Texas, north of the Dallas–Fort Worth area. Smiley had been racing seven years, having run with the Sports Car Club of America and the Aurora Formula 1 series, and having won championships in both. He arrived at the Speedway in 1982 for what he believed would be his third consecutive race, this time in the red No. 35 Intermedics Innovator car, a March chassis powered by a Cosworth engine. On Saturday, May 15, Smiley, on his second and final warm-up lap prior to taking the green flag for an official qualification attempt, drove virtually head-on into the northeast turn outer barrier. According to a Speedway press bulletin he entered turn three and then "lost control, overcorrected into a reverse slide for 280 feet to [the] wall." Pancho Carter, some may recall, hit the wall at about this same point in 1987 and flew upside down for an estimated 100 feet, then slid another 600 feet before stopping with no injury. Smiley's machine became airborne and disintegrated into three sections. The engine section flew 480 feet to middle of north short chute. "The driver," the press report continued, "died instantaneously (12:15 P.M.) of massive head injuries." Smiley hit in close to the same place where Danny Ongais had the year before, but with sufficient raw violence to obliterate the car and himself. The steering wheel flew high in the air, as did Smiley's helmet that sprang from his head at the moment of impact. The wreckage gouged chunks out of the racing surface. Robert Fletcher of Phoenix who owned the Gordon Smiley car had also owned the machine that carried Art Pollard to his death on the south side of the track on the first qualification morning in 1973. Memorial services for Smiley happened on the following Sunday evening at the Chapel Hill United Methodist Church in Speedway, Indiana, at the request of his wife, Barbara. Smiley's burial was at Calvary Cemetery in Omaha in a plot next to his father.

Wall-hitting can become a way of life. Richard Vogler came to Indianapolis in 1983 and the track had barely opened on the first day of practice before he spun in the northeast and rapped the wall a fine one with the left rear and the left front. Two weeks later he hit the northwest wall. Vogler plowed into the first turn wall in 1985, his rookie year in the race. That was on lap 185. A year later he did not last quite as long, slamming into the northeast on his 133rd when a right rear wheel came loose. Returning in 1988, he did it again: straight into the northeast at 159 laps. He had, in fact, bopped the wall in the south chute, gathered the car up and kept going until he found his pit where he picked up some fuel and rubber, then hit the track, still under yellow conditions, when one of his front wheels turned west while the other turned east. Vogler, for his part, went north, directly into the wall. In 1989 he managed not to run into anything and came home eighth. He was back at Indianapolis in 1990 when he slammed the second turn wall, and then hit the northeast six days later. But by then, time was running short. Vogler died, like his father, on a short Indiana track. It happened on live television at the high banked half-mile Salem, Indiana, speedway near Louisville on July 21, 1990, five days before his fortieth birthday, when he brushed wheels with another car on the penultimate lap of a sprint car race, then drove into some out-side fencing while leading the race. Like Gordon Smiley's final accident, the force was enough to cause Vogler's helmet to tear loose from his head. Earlier that day Vogler had established a new one-lap track record of 15.57 seconds. He lived until 10:40 that night at Salem's Washington County Hospital, where the body of 1955 Indianapolis winner Bob Sweikert went after he too was killed at the track. Vogler still won the race, however, because when the race halted, scoring reverted to the previous lap.

Turn three was a crucial factor in 1989, and not only because Jim Crawford, entitled to start fourth, crashed his car there prior to the race with such violence that he ended in turn four, leaving a track littered with detritus in his wake. The more serious, high-stakes incident occurred on the penultimate lap when race leader Al Unser, Jr. and Emerson Fittipaldi, both ultimately two-time winners, bumped at high speed. Unser con-nected with the wall and in what seemed to be a lightning flash spun his demolished car into the lawn. The incident cost him a third Indianapolis win and caused him to score second, the highest-ever performance of a non-finisher. Fittipaldi captured the race, and on his next time around the course Unser was there giving him a double thumbs up. Whether Unser's body language was a politically correct, public relations gesture or whether it was a heartfelt response, or neither one, may never be entirely clear. In auto racing, one picks up the pieces and moves on to the next race.

Irrepressible Canadian Paul Tracy crunched his Marlboro Penske on lap ninety-four of the 1993 race while trying to put some moves on Scott Brayton in turn three. Tracy, to judge from his body language, seemed to blame the incident on Brayton who rolled ahead to sixth place, his best Indianapolis outing in (then) eight starts. Then at 128 laps Jeff Andretti and Roberto Guerrero tangled in the northeast after the latter attempted to overtake the former. The two ended against the outer barrier in the north chute. Both received minor injuries, although Andretti left the acci-dent scene on a stretcher. Arguably, all accidents are freakish, and just as arguably, all accidents are the fault of anyone involved with them. In 1994 highly touted British driver Nigel "if I get an opportunity to win, I'll win"

Mansell was back for a second run on the Indianapolis 500 where he had come in third the year previous. Said stock car standout Dale Earnhardt, "I had such a blast watching him race in F1. Then he comes over to Indy Cars and kicks tail again. I'm not sure I'd want him to come to NASCAR." *Sports Illustrated* called him "the most daring race car driver in the world." Echoed Shav Glick of the *Los Angeles Times*, "in my 25 years of reporting motorsports, nothing I have seen matches Nigel Mansell's talents in switching from Formula One road racing to Indy Car ovals, particularly at Indianapolis where he was running unbelievable speeds on his first day at the track—even though he had never seen it before." Commented *On Track* magazine, "Mansell was magnificent, a model for all of those who think they have what it takes to be the best race car driver in the world." Added Jeremy Shaw of *Road & Track*, "his skill and judgement on the ovals were awe-inspiring; his all-or-nothing qualifying laps on the road courses, equally majestic and entertaining." Sam Moses of *Playboy* said, "On track[s] where he was expected to be vulnerable—the wild one-mile ovals dubbed 'bullrings' for their head-spinning action and potential for the drivers to get gored—he demonstrated genius as he had never done before." Nigel Roebuck of *Autosport* remarked that "the magnitude of his achievement can hardly be exaggerated," adding that "he has shaken everyone with his ability to turn left at colossal speeds. In traffic, particularly, he has no peer on the ovals. Hats off." On it went. "There are athletes who grab pressure by the throat and throttle it into submission," said the *Chicago Tribune*'s Bob Markus. "There are athletes who aim for the moon and reach the stars. There are athletes who give the people what they want and then give them more. Make your own list, but put Nigel Mansell on it."

Mansell, born August 8, 1953, in Upton-on-Severn, England, attended Solihull Technical College and North Birmingham Polytechnic, then began racing in 1976. Early on he broke his neck in a Formula Ford accident, and left a hospital on his own accord after physicians told him that his convalescence would extend to six months, after which he would probably never drive competitively again. By 1978 he had mortgaged his home to pay for a Formula Three car that he intended to race four times. In 1980 Lotus founder Colin Chapman extended him a Formula 1 contract to test cars. A year later, he contracted for three more years with Lotus to drive for its Formula 1 program, then switched to the Williams team with Honda engines in 1985, and in 1987 suffered injuries to his back and spine after an accident in Japan. Having first announced his retirement, he returned to the Williams team in 1991, won the world championship title for them in 1992, then signed with Paul Newman and Carl Haas to drive Indianapolis cars in 1993. Asked what makes Mansell run, Frank Williams opined to *On Track* magazine that it was "the patch of sole-shaped leather on the bottom of his right foot," adding that "He's an incredibly quick driver[;] there's no doubt about that; there's no mess about for him. He gets in the car and just drives it flat out." Beginning on the right foot, he won the pole and the race in Queensland, Australia, that year, his first with Indy-style cars. As writer Stan Sutton pointed out, Mansell is so revered in Great Britain that his likeness graces both a coin and a postage stamp. As to having his face on a coin, Mansell commented, "In our legislation, you have to be dead or in line for a monarchy. I'm pleased to tell you I'm not dead, and I don't want to be king of England." Mansell told *Inside Sports* magazine that "if anyone asks me what I do for a living, I just say I'm a taxi driver."

Nonetheless, Mansell's reappearance at Indianapolis in 1994 did not live up to public expectation, except in his role as taxi driver. Having started seventh, he was still seventh at ten laps, sixth at twenty laps, fifth at thirty laps, sixth at forty laps, thirteenth (after stopping) at fifty laps, tenth at sixty laps, seventh at seventy laps, seventh still at eighty laps, third at ninety laps. Two circuits later, Nigel Mansell could be found in the pit access in turn three with the car driven by rookie Dennis Vitolo perching atop his. Vitolo began by running into John Andretti's left rear wheel, taking flight, and landing atop Mansell Vitolo's who in turn was evidently scalded with boiling water from his cooling system, leapt out of the car, and began rolling on the lawn. Mansell, as per usual in such instances, accepted transport to the infield medical unit where, according to reports, he became so verbally abusive to the staff that someone fined him $1,000. While Vitolo accepted responsibility for the run-in, Mansell boarded his private jet and disappeared.

If one were to limit his Indianapolis experience to that point of view afforded by the northeast turn, one would be rewarded with a generous slice of the Speedway experience without wandering elsewhere. Brazilian Andre Ribiero passed through Indianapolis but once (1995) and like many before him, kissed the northeast wall in the manner that one might kiss a blarney stone or a toad. It happened on the 13th of May in 1995 while he was driving pretty hard and high through that stretch of track in a Honda-powered Reynard and connected with the track's outer limits, slid along it for ninety feet, then away from it for sixty feet, then back into it once more for thirty feet, then banged the wall with the car's right side way over in turn four, then rode that stretch of wall for a time before ending on the track apron. Medical investigation revealed that Ribiero suffered nothing more than customary bumps and bruises.

Peter DePaolo, whose seven Indianapolis finishes ranged all the way from first to thirty-third, published a book that he purportedly authored himself, entitled *Wall Smacker*, in 1934. Today it graces the shelves of all Indianapolis idolaters, provided that they can find a copy. Its title is somewhat self-effacing, inasmuch as it refers to himself and alludes to his Chapter XIII that bears the heading "I Smack the Wall." The wall he smacked was at the inner edge of the north end of the Indianapolis Motor Speedway. "We smacked the inside wall tail-end-to," DePaolo said. "For a second I was out like a light, then came to and saw that the front of the car was not damaged." Having checked the condition of his tires, he shouted to his perplexed riding mechanic, the aircraft pilot and one-time (1921) Indianapolis competitor Riley Brett who, he said, "weighed a few ounces less than ninety-two pounds." Determined to get back into the hunt, DePaolo shouted, "We're still in the lead! Come on, Riley, crank the engine! Hurry up!" to which Brett responded, "Nothin' doin'! I'm through ridin' with you! You're crazy!"

Maybe he was. Other wall smackers have come and gone, although some of them, as noted, have demonstrated a predilection for socking walls repeatedly. In 1996, the first year that the Indy Racing League took over the sanctioning of the 500-mile race, two veteran wall crunchers were up to their old tricks. Johnny Parsons came hellbent through the northeast just before noon on May 11, cut a one and a half spinout that took 400 feet to reach the cement, scuffed along the wall for another 180 feet, then continued another 330 while executing one more full loop. All this cost him a bruised left foot and some substantial left side and rear end damage to his Team Blue Print Racing entry. Mechanics repaired the car, and Parsons, never easily discouraged, held his ground in the race until a radiator failed at 148 laps. Scott Harrington behaved much the same way five days later when his own Harrington Motorsports car pushed high on the track and did the predictable thing: hit on the right side, slid along the track for 120 feet, parted from the wall, slid another 330, connected with the turn-four wall, and stopped mid-track. Had old-timer Riley Brett been onboard with either driver, one might imagine his assertively proclaiming again, "Nothin' doin'! I'm through ridin' with you! You're crazy!"

On May 6, 1997, turn three bit again. This time it was rookie Jeff

Ken Coles Photo
473 Fairwood
Pinckney, MI 48169
1-734-878-2080

Britain's extraordinary Nigel Ernest James Mansell took a third at Indianapolis in 1993, one year after winning the Formula 1 world championship. "I've thoroughly enjoyed the whole experience," he commented. "Next year I hope to go through it with a little more comfort." That didn't happen. Another car drove over his engine compartment, relegating him to twenty-second place. *Ken Coles*

Ward, from San Juan Capistrano, California driving for Team Cheever who, after blowing an engine a half an hour before qualification runs, executed one complete spin entering the northeast, traveled 555 feet, plugged the wall on the car's right rear, traveled another 150 feet, and parked in the north chute. Ward, examined and released, found a good end to the month. Born in Glasgow, Scotland, he came to Indianapolis from motocross where he won national championships in 1985, 1987, 1988, 1989, and 1990, after which he tried four-wheeled competition for the first time at the age of thirty-one in the Firestone Indy Lights series. "I raced motocross. That's what I did," he told Philip Wilson of the *Indianapolis Star.* "Then I moved on to this [Indy cars]. Motocross is a youthful sport. You only have four or five good years, and you're done. That's too young to quit." Ward drove spectacularly in this, his second Indy car race, finishing third behind Arie Luyendyk and Scott Goodyear (like Ward, both foreign-born drivers), leading forty-nine of the last fifty-nine laps, and winning the Rookie of the Year title. Ward's car owner Eddie Cheever, who fell out of the race at eighty-four laps because of a failed timing chain in the car he was driving, told Ron Lemasters, Sr., "I was convinced he was going to win," adding that "We got unlucky with the yellows, and that's just life. But it was one hell of a drive." Ward's motorcycling background invited comparison with former racing bikers Ralph Hepburn, Paul Goldsmith, and "Pelican Joe" Leonard, all of whom also pulled third-place finishes at Indianapolis.

The 1997 race brought other problems in the northeast, however. Robby Gordon stopped in the warmup lane there after his car caught fire on lap eighteen. Like Nigel Mansell at that same place in 1994, Gordon bailed out and began to roll in the grass. Unlike Mansell, he did not hie off to the infield hospital and insult the staff, but instead directed fire fighters on how best to extinguish the fire, climbed back in the cockpit and requested a tow. Then on lap 114, Billy Roe in car No. 50 and Paul Durant in a No. 1 Foyt entry, collided while they were attempting to run side by side through turn three. Both climbed out, unscathed. Roe, an Indianapolis native living in Gilbert, Arizona, had entered the hazardous racing vocation not (as Jeff Ward had) by racing motorcycles, but by turning wrenches variously under the employment of Clint Brawner Racing, Fletcher Racing (both in Arizona), Provimi Racing, Mike Curb Racing, and A. J. Foyt Enterprises. By 1997, however, he was doing none of that, having purchased a firm called The Textbook Company in Mesa, Arizona, and installed himself as its CEO, illustrating that good things can come of developing socially constructive second careers. It was also in 1997 that Arizona governor Fife Symington's friends and counselors encouraged him out of the statehouse after a bank fraud conviction. By 2003 he had become a more or less respected Phoenix pastry chef who, in the words of the Associated Press's Michelle Rushlo, "completed the first six weeks of culinary 'boot camp' and spent another year slicing, kneading and sautéing his way to a culinary arts and restaurant management degree."

To be sure, there were a good many brave souls who peeled, sliced, chopped, kneaded, diced, stewed, and sautéed their way through Indy's northeast turn, especially in 1998 when Danny Ongais, of all predictable people, spun while exiting the corner at just the spot that well might have, but for the grace of God, taken his life in 1981. On this occasion the "Flying O," possibly the "Flying Oh!" as he had become known, hit with his rear and left rear before the car skidded to a conclusion in the north chute at 4:52 P.M. on Monday, May 11. By 5:30 he was in all-too-familiar surroundings, to wit: Methodist Hospital where he was adjudged to be alert and awake, at least, having been picked up unconscious at the accident scene. On the following morning someone announced that "Ongais will not be cleared to drive in the 1998 Indianapolis 500," the explanation being that "he remains in Methodist Hospital after suffering a slight concussion after yesterday's accident." Even so, the medical forces attested that he was "in good condition" and that he would therefore be released before day's end. Although he may not have known it, he would never race again at Indianapolis, having driven in competition there eleven times and placed fourth once and seventh twice, without ever having gone the full 500 miles.

Billy Boat, obviously unintimidated by Indy's walls, connected without personal injury in the northeast on Friday the 15th, 1998, at 11:22 in the morning while onboard one of Foyt's Oldsmobile Dallaras, executing a right side wallsmack that reached its unpleasant conclusion on the grassy apron. That incident was a mere warm-up to a seven car pileup on the race's forty-eighth go-round that absorbed Stan Wattles, Roberto Guerrero, Billy Roe, Mark Dismore, Sam Schmidt, Marco Greco, and Jim Guthrie. It was Guthrie who inherited the worst of it, suffering a broken right elbow, a broken left leg, cracked right ribs, and a cut on his left leg. Everyone involved had an interpretation. Remarked Wattles afterward, "I was between Roberto and the wall. I kept watching Roberto, and the accident happened, and I ran into the back of Dismore. My car was fast and especially easy to drive. I feel bad, especially for my crew. I just feel like crying." Said Guerrero "It was a long chain reaction by the time it got to me,

I hit pretty hard, but when I got out [of the car] in the pits, I looked at it and said to myself, 'There's nothing wrong with it,' so I got back in and did some more laps." Added Billy Roe, "I saw it coming. It was the biggest mess I've seen. I headed for the grass, but there was nowhere to go. I'm very disappointed." Continued Schmidt, "It's just a racing deal," adding that he had a choice between "go[ing] into the grass or hit[ting] Davey Hamilton. I thought we had a top five car. It's pretty disappointing."

Wall smackers Sam Hornish, Scott Harrington, and Billy Boat did their thing again in 1999. Hornish started it all on May 15 when, with smoke trailing his entry into the northeast, he made a ninety degree spin through turn three and then hit something hard in turn four, evading injury. Harrington and Boat each connected hard with the turn three concrete on Monday afternoon, May 17. Harrington was first at 1:45, whacking the cement with the right front corner of his car in both the northeast and the northwest. "The car just didn't want to steer," he confessionally explained to the press corps. "That was our backup car. Now I'm down to one car." At 2:23 fate decreed that it was Boat's turn to plunge into the outer barrier with his right front and right side. Observers reported smoke pouring from the rear of the car before impact. Boat's post accident feelings were similar to Harrington's: "You can get behind here real fast," he said, "and now we've got two bent race cars. I don't really know right now what happened," he continued. "I knew early that I was in trouble. The car never attempted to turn." Asked about his perceived bad luck, he responded, "this place doesn't play favorites." Asked too about his spirits, he answered, "Well, they've certainly been better." Boat, like every other contestant, has his supporters, among them Lloyd Ruby, the eighteen time contestant who never won but who in the opinion of his fellow racer Johnny Boyd had greater mastery over the Indianapolis Motor Speedway than anyone of his time. "Billy Boat," said Ruby. "He's my favorite. He came up the hard way, through midgets. I'm friends with his dad. I'd like to see him do good because he's driving for a mean old man," averring in jesting reference to car owner A. J. Foyt.

On the 20th of the month Johnny Unser, the Cal State graduate from Hailey, Idaho, and son of the late Jerry Unser (brother to Al and Bobby Unser who between them have won Indianapolis seven times and who burned to death at the north end of the track four decades prior), socked the wall in the northeast, drifted low on the course between turns three and four, then hit the wall in the northwest turn with what the track management called "heavy impact." Unser somehow avoided injury. He claimed not to know a reason for the accident. "I was following another car by about 100 yards, and it just pushed up into the wall. We'll look at tapes and download data, and try to find out." He was not alone. A day later John Paul, Jr. cut a half spin in the northeast, connecting with the car's left rear. Paul climbed out of his own volition.

It is difficult to determine whether turn accidents are accountable to the weather, the car, the driver, or some other driver. Rick Mears, who won Indianapolis four times and occupied the pole position six times, had no accidents there until his final appearance. Asked in 2002 how to drive the turns to advantage, he provided a concise but accurate answer: "It's [the line is] mainly high [entering turns one and three, the southwest and the northeast], low in the middle and high out [of turns two and four, the southeast and the northwest]." Continuing, he said, "you want an extremely late entry to have a fast lap. [At] this place especially, the entry determines the exit." In 2000, he had further commented that if "you get your entry wrong, your exit's going to be wrong, so you've got to get your entry right to get the exit right, and that's usually a fairly late turn-in and fairly late apex. I'd always try to get it to where, when I come off the wall, I'd turn the car and get it set and it would work its way back off the fence without ever having to make a correction. If you get that arc right, that was about as close as you could get it. That's what I tried to do. It's very seldom could you make it through there like that without having to make a correction, but it's what you strive to achieve."

It is every bit as easy as that until, of course, one attempts it. Sunday, May 13 dawned bright and clear in 2001. Rookie Memo Gidley ushered the day into motion by whacking the outer limits of turn three and proceeding into a quarter spin that shoved him into the wall with the rear and right rear of his Team Cure Autism Now entry that halted at the inside entrance to turn four. Gidley remained secured to his mount while crews figured out how to return it to the pits. No sooner had Gidley and his car entered the turn sideways than car No. 30 carrying the name "Team Calcium" arrived on the scene driven by Stockbridge, Georgia's Jimmy Kite, who spun to keep from running into either Gidley or any walls that might pose a threat. Remarked Gidley, "It was my second lap of the day. The car got a little loose going into turn three. The impact was limited to the rear crash box and rear wing. I'm fine, and we're going to fix the minor damage and get right back out there."

Likewise Robby McGehee, the six-foot-two, 175-pound St. Louis resident who had the high honor of being the first to pop the new soft(er)

SAFER wall barrier (it happened in the northeast, as bad luck would have it), at 4:36 on Sunday, May 5, which was the Speedway's gala 2002 opening day. There was, not surprisingly, a certain amount of curiosity regarding just how safe the SAFER barriers on all four corners of the track were going to be. When McGehee spun his Cahill No. 10 into what was no longer the turn three "cement" but rather the turn three catch wall, the car hit rear end first then on its right side, briefly tipped on its right side, then turned upright before ending on the fescue between the track and the inner warmup lane. McGehee exited the car with some assistance from the track's safety crew and walked to a waiting ambulance. Bouncing off the SAFER, he said later in a moment of reflection, was "a distinction I'd rather not have." Continuing, he added, "I can tell you it's not soft. I hit hard, but I can also assure you that I'm very glad it was there. I think the angle that I hit made it a lot worse than it would have been otherwise. I have a cut on one leg, and we're just going for more x-rays, but I think I'm fine." On the morning of the following day, Monday, May 6, the Indianapolis Motor Speedway's medical director Henry Bock announced that McGehee (who had broken his lower left leg after a rumble at the Texas Motor Speedway in 2001), had done so again, but that was not the end of his complications. He had not, said Dr. Bock, been cleared to practice (much less compete in) the eighty-sixth running of the Indianapolis 500 because, aside from the rebroken leg, an x-ray revealed small fractures in his upper spine. McGehee then reappeared on crutches wearing a soft cast on his left leg, the outcome of a not-so-soft impact with a soft wall. "I'm sore as hell," said he, "but I'll be fine. It [the car] hit backward and then flipped on its right side." On the brighter side, he remarked, "the fact that I hit the wall that hard, and I don't have a head injury, is a testament that the SAFER wall worked. I think I would have had a head injury for sure, without it. I didn't want to be the test guinea pig for the new wall barrier. I was joking about that yesterday, but here we are." Indeed so. Others were looking on with interest. Said the IRL's operations man Brian Barnhart, "First of all, we're glad Robby is doing well. His crash was a massive impact. We haven't seen anything yet after looking at the preliminary data that has us going in any direction other than forward. Obviously, we're looking for anything to gain information." McGehee, as circumstances developed, was free to buckle back in on May 13, but ultimately sat out the 2002 race.

The articulate comedian Tony Kanaan, behind the switchboard of Mo Nunn's Chevrolet G Force chassis, had taken over the lead in the 2002 race and was well on his way the stealing the whole day when on lap eighty-nine his car slipped as it rounded the northeast corner, did a quarter of a spin, and headed directly for the SAFER, slamming it with the rear and left side and then rolling into turn four. Then driver Rick Treadway stopped at the same place after parting with his right front wing and sustaining damage to the right side of his car that was known that day as the Sprint Kyocera Wireless Airlink Racing Special. The Brazilian bachelor Kanaan, born on New Years Eve in 1974, is capable of expressing himself quite well in English, Portuguese, Italian, and Spanish, and was in his salad days a rollerblading instructor. Interviewed subsequently in Gasoline Alley, Kanaan preferred to look on the bright side of the day. "I'm not exactly sure what happened," he related, "but I think I spun in somebody's oil. But I had a blast. At least I can say that I led the Indy 500. It's just racing," he continued. "We did what we could, but unfortunately we missed it. It's a shame. Next year I hope I get the chance to do it again." Treadway, another bachelor and another aircraft pilot (with a commercial license plus additional ratings in single, multiengine, and instrument rating), happened also to be the son of former Indy car owner Fred Treadway who, with a little help from Arie Luyendyk, won the pole and the race in 1997. His reactions to the lap eighty-nine incident were somewhat consistent with Kanaan's. "There was oil spilled on the track between [turns] three and four," he reported afterward. All of a sudden cars started spinning, and we didn't have anywhere to go. We made light contact with the wall. It was a short day [but] it was a tremendous experience. I'm looking forward to next year." Kanaan salvaged twenty-eighth place, Treadway twenty-ninth.

Excitement in the north end of the Speedway in 2003 mostly waited until fourteen laps from the end when Dan Wheldon, the twenty-four-year-old Emberton, England, bachelor with a portrait of Richard the Lionheart painted on his yellowish helmet, became quite wiggly through the northwest, darted into the wall in the north chute, then went end-for-end and sideways before continuing into the northwest turn upside down where rescue workers tipped his Dallara Honda back on its wheels to allow for easier disembarkation. Other drivers scrambled to keep from involving themselves in his predicament. It was a horrifying accident to behold, although Weldon matter-of-factly told Phillip Wilson of the *Indianapolis Star* that "it looked a lot more spectacular than it actually was," as if to say that it was all within a normal day's work.

Sadly, another lionhearted twenty-six-year-old youngster named Tony Renna, who as a kid was a spring training batboy with the New York

Yankees, died in the northeast turn during a Firestone tire test on a chilly October 22, 2003. The track was cold and so were the tires under his G Force chassis, with which he was relatively unfamiliar. On Renna's fifth lap the car spun at approximately 227 mph into the infield, took to the air, cleared the SAFER wall, and sliced through two steel fence support poles, splitting the car in half. An IRL investigation tentatively assumed driver error to have caused the accident, although there was reportedly evidence that Renna had struck a bird with enough impact to upset the car's stability. A coroner's report called "blunt force" the cause of death. Renna had recently purchased a home in Indianapolis's Broadripple area, and was to have been married in Hawaii a month later. Instead, he became the forty-first driver to die at the Speedway.

Lest one underestimate the human cost of death and injury, Godwin Kelly of the Daytona Beach *News-Journal* visited Joe Renna, the deceased driver's father in Deland, Florida almost a year after the accident. "I've had some very bad days," Mr. Renna said. "In the days after we lost Tony, I had to hold it together for my family. I had to be a strong guy. It's not been easy . . . Losing a child is extremely tough. You know, you never think about that happening. People figure your kids will outlive you." Kids, however, will always be kids. On lap 64 of the 2004 race rookie Eddie Carpenter, 23, stepson of IMS president and CEO Tony George, collided with British rookie Mark Taylor, 26. Taylor's car made a quarter spin in to the northeast turn wall. Carpenter made a half spin and hit with the left side of his machine. There was heavy damage to both cars. Both young men stepped into a waiting ambulance for a ride to the infield hospital.

TURN FOUR: THE NORTHWEST

"It's not that I'm afraid to die. I just don't want to be there when it happens."

Woody Allen

The Speedway's northwest turn, known to some as turn four, is the track's final bend in the road. Moments before the start of the 500-mile race, it is the place upon which all eyes dwell because it is there that all contestants are assumed to be formed up in eleven rows, three abreast. But they never are. The last orderly start was in 1950. Since then Indianapolis starts more resemble a pack of frenzied field mice scurrying at random across a kitchen floor. There is no eleventh row, nor is there a sixth nor even a first. Everyone is out of orthodox alignment possibly because everybody wants it that way, and quite possibly because everyone lacks the driving acumen to pull it off anyway. In 2003 drivers received among their marching orders a mandate that the person on the inside of each row must cross the starting line ahead of the other two contestants in that row. This was more or less done, but it still was a ragged start. Suffice it to say that the days of disciplined Speedway starts ended more than a half century ago and, like dime beer, will not be back. A pace car, maybe several pace cars, bearing an entourage of terrified passengers, escorts all thirty-three cars (or how ever many have survived long enough to receive the green flag) to the starting line while also beating a hasty and safe retreat off the race course. It is a heart-pounding moment. Indy's engines are not especially audible until they are close at hand. Then the earth shakes. Ceremonial bombs explode. Women faint. Clouds of smoke and dust hover in the air. The race, as they say, is on.

Although the northwest is theoretically no different from its opposite (the southeast), it neither feels nor looks that way. Whatever windy conditions prevail, meet the driver from an angle different from what he encounters everywhere else. To exit the southeast is to see a rather broad open area that leads into turn three, the northeast. To exit the northwest is entirely different inasmuch as there are suites and grandstands that hug the track on both sides. Drivers for years have said that the prospect of the main straightaway looks different on race day when people by the hundreds of thousands pack the place on both the left and right, leaving the impression that the track has become substantially narrower. It even sounds different from any other day at the track. Packing thirty-some racing cars on the main straight, be they in or out of formation, also creates terrific vacuum. Racers in the mid-fifties used to claim that one could be swept at high speed down the front straight with one's foot off the accelerator. Those who start in the back are subject to buffeting, severe turbulence, alcohol fumes, howling dust, and debris as severe as anything in Canto V of Dante's *Inferno*.

But like every other bend in the Indianapolis road, the northwest has a copious history, a consciousness of place, and an ambiance all its own. In 1914 the green England Sunbeam factory team six-cylinder entry that French driver Jean Chassagne placed on the pole at Indianapolis with an average speed of just over eighty-eight miles an hour (not the fastest of the thirty-car field that year) is scarcely recognizable as a racing car today. With a dozen cumbersome wooden spokes supporting each wheel, the car resembled more a sporty touring roadster. Appearances to the contrary, however, the Sunbeam was competitive for as long it stayed on the track. With twenty laps and slightly more than thirty minutes of racing time on it, the car and its passengers overturned in the northwest after having blown a tire and spun off the track. Although riding wrench Samuel Morris lapsed into temporary unconsciousness, Chassagne felt the incident insufficient reason to fall out of the chase, and ordered that the car be tipped back over on its wheels, after which he had second thoughts about its road worthiness, and decided with manly reluctance to call it a day. One observer said that the accident was "a spectacular one," although injuries proved to be minor ones, with the mighty Chassagne himself sustaining only a small cut beneath his left eye and another behind his left ear. It was nothing serious. Partly because Chassagne and Morris were spared serious injury, their potentially disastrous accident received relatively little notice, although it was one of the first noteworthy mischances in a long series of incidents occurring in turn four, a place that can be just as nasty as the other three, maybe more.

Chassagne, who resembled certain photographs of Edgar Allan Poe, indeed had a following. "Brooklands fans still thrill," said a press release, "at the recollection of how he wrenched his big twelve-cylinder Sunbeam from the top of the almost vertical banking in order to pass the late Percy Lambert on the inside." The release also noted that he was not always quite so much the "the familiar figure to followers of the racing game," noting that "his early career was spent in the engine room of a French battleship," not the highest of recommendations. Chassagne, by the way, returned to Indianapolis in 1919 when he relief drove for a fellow named Paul Bablot, lasted sixty-three laps, and overturned again. Living dangerously did not appear to have shortened Chassagne's life, that lasted until April 13, 1947.

The French contingent, consisting of Rene Thomas, Arthur Duray, Albert Guyot, mechanic-driver Jules Goux (the champagne-swilling winner from 1913), aviator Georges Boillot, and Chassagne himself, carried $26,500 in prize money with them on their steamship back to the old country after the 1913 event. With appetites whetted they returned to Indiana in 1914 where they found the greater part of mid-America engulfed in water, an inconvenience that obliged Speedway officials to postpone its 500-mile race from a Friday until the following Monday. Devoted racing enthusiasts made the best of it, occupying every hotel room in the city, and responding to the largesse of many Indianapolis residents by sleeping over in the homes of virtual strangers. Then as now, the resident press was skeptical of whether certain spectators came to town for the high purpose of viewing an automobile race, or to use that occasion to surrender one's will and throw a party. "It must have been like this in the good old days of the Roman games," speculated Hector Fuller of *The Indianapolis Star*, "and while those daredevil drivers were risking their lives and making some of the fair sex among the spectators almost ill with the terrible risks they took, there were many others on the ground who calmly went to luncheon and to a bottle of beer on ice."

After Carl Fisher used World War I as a convenient pretext to close the track in 1917 and 1918 so that he could pursue certain higher, more elegant purposes, there were attendance estimates of 120,000 by 1920, a year when the northwest turn appeared to stand out from among the other three in a motor race that seemed comparatively tame. Making the best of it, Lambert Sullivan of *Motor Age* viewed it quite sensibly as "a great race, not spectacular in any sense of the word, but a real trial of the cars entered." Notwithstanding, the old northwest was the site of what little unforeseen excitement came to pass in 1920 when amateur boxer Roscoe Sarles, a race-promoting native of Lafayette, Indiana, who rode with Louis

Chevrolet for two seasons, hurried his Frontenac into the fourth turn wall on lap fifty-eight. In the meantime, Art Klein, who had acquitted himself well as a lieutenant in the air service during World War I, wrecked his Frontenac after forty-one laps, then relieved his teammate Benny Hill, only to crash still another Frontenac in the northwest corner at 115 laps. His car went headlong into the wall, destroying the entire front end, and eventually came to rest mid-track. Unhurt, Klein and his rider Clyde Tatman returned to the pits on foot while track attendants pushed the wreckage, its radiator leaking profusely, off the course. A bridegroom of a few weeks, Klein encountered his wife who intercepted him and seized the opportunity to extract a promise (so said one eavesdropper) to "quit the racing game." Klein held to his vow for one year (while he too served in the aviation corps), and then returned in 1927 for one last try at the 500-mile race.

While Klein was not in evidence in 1921, Louis Fontaine was buzzing around the track in a six-cylinder Junior that became a little unwieldy through the northwest and ended the day straddled barely a few feet from startled spectators, hovering near the inside wall. Jimmy Murphy, the 1922 winner, wrecked his Confederate gray Duesenberg straight-eight later that afternoon in almost the same place, finishing fourteenth in a field of only twenty-three starters. One year later Jules Ellingboe at the helm of another Duesey straight-eight whirled around three times in the northwest on his twenty-fifth circuit and slapped the wall smartly, bending his right rear wheel without doing any injury to himself. News of Ellingboe's moderate misfortune, slight as it was, traveled over radio's magic waves that race day in 1922. Declared one incredulous reporter, "they say that radio fans who didn't join the great throng . . . may actually hear the hum of the engines as the speeding cars make the laps and that all the announcements will go whirring to their ears."

With the proliferation of radios in Indiana came the escalation of speeds at the Speedway. In the 1925 race the number twenty-three Duesenberg driven by Jimmy Gleason in relief of Wade Morton, collided with the wall in the northwest without injury. Having piloted his own white Miller Special to a nineteenth-place finish in 1925 despite a fiery crash in the south chute, twenty-two-year-old Herb (L. Herbert) Jones returned in 1926 to be the youngest driver entered that year. So serious was he about motor racing that he resigned his workaday job at the Haag Drug Company in Indianapolis to pursue what he envisioned as a bright and lucrative career as a driver of fast cars at the two-and-a-half mile

Speedway, where he had agreed to attempt the 500-mile race in fellow driver Al Cotey's baby blue eight-cylinder Elcar. On May 27, a Thursday, Jones registered one qualification lap at 105.67 miles per hour when he caught his left front wheel on turn four's inner wall, whereupon the car rolled over an undetermined number of times before it came to rest on the outer liner. Herb Jones died before a rescue party arrived. Although the Elcar was substantially demolished, mechanics reconstructed it for another qualification attempt, this time at the hands of John Duff, who managed to start last in the twenty-eight car field, bringing the car home ninth.

Popular Jules Ellingboe, whose surprising appearance invites comparison with latter day driver Jack McGrath, had not seen the last of his problems in the northwest. Returned in 1927 in a black and yellow super-charged Miller front drive entered by retired driver Earl Cooper, Ellingboe staged a remarkable, if regrettable, encore by crashing within one lap of the time he did in 1925. His low-slung Cooper Special, the body of which was obscured by four huge wire wheels, was substantially obliterated. *Motor Age* magazine reported that Ellingboe was "so seriously injured that he was taken to the hospital as quickly as possible." Cliff Woodbury, a contender for first place honors, qualified his own Boyle Valve car, propelled by a smallish ninety cubic inch Miller, for the pole position with a run of 120.599 miles per hour, a mile and a half quicker than second fastest qualifier Leon Duray. It was Woodbury's ill fortune, however, to move from first to last (from hero to zero, as some people say) in record time, a feat duplicated in modern times by Duane "Pancho" Carter in 1985, Roberto Guerrero in 1992, Greg Ray in 2000, and Scott Sharp in 2001. As Woodbury rode in third position on lap three, his striking red, white, and blue racer spun in the northwest and somehow landed backwards against the outer wall with a collapsed right rear axle. While uniformed militiamen applied themselves to the arduous task of hoisting the crunched automobile over the wall with use of board planks, Woodbury made a dash toward the pit area. Minutes later, teammate Billy Arnold arrived with his goggles shattered and his eye cut from a fragment of flying debris. Subbing for Arnold, Woodbury motored around the track six times and then turned the car over to O. G. Roberts who kept all four wheels in play until its 146th lap, when Arnold once again stepped into the cockpit. Woodbury, not wishing to allow any grass to grow beneath his feet that afternoon, then replaced Bob McDonough after thirty laps, and drove the car for an additional thirty-four, at which time the car's oil tank developed a pronounced leak. Woodbury's next stop was in the pit of Phil "Red" Shafer where he relieved Shafer and was ultimately flagged off the course at 150 laps, by which time Philadelphia's Ray Keech had finished the 500 miles a winner.

Although it had been a frenetic day for Cliff Woodbury, he was not by any means the only man in Gasoline Alley who passed a more than routinely active few hours. Moon-faced Jules Moriceau, who had gamely driven an even tinier seventy-eight cubic inch Amilcar, totally lost control on the northwest on his thirtieth lap, rammed the wall four times and corrugated the tiny yellow and black racer without incurring any noteworthy injury. Even Harry B. Leslie, governor of Indiana, had his dilemma. Having invited Colonel and Mrs. Charles A. Lindbergh to join him and Mrs. Leslie in the governor's box seats for the race, the newly wedded couple remained missing in action until shortly before race time. To compound everyone's plans, temperatures on race day reached nearly ninety degrees Fahrenheit, although they did not seem to bother Keech who had risen from the relative obscurity of dirt tracking and who had, only a year ago, hurled a racing car over the sands at Daytona Beach at well over 200 miles an hour. On this, his final attempt at Indianapolis, Keech improved on his creditable fourth-place finish the year before and was greeted boisterously as the champion of the seventeenth running of the 500-mile race. Telegrams poured in from delighted radio listeners as far down the road as the chic resort hotels of southern Indiana, attesting that they received reasonably good, static-free broadcast signals from the Speedway.

Hell cut loose through the northwest in 1931 beginning on lap six when Harry Butcher in the Butcher Brothers Buick chassis went through (not over) the wall. Butcher, thirty-five, emerged all but unscathed in the confrontation. Phil Pardee ended his race in turn four on lap sixty. Joe Russo, in the meantime, lost traction there in his white Duesenberg and smashed its tail section while attempting to stay out of Butcher's path. Russo, then a twenty-nine-year-old Indianapolis resident, brought his car under control and continued the chase for 109 laps until an oil leak got the better of him. The worst side of the 1931 race occurred when, as previously cited, Chicago's Billy Arnold, four laps ahead of the field, was flying low on the track and when his crew flashed him a hastily scrawled chalkboard message reading, "All's Well." In reality, all was anything but well. Arnold's next ride down the main straightaway was inside an ambulance after an oil slicked turn four accident severely injured himself and his mechanic "Spider" Matlock, and took the life of eleven-year-old Wilbur

Brink, a boy struck by a wheel from Arnold's racing car while playing at his home on Georgetown Road, parallel to the main straightaway. The wheel fractured Brink's body in numerous places. He received two hours of attention from physicians before being dispatched to City Hospital where he failed to survive the night. On the following morning one newspaper headline read: ARNOLD, COLLAR BONE FRACTURED, PUFFS "FAG" IN AMBULANCE TO ASSURE CROWD. "Just a tough break, that's all," said the baby-faced Arnold from the Speedway's race day infirmary. All, by racing standards, was relatively quiet in the northwest until lap 167 when Tony Gulotta and mechanic Carl Rescigno, then riding second, lost a right rear wheel from their Hunt Special, a gold and green Studebaker entered by D. A. "Ab" Jenkins, the fabled pilot of the speedy Mormon Meteors. It was damned slippery out there. Gulotta and Rescigno slid on that greasy northwest turn, obliterating a large section of the outer concrete wall as they passed none too gracefully over it. Although the men managed to get by with relatively minor scratches and bruises, it was a right rear wheel that, for the second time that day, provided much of the consternation, theirs having bounded into the outer wall, then into the inner, and finally rolling to a rest in a gully a short distance from scurrying infield patrons.

In the 1932 event the first combatants to fall out of battle did so in the northwest. First to go was Alan "Al" Gordon, the hard-drinking proprietor of Club Rendezvous in Long Beach, California, who was at the pedals of the Miller-powered Lion Tamer Special, with Indianapolis's own Horace John Booty along for the ride—and what a ride it was. When the blue and white Lion Tamer "clicked hubs" (as one commentator put it) with another Miller driven by Stubby Stubblefield on the third circuit of the 1932 race, the early traffic was funneling through the northwest corner where the force of the mischance sent Gordon and his companion through a wooden retaining rail along the upper home stretch. They slithered along the grassy strip between the race track and the front edge of old Grandstand H where Gordon and Booty finally brought the beast to book at the north tunnel near the head of the straightaway. In the solemn judgment of AAA officialdom, Gordon himself was personally responsible for the unfortunate series of consequences that brought about Horace Booty's multiple lacerations. "This accident," said one outspoken report, "can be traced to the fact that Gordon did not arrive until Friday previous to the race, had practically no time to practice, and did not understand that coming out of the northwest turn the car always drifts to the outside." So reported the AAA to all who could read. Gordon, who had failed to tame any lions in 1932 at Indianapolis, finished a lowly fortieth in a field of forty, although he became the Pacific Coast champion in 1933. He and riding mechanic Spider Matlock died (Gordon after a few hours, Matlock a day later) after the car they were racing tipped over and crushed them in the south turn of Los Angeles's Legion Ascot Speedway on January 26, 1936. Wilbur Shaw was a participant that afternoon. "As far as sudden death was concerned," he said years later, "the racing fraternity was a hardened group." According to Shaw, it was Gordon who responded to a wave of criticism aimed at auto racing. "What difference does it make?" Gordon is alleged to have said. "We all have to die sometime." The Gordon-Matlock accident closed racing activity at Legion Ascot forever.

Gus Schrader, an aging Iowan who deserved his immense reputation as one of the country's best and most peripatetic dirt track jockeys, but who evidently did not find Indianapolis to his liking, followed Gordon out of competition in 1932. Both Schrader and his riding mechanic Fred Blauvelt, nattily attired in aircraft helmets, white driving uniforms, and black bow ties, lasted but seven laps before their front-drive sixteen-cylinder Miller ran into a wall at the northwest turn near what was then an overhead footbridge where their left front wheel hung on the outer barrier. Neither man was injured, but they were out of business that day. Schrader, a World War I veteran, continued to ply his trade as a dirt track driver both in and out of AAA's dictatorially supervised races, but never again came to Indianapolis as a competitor. There is a photograph afoot of Schrader, buckled in a racing car, shaking hands enthusiastically with a quite young Ronald Reagan, who before World War II earned pin money commentating upon International Motor Contest Association auto races, the so-called "outlaw" (because it was not AAA) racing circuit that performed mostly between the upper middlewest and Florida, sometimes staging hayseed county fair hippodrome exhibitions rather than competitions. Schrader raced unceasingly until the sport killed him at the Louisiana State Fair in Shreveport on October 22, 1941, when he was thrown from his car with such violence that his helmet and shoes were separated from his body.

There were five participant deaths at the Speedway in 1933, including driver Les Spangler and mechanic G. L. Jordan in turn one and driver Mark Billman in turn two. The other two came in turn four, where driver Bill Denver and mechanic Hugh "Bob" Hurst died during a qualification attempt when they leapt the wall in the northwest (reported at the time to be the northeast) turn. Leon Duray's Bowes Seal Fast No. 45 Myron Stevens Miller that bachelor Clay Weatherly of Harmon, Illinois, drove in the 1935 race had a decidedly checkered history, inasmuch as Johnny Hannon lost his life in it on May 21 that year while on a testing run. After crews hurriedly rebuilt it, Weatherly hustled it into the race, albeit in twenty-fifth position, at a speed of slightly under 116 miles an hour. With the storied Rex Mays leading thirty-two cars on lap nine, Weatherly skidded 200 feet through the northwest, pierced the outer wooden guardrailing as Al Gordon had in 1932, and scraped the protective wall in front of Grandstand H. Weatherly and mechanic Edward Bradburn were each dumped out of the car when it rolled along the same grassy strip that Gordon had once inadvertently used. Weatherly died on his way to the infield hospital. Bradburn sustained a broken back and then repaired to Robert Long Hospital for treatment.

By lap seventeen of the 1935 race attention focused again on Al Gordon and what was to be his third and final attempt at Indianapolis when turn four again became the place of his undoing. His Cocktail Hour Cigarette Special, a racy-looking cream and blue Miller with a Weil chassis, slid 600 feet through the northwest with Gordon and mechanic Frank Howard bracing for the worst. The car made its way gradually from the inner to the outer wall and careened into it with enough authority to crack the concrete and come to rest wrong side up atop it. Amazingly, the mishap played out with no substantial injury to either occupant, even though Howard fell out of the car. "It just got away from me; that's all," said the plucky Gordon at the Speedway's ever-active infirmary. Mrs. Gordon, not quite so placid, rushed to her husband's cotside where she discovered him sitting up, sucking on a large cigar, and declaring that he wanted to reenter the race. Instead, he and Howard returned to the conviviality of Gasoline Alley where they poured a drink for themselves and for movie idol Richard Arlen (whose latest film, called *Let 'Em Have It*, had just been released) who passed the afternoon as a lap scorer in Lou Moore's Foreman Axle pit until the car lost an engine at lap 116.

Wilbur Shaw crossed the finish line a winner at Indianapolis in 1937 when Springfield, Illinois, rookie Floyd Davis, the co-winner of the race with Mauri Rose in 1941, crashed in the northwest on his 190th lap. Earlier in the day AAA observers observed that the exhaust pipe on Davis's striking blue and silver Thorne Engineering Miller had worked itself loose, and that renegade riding mechanic Dee Toran was holding said pipe in place to forestall its falling by the wayside. After they spun, some predictable things happened. One was that the car bucked Toran out of his saddle and left him to fend for himself in the middle of the race track with a bunch of crazy racers aiming in his direction. Another thing was that Davis and Toran were both at least momentarily rendered unconscious. After 1941, Davis never returned to the Speedway as a driver. Toran, a veritable terror in midget cars after World War II, later received a manslaughter conviction in the June 10, 1947 death of fellow Connecticut driver Alvin "Jeep" Colkitt at Bridgeport.

When Davis and Rose won the race in 1941 the mayhem at Indianapolis had acquired its now familiar carnival aura, especially across the street from the Speedway's southeast property line where all night rowdiness caught the attention of track management. However, if one had grown weary of watching cars go around the track, there were other wholesome diversions around Indianapolis. The Fox burlesque house on North Illinois rolled out its all new "Speedway Follies" featuring "25 Beautiful Baby Dolls." Thrill seekers with somewhat different tastes in entertainment could elect the Riverside Amusement Park a few miles east of the Motor Speedway at Thirtieth Street and White River where the featured attraction during race month was the inimitable Pasha Alexandra, the Egyptian Miracle Man buried alive nightly (twice on Memorial Day and Sunday) before the eyes of awe-struck tourists latterly arrived in the big city where they uncovered a cornucopia of entertainment possibilities, not the least of which was Horace Heidt and His Pot O'Gold Stars at the Lyric Theatre, also on North Illinois.

When finally it came time for the 1941 race, spectators in the northwest end experienced a sobering moment late in the afternoon when thirty-two-year-old Everett Saylor, a relatively obscure former public school teacher from Dayton, Ohio, spun his red and silver Weil chassis owned by Cincinnati physician Mark E. Bowles on lap 155. The trouble began when Saylor dipped his car low in the apron of the turn, then continued through an inner guardrailing, then into a parking barrier wall situated well off the race course. After roaring into that barrier his dirt track racer rolled over and heaved itself into a parked car while frantic bystanders fled in every direction except northwest. For the critically injured Saylor it was the end of the line at Indianapolis, and although he recovered in time he never again returned for a rematch at America's premier motor race. By the time clean-up crews had removed the wreckage of Saylor's car, Mauri Rose was self-contentedly igniting his pipe in Victory Lane and receiving the five-year-old Borg-Warner Trophy with its removable lid.

Rose proceeded to pass the evening by taking his car out for a leisurely drive, at which time he paid a call on Saylor who was liberally bandaged within the sanctimonious confines of Methodist Hospital. Seemingly unruffled by his first win at the Brickyard, Rose, somewhat incognito, was dressed in a business suit the following morning at 7:30 when he left home for another routine day at the Allison plant across from the Speedway. As events unfolded, Saylor died as a result of a compound skull fracture a year and a day later in a Cape Girardeau, Missouri, racing accident. His gravestone at Dayton's Willow View Cemetery reads, "Everett E. Saylor/1909–1942/ [profile of a driverless race car pointing left]/ Always a Champion."

"The 2½ mile brick Speedway with its patchy asphalt covering is no longer adequate in its present shape, contours and banking for the modern racing car," warned John Bentley of the British motoring journal *The Autocar* in 1949. "To misjudge the turns at Indianapolis," he continued, "you may land on the inside apron, upside down, as Charles Van Acker's Redmer Special did this year during the 11th [10th] lap, or you may end up facing the other way, with both rear wheels ripped off, as did Duke Nalon on the 24th lap." While Bentley's admonitions were at least thirty years premature, he was still correct. There was no gainsaying in 1949 that Van Acker, a jolly Belgian-born machinist from South Bend, Indiana, and sometime Notre Dame undergraduate, had indeed spun his wife's No. 10 while attempting to worm his way through the northwest. Van Acker's beefy wire-wheeled car, a red, white, and silver Offy, powered Stevens chassis, rebounded from the inner guard railing thirty-five feet farther down the track. Then after the big machine rolled over one and a half times, it came to a tentative stop on the inner guard railing without crushing its occupant. A posse of fast-moving firemen righted the car, and Van Acker crawled out, unharmed but not unshaken. Showman to the end, he waved triumphantly to the appreciative crowd. It was his final Indianapolis appearance after three starts.

Tony Bettenhausen, who drove all but one Indianapolis 500 between 1946 and 1950, drove a cigar-shaped Offenhauser-propelled Mobiloil Special in 1951 cared for by Lou Moore. On lap 178 he spun coming through the northwest turn and slid into the infield, where, after some help from a tow truck, he got his engine running and motored back to the pits to find he was out of contention for the afternoon. Dark horse Floridian Lee Wallard in a brakeless, deep blue Belanger Motors dirt car that Bettenhausen had turned down on grounds that he felt it uncompetitive, won the race.

Bettenhausen, meanwhile, scored ninth in a race that had only eight cars still in contention at the conclusion, one higher than the fewest number finishing Indianapolis—seven, in 1966.

Another Floridian, Bayliss Levrett (original spelling *Levriett*), then living in Glendale, California, was a way-back finisher in the 1949 and 1950 races, but showed up at Indianapolis in 1952 in a Kurtis 2000 dirt car chassis that he had assembled himself and sold to Verlin Brown of the Brown Motor Company in Richmond, Indiana. On Saturday, May 10, Levrett lost contact with the car while he was making his way through turn four. Norman Werking, on assignment for *Automobile Topics*, was on the scene and reported that Levrett began his difficulties that day with "a long series of bumps against the outside retaining wall." Having scuffed the cement as many as ten times, Levrett began "bouncing back and forth like a billiard ball going into a pocket," after which he fell partly out of the seat and dragged for a hundred feet. The car then turned sideways in the center of the track while flames from its punctured fuel tank reached a height of twenty feet. Levrett attempted to tear his flaming clothes away. Suffering first- and second-degree burns on his wrists and ankles, he soon announced his retirement from automobile racing, and managed to recover with surprising rapidity, living to the age of eighty-nine, although in compromised health, with his scars still evident.

Part of the drawing card for the annual spring rites in 1952 was the presence of Alberto Ascari, born July 13, 1918, a second-generation Grand Prix driver who had prevailed in thirty-one international races dating as far back as 1937 and who had won the world driving championship in 1950 as a member of the Ferrari racing team. The likable Ascari, who seemed amenable to the press corps at Indianapolis, was also reputed to be, in the words of one commentator, the "greatest foreign threat in nearly decades." After qualifying for the nineteenth starting position in a red Ferrari whose torque was reportedly inadequate to accelerate out of Indianapolis's four turns, Ascari showed his stuff by charging into eighth position at the fifty-mile point. Moving through the northwest, however, Ascari became uncomfortably aware that his right rear wheel was about to fold, which it did. In the meantime, the Ferrari commenced an 850-foot slide that carried it to the track apron and then over the lawn where it spun in a clockwise direction, finally ending halfway on the apron once more. Although Ascari reentered a year later, neither he nor his car arrived for another Indianapolis assault. In those fast times, the odds of dying behind the wheel were better than even. After surviving an inadvertent plunge into the picturesque harbor at the Monaco Grand Prix, Ascari died after a testing accident at Monza on May 26, 1955, four days before Bill Vukovich perished at Indianapolis.

A year later, in 1953, Germantown, Pennsylvania's forty-two-year-old Len Duncan, a seemingly indestructible man with an interminable racing career as driver and chauffeur (after having been wounded in the Navy, he was Harry Truman's coachman when the president visited England following the Potsdam Conference), spun his Central Excavating Special in turn four on the final day of qualification runs. Although Duncan, born in New York City, was uninjured, the same could not be said of his car. "I still remember taking the President to Buckingham Palace," Duncan told writer Len Calinoff. "They gave me a big Buick convertible, and Truman was sitting in the back seat. Next to me was a secret service guy, and he had a violin case on his lap, and you know what was in the case. It was a gun that went *rat-tat-tat*. So here we were going down one of the main streets in London, and the crowd starts to converge on the Buick to see Truman. All of a sudden, this secret service man opens the case, and I say to myself, 'geez.' If someone wants to shoot the president, here I am in the front seat. I was more scared than the first time I drove a big car at Ascot in 1928 or was it '27? I still remember stalling the car every time we came to a stop, and I heard the President say to me, 'Son, after the war you had better take some driving lessons.'"

During the race itself, quiet Don (Donald Lloyd "Fritz") Freeland, a 190-pound California roadster and sprint car specialist from Redondo Beach competing in the first of his eight races at the Speedway, grazed the wall on the northwest turn and spun crazily toward the infield where he finally regained control of his Bob Estes Special, a Watson dirt car. "The driver does not appear to be injured," said an on-the-spot dispatch. The door of opportunity had opened wide for Freeland when Estes's former driver Jim Rigsby died a well publicized death when his car rocketed out of turn three at the half-mile Dayton, Ohio, speedway on August 31, 1952, and flew higher than the old trees that surrounded it. Estes's first replacement driver, Joe James, the engaging Californian widely believed to be marrying into the Hulman Speedway family, got himself killed in another Estes car after a November 2 accident on the San Jose mile dirt track. Freeland, born the son of a Bakersfield letter carrier on March 25, 1925 in Torrance, and educated at a Los Angeles trade school, entered the Navy the day before his eighteenth birthday, became a motor machinist and Diesel mechanic, and received his discharge papers on January 18, 1946, just in time to hit the race tracks, beginning at the infamous Ash Can Derby track in San Bernardino where Troy Ruttman began racing as well. Freeland acquired the habit at the old Carrell Speedway (so named for a certain Judge Carrell whose property it was) in Gardena when it opened that October. He tried midget racing briefly at two short (in time and distance) board tracks at the Los Angeles Coliseum and at the Rose Bowl, then motored east to race hot rods with the old Hurricane group in Chicago. Like other returning war veterans who traded one kind of helmet for another, Freeland, a top line driver who never seemed to win races, immersed himself in the racing life and is alive today. "All my friends are gone, for Christ's sake," said Freeland at sixty-five. "I was real buddies with Jimmy Reece and Jerry Hoyt [both deceased]. At first, losing friends didn't bother me all that much. Then I'd be looking at a group picture, thinking to myself, 'he's not here; he's not here; he's not here.' It sort of got to me."

The cream of the 1953 rookie crop, however, was ectomorphic Jimmy Daywalt who adored public attention as much as any Speedway performer before or since his time. Returned in 1954, Daywalt never ran worse than fourth at fifty mile intervals, while visions of the Borg-Warner winner's cup danced in his head until his 111th tour of the track when he contacted the wall in the northwest, coming off it backwards and taking Pat Flaherty (relief driving for Jim Rathmann on that miserably hot afternoon) with him. While there were no injuries to report, Daywalt returned to Gasoline Alley in tears, believing that his one chance ever to win Indianapolis had eluded him. He was, as events turned out, quite correct in his assessment, as was a one-legged driver named Cal Niday, known to some of his pals as "Wooden Leg," a mustachioed ex-barber from Pacoima, California, who had more than thwarted expectations with which to deal. With the death of Billy Vukovich on the backstretch out of turn two that year, relatively little attention came to Niday, a midget car expert who struck the wall on the northwest turn slightly north of Grandstand H, and ended nose down in an infield incline with his front wheels against a spectator fence. He had slammed the wall in such a way that his head was pitched to the right side of the cockpit and into the wall. Listed in critical condition with a skull fracture that affected his vision, a crushed chest, a ruptured liver, multiple lacerations, and third-degree burns requiring skin grafts on his leg, Niday had run his last race. His car was a deep yellow Kurtis 500B D-A Lubricant Special that had been riding among the race leaders at 171 laps. Niday later declared that, had he not crashed, he had a realistic chance of winning Indianapolis.

Calvin Lee Niday, born April 29, 1914, in Turlock, California, enrolled at Turlock High School where he lettered in basketball, track, and football. He had a football scholarship awaiting him at Washington State when as a high school senior he lost his left leg in a motorcycle accident that occurred on his way home from a football game. So instead of Washington State he went to Molar Barber and Beauty College from which he was graduated in 1935. Niday began racing in 1937 while on tour with a troupe of stunt bikers who called themselves the *Hollywood Hell Riders*, in whose august company he broke his remaining leg in Ord, Nebraska, and passed nine months of hospital time contemplating the ceiling. Niday teamed up with Duane Carter, who took him east as a stooge (racing parlance for a menial helper) and warmup man. After stints with Ronnie Householder and Pee Wee Distarce, Niday found work in Hollywood motion picture studios in the war years. He married the former Elsie Crandell (once married to Indianapolis driver Frank Wearne) on May 31, 1942, and their son Gilbert, known as "Buster," was born in 1945. Niday somehow raced motorcycles during the war, winning five of seven events, and became president of the Southern California Motorcycle Club that he said included their excellencies Ward Bond and Clark Gable in its membership roles. Following the war he raced midgets from one end of California to the other, grabbing more wins in San Diego, for example, than any driver of that period. He went on a racing spree in San Antonio with Johnnie Parsons, Bill Vukovich, and Andy Guthrie, winning two of three feature events before shipping off to Australia with Perry Grimm, winning what could be won at Brisbane and Sidney. He then raced the length and breadth of America, but did not embark seriously on the Championship Trail for Indy cars until the 1953 and 1954 seasons, where he did not find the successes he had in midget cars. Niday attempted an Indianapolis comeback in 1956, but discovered that his vision had not corrected sufficiently to race there again, although he did undertake the Pikes Peak hill climb and tried his hand occasionally with midgets and sports cars. The Nidays lived in Hawaii for some time in the 1960s. Calvin died in a freak accident at the Willow Springs track in California during a vintage racing car exhibition on Valentine's Day 1988 when the car he was driving tipped over, throwing him on the track, after which he developed an irregular heartbeat and suffered heart attacks en route to a hospital.

There used to be myth surrounding the Indianapolis 500 that its races pitted the thirty-three (or whatever the number happened to be in a given year) best drivers on the face of the globe. That, of course, was a patently absurd claim, although to be sure the Motor Speedway has showcased some of the world's best driving talent including, but obviously not limited to, Anthony Joseph Foyt, certain members of the Unser family, Wilbur Shaw, Rick Mears, Rex Mays, Jim Clark, Graham Hill, Juan Montoya, Bill Vukovich, Ted Horn, Mauri Rose, Louis Meyer, John Rutherford, Bill Holland, Troy Ruttman, Mario Andretti, Rodger Ward, Peter DePaolo, and whomever else one cares to nominate. One could also assert that there are enough names (e.g. Bob Bondurant, Chris Amon, David Coultard, Nino Farina, Richie Ginther, Mike Hawthorne, Bruce McLaren, Stirling Moss, Tazio Nuvolari, Carlos Reutemann, Keke Rosberg, John Surtees) who did not compete there, to form a decently respectable automobile race. "You don't always have the thirty-three best drivers at Indianapolis," 1983 winner Tom Sneva acknowledged. "There [are] so many good, talented race drivers around that don't get the opportunity because they do not have the financial backing, they don't have the right people behind them or right sponsorship situation, and they never get a chance to show how good they really are."

Far lesser names, however, have tried and succeeded, or tried and failed. American audiences are understandably partial to home-grown talent, and many such drivers came off the sometimes obscure county fair dirt tracks. Such was a man named Marvin Pifer, a six-foot-two, 200-pound man who came from Adrian, Michigan, where his father was the town fire chief, and who died in 1974 of heart failure (supposedly complicated by multiple sclerosis) at the age of forty-six. Pifer began driving with the Central States Racing Association while assuming the identity of his older brother Aldun between 1946 and 1948, then escaped to Tampa in the company of the mysterious outlaw driver Harry King who summered in Michigan and wintered in Florida. Pifer began racing with the American Automobile Association in 1950 until he was inducted into the Army that in turn pointed him toward Korea. Upon his return he is alleged to have triumphed in twenty-three of twenty-five outlaw automobile races conducted under the banners of the CSRA (the Central States Racing Association) and the International Motor Contest Association. When he was not winning races, he was driving fire trucks under his father's auspices. On the recommendation of Hoosier favorite Pat O'Connor, Pifer joined the Indianapolis Motor Speedway's freshman class of 1956 that included Edgar Elder, Johnny Kay, Leroy Warriner, and Buddy Cagle—none of whom ever drove in competition there. Assigned to the red Commercial Motor Freight Special, a dirt track car entered by Karl Hall of Orleans, Indiana, Pifer turned laps in excess of 138 miles an hour, a speed that would probably not have earned him a starting position at Indianapolis that year. On May 10 he put the car into the wall in the northwest turn, resulting in a skull fracture and some lesser medical consequences that nevertheless occasioned a lengthy hospital confinement. Afterword, he returned to Adrian where he continued driving on the shorter tracks, and ended his racing career, with well over a hundred wins, on the Michigan State Fairgrounds mile dirt track in 1960. Back home again, he expanded his automotive repair business to open Jeep and Triumph dealerships.

During the running of the 1956 race, little known Air Force veteran and three-time Colorado midget car champion Keith Andrews, a Colorado Springs garage owner and a divisional winner in the 1954 Pikes Peak hill climb, drove Detroiter Harry Dunn's 500B Kurtis roadster, and while there was hardly anything unusual about the car in this, the heyday of roadster-dom (said ex-driver Sam Posey, "the design of the Indy cars had stagnated around an unsophisticated car called a 'roadster' which all the teams ran virtually unchanged year after year") at Indianapolis, there was some-thing unexpected in the car's right front Firestone that exploded in the northwest on Andrews's ninety-fourth lap. He spun, righted the old tub, and headed back to the pits for a new tire and a new issue of fuel. It could hardly be said that racing luck smiled on him that day, inasmuch as the car later stalled at the south end of the track. Nor was fortune riding with him in 1957 when he died at the age of thirty-six while testing a car entered for Italian driving champion Nino Farina. It was on May 15 at 11:25 A.M. that Andrews again lost control in the northeast just as he had turned a lap in the 136 mile an hour bracket when the roadster went below the white line, fell into a 360-degree spin, skidded 755 feet into an inside retaining railing, rebounded 300 feet toward the white line, spun again three quarters of the way around, and slid another 450 feet into the wall, pushing the steel guard railing two feet. The sheer force of the accident drove Andrews into the steering wheel, breaking his neck. He was the forty-first individual to lose his life at the track, survived by his wife Glenice and two daughters.

The passing of unobtrusive Keith Andrews prior to the 1957 race seemed to set a precedent for other turn four difficulties. Rookie Mike Magill, the thirty-seven-year-old former stock car driver and war veteran, spun the Dayton Steel Foundry car toward the end of the northwest corner.

Enthusiastic Al Herman of Allentown, Pennsylvania, driving the same Dunn Engineering car that Keith Andrews looped the previous year, was ten laps ahead of Magill when the accident took them both out. Magill and Herman appeared at the Speedway in subsequent years with somewhat better, if less spectacular, results. Harry Dunn's roadster, however, had a fatal attraction for the northwest, crashing there in 1958 for the third time in as many years. Occupying the cockpit that time was Springfield, Illinois's Chuck Weyant, a native of St. Mary's, Ohio, and the divorced owner of the Finish Line Tavern in Springfield, a short distance from the Illinois State Fairgrounds. Weyant, in any event, followed Al Herman's skidmarks to a fault by stuffing the Dunn car into the northwest wall. If ill luck indeed comes in packages of three, Harry Dunn's trilogy of misfortune had run its cycle for the nonce. When he returned gamely in 1959 with Herman again at the controls, the car ran all 200 laps and finished an ominous thirteenth.

In preparation for the 1961 Indianapolis 500 mile race, Dr. Thomas A. Hanna examined seventy-six aspiring drivers. Their average age, he deduced, was thirty-three and three-tenths years, their average weight was 165 pounds, and their average height five-feet-ten-and-a-half inches. Three of them wore glasses while driving, and twenty had removable dentures. Fifty-nine of the men identified themselves at Protestants, seventeen as Catholics. All but three said they were married. "Steady Eddie" Johnson from Cuyahoga Falls, Ohio, who seemed not to square too well with Dr. Hanna's 1961 driver profile, was under contract to drive for wealthy Troy, Michigan, industrialist Jim Robbins in whose car Johnson had finished sixth in 1960. At the age of forty-two when most drivers give at least fleeting thought to retirement, Johnson had no such intentions. His on-track steadiness had served him well in every Indianapolis race since 1952, and he would continue his knack for avoiding trouble on the Speedway until the 1966 competition, his last. All drivers have accidents. Johnson flipped a midget over a hub rail at the Akron, Ohio, track. Had fellow drivers not pulled him from his burning car, he probably would have died then and there. Instead, Johnson did considerable hospital time while being treated for third-degree burns on his hands, arms, and lower face, while most of the rest of his body suffered second degree burns. But in 1961 he was not only the oldest man in the race, but also shorter (five-feet five-inches) and lighter (at 155 pounds) than the good doctor's driver profile. Johnson qualified the Jim Robbins Kuzma chassis (known as "Johnson's Jet") for the 1961 event with a four-lap run of 145.843 miles per hour. While no handicapper would have put money on Johnson's nose as a potential winner, he seemed a candidate for a top-ten finish.

Circumstances turned out otherwise, however, and Johnson registered his first and only Indianapolis crashout when, at 2:20, starter Bill Vanderwater frantically waved the yellow bunting while caution lights turned yellow at stations around the course. The trouble was in the northwest where, at 127 laps, Johnson had brushed wheels with Arizona's Wayne Weiler, then began a protracted slide toward the inner edge of the track where he met with the inner retaining wall. Parked on the middle of the track, Johnson waited momentarily while cars swerved to miss his disabled racer, then hopped out of the car and over the wall to safer territory. By 2:25 a red rescue vehicle was at the scene, being motioned backward by a United States Auto Club functionary stationed in turn four. But as the truck moved in reverse, a man fell from the back of it. The driver continued in reverse, over the man's body, and then about five feet past him. The victim was John Masariu from nearby Danville, Indiana. Ironically, the entire incident went mostly unnoticed in this, the Golden Anniversary running of the 500-mile race. The winner was A. J. Foyt, a second generation Houston driver half Johnson's age, who connected with Victory Lane after four Speedway attempts. Johnson (1919–1974) and his car owner Jim Robbins died in separate airplane crashes.

Although the eyes of Texas were upon Foyt in the oily 1963 race that went to Parnelli Jones, they were also on the rest of the sizable Texas contingent that included Jim McElreath, Ebb Rose, Johnny Rutherford, and Lloyd Ruby. With consistently wretched luck that worked at cross purposes with his immense talent, Ruby remained a sentimental favorite at Indianapolis for the remainder of his long career in the saddle of potentially winning machinery. Having finished in the first ten in each of his first three tries, he retired from action in the Zink Trackburner at the 1963 race in the northwest bend at 126 laps when he spun and caught the wall with his left rear wheel about twenty-five feet north of Grandstand H. The car then slid along the track and stopped on the infield lawn. In eighteen consecutive Indianapolis starts between 1960 and 1977 his third place in 1964 was as close as he would come.

Like Ruby, unbridled Jim Hurtubise, a Depression-era kid from North Tonawanda, New York, always attracted great spectator enthusiasm in spite of poor results at Indianapolis. It was on the fifteenth day of May in 1965 that Hurtubise was rounding the northwest turn during a practice run in a fluorescent red Kurtis four-wheel drive car ominously christened the Tombstone Life Special (after an Arizona insurance company) when supposedly the throttle stuck. The result was a totally demolished car missing both right wheels, the outcome of a wallbanger that followed a 380-foot slide through the Speedway's fourth corner. Hurtubise himself was preserved from disaster both by divine providence and by Firestone's newly developed fuel cell that prevented his right side fuel tanks from rupturing. The specter of fire was a particular threat for the thirty-two-year-old hell-on-wheels who had spent the better part of the previous year bedridden in the United States Army's burn center in San Antonio, recovering from devastating burns suffered during a 100-mile championship car race in Milwaukee. Undaunted by his pre-race spill in 1965, Hurtubise climbed resiliently into a latter-day Novi but went out of the contest in one lap with what were reported to be transmission problems. Jim Hurtubise died on January 6, 1989, from heart failure while living in Port Arthur, Texas. His age (fifty-six) was his racing signature, his having driven cars for years carrying that number. Hurtubise reposes today at a mausoleum in Indianapolis's Crown Hill Cemetery.

Riding in third position in the 1966 race in a Lotus Ford that appeared at a distance quite like Hurtubise's Tombstone Life Special, eventual four-time winner Al Unser of Albuquerque, New Mexico, parted with a wheel on lap 161, struck a car driven by Joe Leonard, and lost traction in the northwest, coming to a stop against the wall where he unfastened himself and departed the bright red car unhurt. When the race ended, the first two finishers were stylish imports: British rookie Graham Hill was first, and Scotland's Jim Clark second by half a mile an hour to Hill's winning average of 144.317 miles an hour. In retrospect, the race might just as well have gone to Clark, an imbiber of Scotch and grape juice, had he not spun on two occasions in the northwest while leading the event. On his sixty-fourth circuit he momentarily lost control of his STP Gas Treatment car, another screaming red creation, and narrowly missed the inside wall. Somewhat the same thing happened on his eighty-seventh lap when he spun around three times as he entered turn four.

Columbia, South Carolina's Lonnie LeeRoy Yarbrough (1938–1984), who died in a mental hospital, identified himself mostly with NASCAR where he competed between 1960 and 1972. Comparatively unaccustomed to open wheel racing cars, he came to Indianapolis three times without a great deal of beginner's luck. Having originally been entered at Indianapolis by tire dealer Gene White, Yarbrough finally qualified for the race in 1967 in a Ford V-8 Rolla Vollstedt chassis entered instead by Michigan's Jim Robbins. When the race got underway Yarbrough made it around the course once, then spun in the northwest on his second lap. He was able to crank the car over and restart, only to have the race stopped entirely at eighteen laps because of driving rains. When the procession got back underway the following day, Mario Andretti dropped a wheel in the northwest. To avoid running into him, Yarbrough spun again followed by Lloyd Ruby (replacing George Snider) in a Vel's Racing Team Mongoose. Both Yarbrough and Ruby slipped off the track sideways and each hit the dirt banking that Cal Niday had run into at the north end of the course. All drivers bailed out unhurt while their cars remained parked in the lawn for the remainder of the day, which went to Foyt, making him the fourth three-time winner in Speedway history.

It was the leader's 124th lap in the 1968 race when rookie Bill Vukovich, son of the 1953–1954 Indianapolis champion, collided with Mel Kenyon. Vukovich spun in the northwest and came to a halt at the head of the main straight, backwards. Kenyon continued on as if nothing had happened, just as John Rutherford arrive on the scene and hit his brakes, only to be shoved from behind by fellow Texan Jim McElreath. Although Rutherford spun around, both he and McElreath (nursing a badly crunched nose cone) regained momentum enough to limp back to the pits for some heavy repairs. Smallish (145 pounds) Oklahoma born Mike Mosley who during his career won three Indianapolis car races after starting last, whirled low on the turn four apron, regained control, and followed the others pitward. The only visible evidence of foul play at this point was a considerable quantity of dirt and other detritus on the track. Vukovich, who for reasons of personal security hastened over the outside wall, had a change of heart, returned to assess damage to his Shrike into which he rebuckled himself, and accepted a shove back to his pits where he took on fresh rubber and charged back into the fray, finishing seventh, a lap ahead of Mosley.

Late in the steamy afternoon of May 21, 1969, it appeared that for all the world, Mario Andretti's prospects for winning the Indianapolis 500 were on the slim side. While clicking off laps at 172 miles an hour that would have handily captured the pole position that year, it chanced that a right rear hub failed as Andretti screamed his fluorescent red four-wheel drive Lotus Ford through the northwest bend, crushing the wall with considerable might at the exit of the turn and transforming a sleek, high technology racing car into what Andretti's accomplished chief mechanic Clint Brawner chose to call a "twisted wad of expensive junk." Considering the seriousness of this celebrated wall-slam, Andretti could count himself fortunate for having received only facial burns and multiple body bruises. "As long as I can get out of something like this," Andretti told Brawner, "I have to feel lucky as hell."

Following the accident Brawner uncrated Andretti's back-up car, a Brawner Hawk that Andretti was openly unenthusiastic about driving. Qualifying at 169.851, Andretti started his fifth 500-mile race at Indianapolis in the middle of the front row and came home the winner. For Brawner, who first saw the Speedway in 1938 and had been plying his trade there for nineteen Mays, it was his only win there. Having prepared cars for Jimmy Bryan, Bobby Ball, Troy Ruttman, Eddie Sachs, Bill Vukovich, and Bob Sweikert, Brawner worked with the best oval track drivers in the game, and over the years won fifty-one Indy car races. Threatened by skin cancer for much of his life, he died two days before Christmas in 1987 and is buried in Phoenix's Greenwood Memory Lawn cemetery, a short stroll from the graves of Bryan and Ball. Andretti's Indianapolis win was also a first for the car's sponsor, controversial and rotund Andy Granatelli who had once made an abortive bid for himself as an Indianapolis driver. "The instant Mario cleared the checkered," Brawner said, "Granatelli had taken off on a dead run, whooping at the top of his lungs toward the winner's circle." Brawner, who first feared that Andretti had died during his horrendous pre-race crash in turn four, had put in an ironic, enervating month at the track. For Andretti, it was not his last run-in with the northwest wall. The following May 11, when on another high-speed chase the suspension folded on his 1970 McNamara, almost destroying the seemingly charmed Andretti who retired from racing in one piece in 1994. Returning for a test run in 2003, he nearly killed himself again at the south end of the track when his car took wing for what may have been one of the longest airborne rides in Speedway history, and landed on its wheels, shiny side up.

Nor was the northeast good for Mike Mosley, who had technical difficulties there in 1968 and was plagued again in 1971 and 1972. At 159 laps in the 1971 chase, Mosley's three-year-old made-over Gurney Eagle powered by a turbocharged Ford engine parted ways with a right front wheel, without which the car did not behave quite as well, spinning into two parked racing cars that had been driven by Steve Krisiloff and Mark Donohue. Bobby Unser, at the stick of Dan Gurney's Olsonite Eagle, swerved to stay out of Mosley's wake, and rammed the wall in a blast of flame. The emerald grass stains on Mosley's helmet, meanwhile, were indisputable evidence of his having flipped over in the melee. Medical authorities judged Mosley to be in serious condition with a broken arm and a broken leg. After Vukovich looped his car and then continued through the turn, Gary Bettenhausen voluntarily stopped his blue, wedge-shaped Thermo King Special to pay his respects to the injured Mosley, then continued on to place tenth, his best run in four starts. Although he recuperated in time for the 1972 race, Mosley's fortunes were no better. Leading at fifty-six laps, his turbocharged Offenhauser parted with another wheel and caught the wall toward the end of turn four. By the time he extricated himself and rolled on the track to extinguish the flames on his driving suit, his Vivitar Special had parted with another wheel. Condemned once again to pass a dismal summer recovering from burns, Mosley's 1973 reappearance netted him a tenth place. Mosley, a high school dropout from Fallbrook, California, an hour's drive south of Los Angeles, was in some ways a strange, complex man who, though he won five Indy car races, seemed fundamentally unenthusiastic about auto racing. In the opinion of some who knew him, Mosley actually feared competition, although no one who saw him in action could be convinced of this. "Mike didn't have racing in his blood," his widow Alice May told writer Joe Scalzo, "and he wasn't racing for the money. He never thought about becoming rich. He wasn't in it for the glory, either. But he'd been an Indianapolis driver, and he was too proud to go pump gasoline for six dollars an hour. It was race or starve, so he raced." Mosley said as much in 1968 when he told a USAC interviewer that "when I was living in Indianapolis there were several times when I was nearly broke; and every time I was nearly out of money I'd go out and run a good race to make some money." Corroborating that Mosley comment, one of his Indy mechanics (later USAC CEO) John Capels commented that Mosley "didn't want to race any more than was necessary." His crew members at Indianapolis recall that after a day at the track, he would stuff his sweaty driving suit in a bag, and evaporate. Emotionally withdrawn, Mosley seemed incapable of dealing with two of racing's enervating realities: the press and the public.

On March 3, 1984, Mosley took his son Michael Dean out for a day of off-road roughhousing with a three-wheel all terrain vehicle and a motorcycle in the desert at the state park in Borrego. On the return trip in their 1975 four-wheel-drive Chevy van with trailer, Mosley missed a turn on Highway 79 near Aguango about twenty miles east of Fallbrook and, partly because there was no guardrailing, plunged (as others before him had) into a steep fifty-yard ravine where the impact sheared the fiberglass top off the vehicle and threw both occupants out. Mike Mosley, thirty-eight, died when the van toppled on him. A nearby resident rescued Michael Dean just as the van exploded. On March 7, on board a sailboat owned by family friend Walt Pekula, Alice prepared to fulfill Mike's request to have his ashes spread in the Pacific near Newport Beach. When she suddenly felt unable, Mike's brother Doyle completed the task. Friends erected a monument in Victorville to Mike Mosley, and raised approximately $30,000 for Michael Dean, most of which disappeared in a market decline. He, in turn, resolved by 1996 to enter the racing business himself, but has since fallen from public view.

The 1973 Indianapolis race proved to be the final one for Peter Revson, a man in most respects dissimilar to Mike Mosley, who in five starts either finished well or did not finish at all. With three laps down, Revson smacked the wall in the northwest without injury to himself. Overeager to remove Revson's Gulf McLaren from the track, the rescue team that suspended the yellow car from a cable on the back of a wrecker managed to drop it. Revson, in the meantime, assembled his gear and departed the Speedway en route to Monte Carlo with notions of breaking the bank at the annual Grand Prix. On March 22 of the following year, he lost his life while testing a car at the Kyalami circuit in South Africa. Born in New York and educated at the Williston Academy followed by two years at Cornell, the dashing bachelor advanced in racing not as Mosley had on the dirt tracks of California, but in various classes of sports cars beginning in Hawaii in 1960. At the Speedway in 1971, he was second only to Al Unser in the final tally.

Tuesday, May 18, 1976, Edward Wayne Crombie, not one of the more familiar figures in North American racing, crashed at about 160 miles an hour in the northwest turn during his driving test in a car of uncertain origins that he entered himself. Crombie slid 450 feet toward the inside wall, connected with his right rear wheel, then whizzed another 225 feet, clobbering the wall again for good measure. The car finally stopped near the pit entrance on the main straightaway. It was a paradigmatic turn four accident, one that would happen many times in the future, and a reminder that generic Indianapolis accidents tend therefore to repeat themselves. Since all tests were to be completed by the following day, Crombie was out of contention as an Indianapolis starter. A thirty-year-old ex-crew member at Indianapolis, Crombie came from Williams Lake, British Columbia, and had been racing only four years in super modified cars in the Pacific Northwest as well as in upstate New York at Oswego, winning as many as eight races in a season.

Fearless Danny Ongais had one of his numerous unpleasant moments at the Speedway on the 16th of May, 1978, while driving his backup Interscope racer. The black No. 25 car became uncontrollable upon exiting the northwest, went every way except straight ahead for 460 feet, tagged the wall with the left rear wheel that disengaged and appeared to ignite a flash fire. Taken to the infield for medical observation, Ongais received treatment for what historian Jack Fox called "a good shaking up, back bruises and a cut tongue." At the time of the accident Ongais was using an engine belonging to the Gene White car to be driven by Lloyd Ruby. The engine, however, went up in smoke. A hard man to discourage, Ongais got back on track by race day, blew another engine and came in eighteenth. For Ruby, it was the end of the line. After eighteen consecutive races, he never competed there again. It should be noted that Ongais let another year pass before coming back to the track with the same racing team and smacking the northwest once again, only with still worse consequences. This time it was on Saturday, May 12, 1979, at 4:43 when he did the same thing he had the year before, except with more gusto and more damage. Having turned the track in the 191 speed range, Ongais slipped into a half spin exiting the northwest, slid down the track for about 550 feet, throttled the inside guard wall, faded into another half spin and slipped another 150 feet, popped the inside wall again, then coasted for another 100 feet or so. When help arrived, Ongais was out cold in the car, with wreckage wrapped around him like a fiberglass tortilla. Having regained consciousness, he had still to wait for twenty-two minutes for rescuers to unwrap the car. Ongais was checked over in the usual manner after commenting about more than routine discomfort in his lower neck, then was packed off to Methodist Hospital for more investigation. Once again, Ongais bounced back, started twenty-seventh and finished fourth, his career best at Indianapolis.

Ongais was not alone in having turn four problems that year. Difficulty befell Todd Gibson seventeen days later. At forty-two, Gibson was no novice at Indianapolis in 1979, having come there as a chief mechanic for the amazing Jan Opperman three years before, when Opperman managed a seventeenth-place finish. Gibson, racing out of Richwood, Ohio, had won more than 450 feature racing events by this time, and even tried Indianapolis cars twenty-one times at venues like Trenton, Milwaukee, and Phoenix, but never raced at Indianapolis. Tom Sneva, at the other extreme, raced at Indianapolis eighteen times, and won the 1983 race. But in 1979 the turn four that bit Todd Gibson during a practice session bit Sneva all the same. It happened toward the closing laps of the race with eleven circuits remaining when his No. 1 Sugaripe Prune Special, Jerry O'Connell's year-old McLaren Cosworth that started second, lost a rear wing while moving through the third turn, scattered shrapnel through the north chute, then clubbed the wall, but hard, in the northwest. Sneva appeared to be momentarily unconscious, then vacated his heavily damaged car with assistance. Back in Gasoline Alley Sneva's wife Sharon awaited him in tears. Known as "The Gas Man," Sneva was the first person officially to turn a 200 mile an hour lap at the Indianapolis Motor Speedway. Besides winning the race, he was a three-time (1977, 1978, and 1980) runner-up, and a three-time (1977, 1978, and 1984) pole winner. Racing was good to Tom Sneva. As to winning Indianapolis, he remarked in 1998, "at the time, it was a big deal, but I didn't know how big a deal it was. It was a big event, but it was something I had been trying to do for a bunch of years. That Indy winner tag behind your name opens a lot of doors for the rest of your life. It gets you into places where you can talk to people and do things you wouldn't otherwise be able to do. It's more important to me now than when I was still active."

Gordon Smiley, who was killed in a turn three accident in 1982, at least twice had his problems with the northwest the previous year on the fourth day of the race month when he blew a right rear tire and spun without colliding with anything, and then again on lap 142 of the race itself, when, attempting to pass Tony Bettenhausen (the younger) in turn four, the two touched wheels, sending Smiley into the cement backwards, after which he blamed the problem on Bettenhausen during a radio interview. On the following day Tony's contentious brother Gary confronted Smiley, the two nearly came to blows over the incident. With racing experience largely confined to sedans, Formula Fords, and Super Vees, automotive journalist Patrick Bedard, no doubt wanting to discover for himself "what it's like out there" (as the cliche went), arranged to drive at Indianapolis in 1983 in a new March Cosworth as teammate to Scott Brayton, and managed to start seventeenth and drive forty-two laps before something unnerving beset him while exiting turn four when he scraped the outer wall, then contacted it a second time, finally coming to a stop with the nose of his Escort Radar Warning car pointed to the wall with minimal damage. Turn four fended off several other cars that year, among them the likes of intrepid Bob Harkey who, after a six-year layoff, had a mind to return to competition in a 1981 Coyote with Cosworth power. He was surging through the northwest on May 12 when his left front wheel tagged the right rear wheel of Mike Mosley's new March Cosworth. Mosley felt some sort of impact on his right rear corner, but continued moving. Not so Harkey, who slid into the wall with the right side of his machine, and stayed there for another thousand feet, emerging from the altercation with a broken hand and wrist, multiple broken ribs, a broken neck (in two places), a broken collarbone, and a bruised lung. Harkey, a former aircraft stunt pilot and midget racing champion, had closed out his driving days. So too, five days later, future NASCAR staple Ken (Kenneth William) Schrader who had been racing whatever car he could find since 1971, approached turn four excessively low (in the view of at least one observer), broke into a spin, slipped and slid 300 feet, and creamed the wall on the car's right side. Schrader visited the infield hospital where physicians released him after examination, although his blackened eyes clearly showed that he had sustained a considerable impact. His car was a 1982 March Cosworth entered by Usona Purcell and cheerfully called the Friendship Special, although after the wall contact owner and driver became unfriendly and parted ways. At the time, at least, Schrader, a St. Louis native who had gone to high school in Ballwin, Missouri, seemed to be a good Indianapolis prospect that never came to fruition. In 1982 he won the hard fought USAC dirt car title, and in 1983 he was the group's sprint car point man. Schrader's revenge was to take his talents to NASCAR where he has since made an everlasting home for himself.

Patrick Bedard, still finding out about Indianapolis, had somewhat the same fate befall him in 1984 as he had in 1983, only far worse, albeit he lasted twenty more laps to find out this time. Having run far below the pace set by the race leaders, Bedard's March C-29 Buick V-6 suddenly took to the infield in the north chute, careened into a earthen mound and disintegrated, its engine hurling in one direction, and a veritable shower of broken race car pieces distributing over lawn and track. Bedard might well have been killed, but instead came through it all with a concussion and broken jaw. Because of debris and confusion at the accident site, Danny Sullivan, who won the following year's race, punched into the back of Roberto Guerrero and managed to put himself out of competition for the day. Then, exiting the northwest in 1984 on lap 104 was two-time winner Gordon Johncock, who tagged the wall on the exit of turn four and went full tilt onto the pit lane where he ran into something unmovable and rebounded toward the outer grass strip and retaining wall of the lane, nearly running down at least one pit man. People on duty there scattered like fleas. The incident caused Johncock to be pinned in the car with a broken ankle. Back on May 12, Dublin-born Derek Daly in the No. 61 Provimi Veal car looped once exiting that same bend, floated about 360 feet toward the outside wall without connecting with it, then changed direction as it coursed about 400 feet toward the inner barrier just north of the pit entrance. Neither driver nor machine were appreciably damaged. An hour and a half later Stan Fox lost Ralph Wilke's Pabst entry at the exit of four, whirled around two and a half times covering about 620 feet, darted across the track, and rammed the rear of the car before it quit moving at the entrance to the pit lane. Then about four hours later Steve Chassey felt the bottom drop out of his Genesee Beer Wagon car in the northwest, hung on while it traveled 300 feet and pasted the wall with the car's rear end, substantially damaging it and giving Chassey a shin injury to boot. More of the same happened late the next day, May 13, when John Paul, Jr., hustling the No. 12 VDS car, skidded out of control for 300 feet, smacked the wall, then kept moving for another 580 to do what his colleagues had done by bopping the inside wall near, yes, the pit entrance.

Obviously, such things can happen to anyone. Dutch import Arie Luyendyk, for instance, was moving pretty well until lap 188 of the 1986 classic when, chasing tenth place, he blew a tire coming through the northwest, spun, scrubbed off a certain number of miles per hour, than banged backwards into the inner liner just north of the pit entrance in that, his sophomore year. They come. They go. A second-generation Canadian driver named Ludwig Heimrath, Jr., then living in Spanaway, Washington, came to town in 1987, 1988, and 1989, made the race on all three occasions, and then vanished. In his second showing he was doing decently well until lap twenty-eight when in the north chute he happened to notice that one of his wheels was missing. That significant problem developed as a result of his having stopped the previous lap for three tires and a little fuel. The consequence of all this was a spin with no "contact" a euphemistic code word that race management uses when someone runs into something adamant. Raul Boesel, a long-time Indy car competitor who never won an Indy car race, had the same sort of trouble there in 1988, except that he crunched into walls three times on the fourteenth of the month, damaging all zones of Doug Shierson's new March Cosworth. Then first-year man Scott Charles Atchison, a 140-pound Bakersfield, California, bicyclist and motorcyclist who in those frothy days logged 200 miles a

Canadian Jacques Villeneuve, younger brother of Formula 1 great Gilles Villeneuve, tasted the wall in the northwest turn in 1984, suffering head injures and destroying his car. Gilles's son, also named Jacques, won the 500 in 1995 and became Formula 1 world champion in 1997. *John Mahoney*

week on two wheels, clobbered the northwest on the nineteenth of the month with a 1986 March Cosworth sponsored by the International Association of Machinists and Aerospace Workers. There were no reported injuries, although Atchison never eventually competed in an Indianapolis 500. On May 21 Pancho Carter's 1986 March Buick lost pressure in one tire and brushed the turn four whitewash while in sight of the checkered flag signaling the completion of a qualification attempt, after which he connected with the inside wall and finally came to rest on the main straight in front of the scoring pylon. On lap thirty-two of the 1988 race Tom Sneva, a man never too shy to bite a wall, nor too shy to be bitten back, struck and was struck, once more. Unsteady through turn four, he drilled the wall and then did the formula thing: rebounded from the outside, smashed the inside, and trickled on down to the opening of the pit lane, scaring the daylights out of fleeing pit workers. One remembers carefree

Kevin Cogan as the imperturbable guy who seemingly materialized out of nowhere to capture a surprising fourth place in 1981, and then came within a quarter of a lap of winning the 500-miler in 1986 but accepted second place after some serious dicing for position at the north end of the track.

It was a spectacular, Hollywood-style conclusion to the day. Behind winner Bobby Rahal and Cogan came high flyers Rick Mears, Roberto Guerrero, Al Unser, Jr., Michael Andretti, Emerson Fittipaldi, Johnny Rutherford, and Danny Sullivan. It was Cogan's greatest day. His nadir, however, had arrived in 1982 when he started second (middle of the first row, if there was a first row) when, a hundred or so yards before the starting line Cogan's Penske-owned Norton Spirit cut right and speared A. J. Foyt, swung left and rammed the inside straightaway wall, and was in turn speared by no less of an Indianapolis presence than Mario Andretti. While that was transpiring, far back in the pack rookie Dale Whittington unaccountably veered to the inside and nailed Roger Mears. The result was that Cogan, Andretti, Mears, and Whittington did not manage to reach the southwest turn before being eliminated for the day. It was a disgrace. Asked by reporter Jan Shaffer whether the 1982 Speedway incident tarnished his reputation, Cogan replied, "There's no question about it. I think [Roger] Penske found it impossible to re-sign me. For Roger, it's a business decision. They introduce Kevin Cogan, and 70,000 boo. I'm sure Miller or Penzoil wouldn't like it."

In 1989, however, Kevin Cogan looped in turn four on only the third lap, banged the inside wall, and then bolted as others had, to the opening of the pit area. It was no laughing matter, since Cogan's new March Cosworth, also underwritten by the Machinists' union, was so completely obliterated that it might well have been carrying an onboard bomb that detonated. Not only was Cogan not dead, but after rescuers removed the engine from his lap, he struggled out and marched (if one will forgive the pun) away as one might leave a boxing ring. The cleanup process required nearly thirty minutes of track crew time. After a dozen Indianapolis races, Cogan rather disappeared from racing circles, leaving a vocation that he had begun at the age of eleven when he raced dune buggies against family retainer Parnelli Jones.

A USAC short track champion, the precocious Steve Butler, also nearly wiped himself out at the northwest turn in 1989 on the tenth of the race month when his Stoops Racing Team Lola spun once, traveled 380 feet before darting into the white cement, then rebounded for another 520 feet or so to the inside barrier, and halted, like so many others had, at the maw of the pit lane. Another would-be starter was Steve Saleen, who on May 20 did close to the same thing, exactly on script: lost handling entering turn four, made one complete spin, slammed the outer wall nearly head on, slid along it for a distance, and came to a stasis almost where Butler had. Saleen accepted a ride to Methodist where medical authorities elected to take him prisoner. Born in Inglewood, California, in 1949, Saleen had been graduated from Whittier High School and studied at the University of Southern California. Back home, aside from his racing Super Vees and Formula Atlantics, he was best known as the designer and manufacturer of the Saleen Mustang, a customized version of Ford's famous muscle car.

Unheralded Jeff Andretti, the younger of Mario's two sons, came to the Speedway in 1990 and had his difficulties, particularly in the northwest. Having raced karts, Pro Fords, Formula Fords, Super Vees, American Racing Series, and Formula Atlantics, he was nevertheless bumped out of the 1990 Indianapolis 500 and listed as second alternate, although for many decades alternates never competed at Indianapolis. He too added his name to that honor role of men who shot the wall, losing touch with his car that hit on its left side, spinning crazily across the track, and making an unanticipated visit to the pit entrance. Andretti staged an encore nine days later when he lost it again in turn four, executed another full spin that lasted for 600 feet, then gathered the car up and steered it back to the pits after having hit nothing at all. On May 18 came Bernard Georges "Bernie" Jourdain, the Mexico City businessman and former employee at Volkswagen of Mexico, who reexecuted that same wall-smacking rite that separates Indianapolis drivers from the rest of the human race. Jourdain won rookie of the year honors at the Speedway in 1989 when, after having had the slowest qualification speed ranking in the field, he advanced to a ninth-place finish.

The ritual did not, of course, cease merely because it was May and 1991. Quite the contrary. In one of the northwest's all-time worst episodes, Frank Arciero's 1988 Penske Buick V-6 with earnest Mark Austin Dismore (initials MAD) from Greenfield, Indiana, on board emerged high out of turn four, slid 380 feet into the cement, cut 900 feet across the track to the pit entrance, then 220 feet to the outside pit wall where the three-year-old car broke into two pieces, littering the track with debris. Dismore remained all the while in the tub of the demolished car, with fractures in his neck, right knee, and right wrist, along with numerous other foot injuries. Surgeons at Methodist hovered over him for six hours in an operating room, and declared him in stable condition afterward. Not many men over the seasons burned with such desire to race at Indianapolis as did Dismore, born October 12, 1956. His father Emerson originated a company known as Comet Kart Sales three years later in Greenfield, about twenty miles east of the Speedway, and in time son Mark became its manager, expanding the facility to 20,000 square feet and the business into the world's largest go-kart business. Dismore himself began his racing activities with karts in 1968, and by 1983 worked his way into Super Vee competition, then USAC midget cars in 1987, followed sequentially by Corvettes, Toyota Formula Atlantics, then to CART championship Indianapolis car competition. Unbowed by his 1991 Indianapolis crash, Dismore hobbled back to Gasoline Alley in 1992 looking for another car to drive. He found two, neither sufficiently fast to make the cut. In conversation with a *Speednet* reporter about his 1991 problems, Dismore said, "I have some frame-by-frame pictures, and it turns out that I bent the lower wishbone after brushing the [north] short-chute wall," adding that "I remember thinking I should slow down and come into the pits, when it [the race car] took off." He did not qualify for his first Indianapolis 500 until 1996, which was also the first race for the newly formed Indy Racing League, and has been a regular at the Speedway until he ran the 2002 race. Although Dismore won the second of two Indy car races at Texas in 1999, possibly his greatest day in the sport was winning the Rolex 24 Hours of Daytona in 1993 in a Dan Gurney-prepared Toyota GTP car with driving partners P. J. Jones and Rocky Moran.

There was no question that Dismore's wall shunt constituted most of the horror at Indianapolis in 1991, albeit more corner excitement followed as it inexorably would. Randy Lewis, for instance, brushed the wall in the northwest while he was contemplating the green flag for a qualification run on May 11. He proceeded down the track and into the first turn before cracking the outer barrier and stopping in the south chute, leaving a totally destroyed racing machine in the middle of what appeared to be a short-lived firestorm of destruction. A day later Dominic Dobson, the Stuttgart-born former driving instructor at the Bondurant competition school broke his left thigh after a quarrel with the northwest wall into which he careened and sallied all the way down into the north pit area. No sooner had he been extricated than he began discussing the prospects of driving with a broken leg, regardless. That had been done before, as in the case of Steve Krisiloff in 1975. Indeed, some drivers, including the first of two Al

Millers, Bill Schindler, and Cal Niday have competed in the race with a leg missing. Dobson's car was far worse than his body, however, and Dobson indeed found a carbon fiber leg brace and a backup car with which he ran the race.

After Dobson's crackup came a similar one at the hands of one Dean Hall, a rather unlikely contestant at Indianapolis, who apparently drove into the northwest on the low side and socked the wall with the left front of Kent Baker's 1989 Lola Buick, destroying it. Baker afterward good-naturedly referred to his race car as "a piece of toast," which it assuredly was. Hall, who began his racing career in 1986, was perhaps better recognized as an expert skier and free spirit who clocked-in at 120 miles an hour on the slopes of Silverton, Colorado. At least one of his fellow drivers referred to him as "that skier." Hall claimed to have won 46 percent of the automobile races he entered in Formula Fords and Formula Atlantics. His only run at Indianapolis came in 1990 when he scored seventeenth. The other somewhat unlikely prospect to clap the wall in 1991 was Los Angeles bachelor and Indy car beginner Ted Prappas (Theodore Panos Prappas) who on the eleventh of the month clapped it once, slipped another 720 feet, and clapped it again. Prappas carried the Greek, British, and American flags on his helmet, acknowledging that he was an American, his father was Greek, and his mother British. She, incidentally, was at the time the business agent for actor Jimmy Stewart and singer Mel Torme. Prappas, curiously enough, claimed that he had never won an auto race in a car painted other than in black.

The star newcomer in 1992 was thirty-nine-year-old Nelson Piquet Souto Maior, known simply as "Nelson Piquet," the fourth child born to Dr. Estacio Souto Maior, a physician who became Brazil's Minister of Health. Piquet was himself a busy bee in those days, what with his Pirelli, Suzuki, and Mercedes-Benz dealerships; his PROCOM sports promotion company that organized golf and motocross events in America, Europe, and Japan; and his Piquet Racing organization that promoted International Formula 3000 events. At the time of his arrival at Indianapolis, Piquet had twenty-three wins and twenty-four pole positions in Formula 1, with 204 career F-1 starts under his belt, then second only to Riccardo Patrese's 224. Piquet captured Formula 1 championships in 1981, 1983, and 1987. But all did not go well for the Brazilian bachelor who, at the controls of John Menard's No. 27 Conseco 1992 Buick V-6 on Thursday, May 7, did exactly what others had done, and did it in the same way: exiting the northwest turn, he lapsed into one complete spin that carried him 400 feet, head on, into the outer limits, whereupon he slid another sixty feet along said wall and fell into a one-and-a-quarter spin, ripping down the track 760 more feet before rolling to a stop in the middle of the front straightaway. The racing car sustained considerable front end damage. As for Piquet, he was whisked off to Methodist with a concussion as well as multiple fractures of both lower legs and feet. True, that had happened a few times before, but not with such catastrophic consequences. That same afternoon he underwent orthopedic surgery.

This was no ordinary incident, but rather a celebrity wall smack, comparable to hearing that Fred Astaire clumsily slipped on a banana peel and tumbled down a flight of steps. USAC technical director Mike Devin said that although Piquet had driven over "a small piece of aluminum" on the backstretch, having done so did not "seem to have any bearing on the accident." It came to light that at the time the wreck occurred the track was under yellow (caution) condition for possibly ten seconds, and that a spokesman at the Goodyear tire company said that Piquet's tires were "flat spotted inflated," meaning that they had lost no air. Piquet's chief mechanic Darrell Soppe concurred with Devin, adding that "the yellow was out for a long time before he hit the wall," saying too that "It's a real shame. He's a neat guy and a real professional." On the following day there was a briefing with Speedway medical director Henry Bock, and noted Indiana orthopedic surgeon Terry Trammell, during which the press heard that Piquet had undergone six and a half hours of surgery concluding at 12:30 A.M. at the hands of physicians Trammell, Tom Southern, and Dean Maar who together listed Piquet in fair condition after his suffering a badly broken left foot and ankle, a broken and dislocated right ankle, a lacerated right knee, and injuries of a lesser nature to his left elbow and wrist. "There were devastating injuries to his left foot and ankle," Dr. Trammell added. "We were able to reconstruct the left foot and ankle, and we used a device called a Ilizarov to help hold the forefoot to hindfoot of the leg," adding that "circulation to his feet is excellent." Piquet was to roll back into surgery on Sunday (two days later) for what Dr. Trammell described as "housecleaning, to make sure there is no debris in the wounds and muscle." Asked whether amputation had been under consideration, Trammell replied in the affirmative, concluding that his surgical patch-up would take him the better part of a year from which to recover. "To what degree he recovers, it's too early to say," continued Trammell. After Sunday's surgery, there were yet several more hours of operating time on Wednesday. Piquet, still an Indianapolis rookie like any other

Speedway first-timer, returned in 1993, where he spun out again early in the month, started in the thirteenth position, and fell out of the running after thirty-eight laps, finishing thirty-second.

Tom Sneva and Woburn, Maine's rookie Brian Bonner both spun in the Piquet place during the 1992 race without much damage or fanfare. The battered wall along the fourth turn at Indianapolis remained unassaulted for nearly a year until, on the fourteenth of May in 1993, along came Didier Theys all the way from Nivelles, Belgium, to give it a hearty pop in a purple 1991 Lola Buick V-6 owned by health spa entrepreneur Ron Hemelgarn. There was nothing especially unique about the miscue, Theys's having spun one time into the inner wall, off which he rebounded and parked in the midst of the front straightaway. He acquired a bruised left thigh that medical personnel insisted upon evaluating for a succession of days. Other than that, Theys was free to hit the track (but not the walls) again, which he did for 193 laps, finishing twenty-second in the race.

Canadian hockey enthusiast Donald Scott Goodyear, who had started the 1992 race in last position and came within .043 miles an hour of overtaking winner Al Unser, Jr., and who actually finished first in the 1995 race until he was penalized for passing the pace car (about as inadvisable as playing bumper tag with a police cruiser), was the first man on his cell block in Gasoline Alley to rap the northwest in 1994. And what a produc-

Brazil's Nelson Piquet on the move in a Lola Buick during a 1993 Indianapolis practice run. The previous year he had all but destroyed his lower extremities and suffered a concussion in a crash. *Ken Coles*

Three time Formula 1 world champion Nelson Piquet's Indianapolis career lasted for a total of thirty-eight laps in the 1993 race. He is pictured here on the right in conversation with Ireland's Derek Daly, a six-time Indianapolis competitor. *Ken Coles*

tion number it was, looping out of control on the fifteenth of May, slipping and sliding an amazing 1,200 feet in his backup Budweiser King Special, socking the inside wall with the left side of his machine, then flying out of control for 245 more feet and running smack into the fifteen-foot long and seven-foot wide attenuator (think of a huge shock absorber capable of softening an immense frontal impact) with the right side of his car at the point dividing the track from the pit road, then tearing into the pit area with another half spin and into the outside pit wall where he eventually stopped. All that happened in a few seconds at about 4:20 in the afternoon. After having been scrutinized at Methodist for back pain and some problem with his left thigh, Goodyear received his walking papers at seven that evening, and headed back to the track.

Among the rookie class of 1995 was Davey Hamilton of Boise, Idaho, son of Ken Hamilton who came to Indianapolis back in 1981, and logged three of four qualification laps before being waved off the course. Davey Hamilton, who later worked at his father's painting company, began racing by running six-cylinder cars at Boise in 1979 and winning a bunch of races, particularly in the west and southwest, and at the annual desert clan-gathering Copper World Classic every spring in Phoenix. At the Speedway in 1995 Hamilton strapped into the purple No. 95 Delta Faucet car, a 1994 Reynard Ford-Cosworth XB that on the tenth of the month rode him smack into the whitewash in turn four and took him a few seconds later near, but not into, the attenuator at the pit opening. All this occasioned hospital time, however, for treatment of a concussion, severe contusions on his left knee, and serious bruises to both knees, followed by surgery to repair a broken right ankle. Davey Hamilton did not race at Indianapolis that year, but he did for the following six, until he sustained even worse foot and ankle injuries at the Texas Motor Speedway (after a record forty-eight consecutive Indy Racing League starts) in June 2001 that have kept him out of racing since.

Hamilton's Indy crash preceded a similar one that befell Mexico City's Formula 2 and 3 champion Carlos Guerrero (Gonzalez) nine days later when his Viva Mexico Lola Ford Cosworth went through the usual turn four pattern of executing one full spin, cracking the outside cement with the right rear, then darting across the track to pop the inside limits before stopping against the inside pit wall. At the time of the mishap Guerrero had only one championship car race behind him. Small wonder that crews are wary of pitting their cars on the north end. Johnny Unser, son of the late Jerry Unser who was killed by a 1959 Speedway accident, gave them a fright in 1996 when he did a half spin up in turn four, hit the outer wall a ton, then connected with the inner, completing his run inside the pit entrance.

In 1996, the first of the Indy Racing League–sanctioned races, there came a turn four initiated accident more wicked than Nelson Piquet's in 1992. Just as Buddy Lazier crossed the finish tape the winner of the eightieth running of the Indianapolis 500, there was a three-car northwest turn accident in progress, involving good-hearted but accident prone Roberto Guerrero, who spun his Pagan Racing No. 21 1995 Reynard Ford Cosworth and collected car No. 8, the Team Scandia 1994 Lola Ford Cosworth driven by twenty-six-year-old Italian sophomore starter Alessandro Zampedri of Monte Carlo. Zampedri had started the race in seventeenth position and had winning on his mind all race long, never having dropped past eighth position at any ten lap interval, and having assumed the lead at both lap 170 and 180 in the 200 lap race. He dropped to second place on lap 190 with ten circuits remaining and was hot on the trail of Buddy Lazier when on the final turn he tangled with Guerrero and his own teammate, Eliseo Salazar in the No. 7 Team Scandia car.

In other words, the race ended in triumph and destruction as is not even slightly unusual at Indianapolis. Roberto Guerrero underwent examination and was released from the infield medical station. Eliseo Salazar visited Methodist for scrutiny and X rays of his right leg. A copter hustled Alessandro Zampedri off to Methodist to address some open lower-leg fractures, multiple compound fractures of both feet, and dislocations of both ankles. Orthopedic surgeon Kevin Scheid reported later that Zampedri's left foot had been all but amputated. A team of physicians led by Dr. Scheid operated until midnight. Early in June, Zampedri underwent surgery five times at the hands of plastic and reconstructive surgeon William Sando. A hospital spokeswoman told the *Indianapolis Star* that Dr. Sando referred to the procedure as a "free flap transfer," meaning that he had removed some flat muscle tissue from Zampedri's back and transferred it to his left foot. It was a task that presumed through microsurgery to reconnect vessels to the newly introduced muscle tissue. Dr. Scheid also commented that Zampedri's injuries "were similar to those suffered by Nelson Piquet" except that "this case was more challenging." Dr. Sando commented that the microsurgery was such that "we had to sew arteries and veins with a diameter about the size of a pencil lead into place using a thread with a diameter about one quarter the size of a human hair." The following December Zampedri, propped up by aluminum walkers after two more operations, met the press to declare that he would enter the 1997 Indianapolis 500. "Leading Indianapolis was the highest of highs in my entire life," said he, "and I want to feel that again."

When entries came in for the 1997 race, Team Scandia again listed Zampedri as the driver for two (including a backup) of its eight cars. It has been "a very tough year for me," he said. "I had to go through nine surgeries with lots of relapses." He had been in rehabilitation for eight hours a day until December, then cut back to six. On Saturday, May 10, Zampedri turned four qualification laps at 209.094. On Saturday, May 18, he found himself bumped out of the race by faster qualifier Paul Durant. Zampedri then completed a four-lap qualification run of 211.757 while rain droplets fell gently over the track, putting himself back into the race, and bumping woman driver Lyn St. James who in turn was re-added to the program after consternation about a rule interpretation, resulting in there being thirty-five cars in the race instead of the usual thirty-three. It then came to pass that Zampedri need not have made the second run, since all but one qualifier would start the race anyhow. "The last two weeks," he said, "have been the longest in my life, not the last year."

While Zampedri's recovery and return to the 500-mile race was as remarkable as Nelson Piquet's, both drivers enjoyed only Pyrrhic victories. Piquet finished next to last in 1994; Zampedri finished dead last in 1997 after his car developed an oil leak in a race that took three days to run after a series of rain delays. The northwest turn, in the meantime, had bitten others that month, beginning with Scott Sharp who careened into it on May 7 in one of A. J. Foyt's entries, and didn't stop until he had crossed the start/finish line. Sharp appeared to be in a dazed condition when medical help arrived and proceeded to load him into an ambulance. Sharp's wife then arrived on the accident scene, after which some words passed, whereupon Foyt picked the woman up bodily and carried her off the track. Meanwhile, Sharp's injuries seemed to be limited to a bruised right knee. "I can't worry about future crashes," said the always upbeat Sharp. "My job is to stand on the button." Two more days passed before John Paul, Jr. became the northwest's next victim, but he did not fare nearly as well as his colleague Sharp had, inasmuch as he, complaining about pain in both legs, received news at Methodist that he indeed had multiple fractures in his lower right leg and heel. When the hospital released him after two days

Italian ace Alessandro Zampedri, pictured here as a rookie in 1995, had three shots at the Indianapolis 500. On his final lap in 1996 he tangled with another car, resulting in the near loss of his left foot. Having convalesced for nearly a year, he returned in 1997 but retired before completing the first lap. *Ken Coles*

Paul had casts on both legs, with the prospect of six to eight weeks of wheelchair time. Later that summer Jerry Garrett of *Car and Driver* magazine visited Paul in his West Palm Beach home, and found him in another wheelchair, gazing forlornly out a window. Garrett recalled that following the accident Paul had awakened hours later in a hospital "with a shattered left foot, a splintered right leg, a gashed chin, and a huge black eye." Asked what occupied his mind, Paul answered, "the mortgage."

Of course the 1997 race went on without him. On lap twenty-three wall smackers Steve Kinser, Eliseo Salazar, Mark Dismore, and Roberto Guerrero piled up in the northwest under yellow flag conditions when they became aroused over what they thought would be a green flag. At least there were no injuries to report, nor were there in 1998 when sprint car specialists Jack Hewitt and Jimmy Kite tested their fortitude against the walls in the northwest. Hewitt rapped it once, Kite twice. John Paul, Jr., out of his wheelchair and back in the race, led for thirty-nine laps, but finally fell back to eighth at the finish line.

"The electricity around this place is still here," said Johnny Rutherford wistfully. "The halo of energy still hangs." A loud thud that emanated from the pit entrance at 5:20 on Friday, May 19, 2000, bore audible witness. It was the dreaded, if unfamiliar, sound that metal and fiberglass made when they collided at high velocity with the new PEDS-2 barrier. The driver, a forty-six-year-old Japanese man named Hideshi Matsuda had spun the Oldsmobile-propelled Beck Motorsports Dallara chassis in the northwest and slid out of control into what would have been the end of the pit wall, had not the PEDS-2 been operational, replacing the original PED barrier. He reported as demanded to the infield care center where authorities tactfully notified him that he had not been injured. Scott Harrington had much the same medical experience at around half past noon the following Saturday after he spun and slammed both walls.

Lest there be some stigma—some dreadful onus attached to running full throttle into walls whenever opportunity presents itself—Tyce Carlson gave both his car and the wall a sound thumping one Saturday afternoon in May 2001. Tyce visited the hospital and was permitted to leave of his own recognizance, but at the same time was not permitted just yet to be back on the track. About an hour and a half later Jim Guthrie, owner and proprietor of Car Crafters Collision in Albuquerque, collided with the fourth turn wall and did not stop until he passed over the finish line, fortunately without personal injury. Asked why he slammed the wall, Guthrie replied, "it [his car] didn't turn." Asked about his quest at Indianapolis in

2001, said he, "Done. Done. The sponsorship potential is gone. We had to be in the show [to receive sponsor support]. We're only about $100,000 down [with expenses] and a totaled car. This is worse than a broken leg." On lap eighteen of the 2001 500-mile race, eventual IRL season champion Sam Hornish of Defiance, Ohio, spun exiting turn four on cold tires and took Al Unser, Jr. with him, although the two cars never touched. Hornish returned to his pit for new tires and finished the race in fourteenth. Unser, out for the day, scored thirtieth. Before the day ended, Cory Witherill found himself out of control in turn four on lap 134, skidding down the track until he came to the attenuator at the opening of the pit lane.

Bruno Junqueira, the guy from Belo Horizonte, Brazil, who claimed fifth place in the 2001 race, started on the pole in 2002, but not before running his mount into the wall in the northwest on Thursday, May 16 with slight left-side damage. He fell out of competition on lap thirty-one with a gearbox malady. On lap 173 Tomas Scheckter, the sometimes difficult son of 1979 Formula 1 champion Jody Scheckter, struck the SAFER buffer in the northwest and slid a good distance down the front straight, stopping beside the outer wall after having led for eighty-five laps, more than any other contestant. It marked the third consecutive year that a newcomer had taken charge for the most laps, Juan Montoya having led for 167 in 2000, and Helio Castroneves for 51 in 2001. Said Scheckter after the race, "I had no control over the car."

Neither did Billy Boat when he exited turn four on Saturday, May 10, 2003, at 10:02 A.M. in a bright yellow Panther Racing Dallara Chevrolet and turned a 180-degree right-hand loop, then did another 180 left-hand one. Just at the moment when he seemed to be under control he rammed the safety attenuator at the end of the north pit wall, took to the air, and did two 360 bronco-busting whips across the track before banging to a halt against the outside wall on the main straight. He was sent off grounds for additional medical evaluation. Fighter to the end, Boat was back on track by Wednesday. Having started the race in twenty-ninth position, the car lasted seven laps when an engine expired, leaving Boat with no choice except to park the car on the backstretch.

In the 2004 contest, the track's 88th May race, the northwest continued to measure out its mayhem, as for example on lap 10 when A. J. Foyt IV brushed the wall, motored on down the straightaway into turn one where he spun the car into a SAFER barrier. Continuing at speed after a wall tap was a rookie misjudgment, something that Foyt acknowledged afterward. "I thought everything was OK," he said, "but when I got into

[turn] one, I found out it wasn't. It was pretty stupid on my part." He wasn't alone. On the 105th circuit rookie Darren Manning who replaced the late Tony Renna in one of the Target Chip Ganassi Panoz G-Force cars, collided with seven time Indianapolis contestant Greg Ray. Both did a quarter spin to the left, clipped the attenuator at the opening of the pit lane and gathered up Sam Hornish who had high expectations, ending the day for all three. On lap 131 rookie Marty Roth maneuvered too high in turn four and touched the barrier with the right side of the car, then continued down the straightaway, slamming the inside wall. Indianapolis for these four and for the hundreds of others who preceded them over the Hoosier decades was little more than a tangled web of frustration borne of failed aspiration.

Afterword
It's Entertainment

Sua enique voluptas

("everyone has his pleasures")

Lest it be forgotten, attractions other than car racing have transpired over ninety-six years at the Indianapolis Motor Speedway. Babies have been conceived and born, people have keeled over with coronaries, balloons have ascended, privies overturned, ordinary folks busted and booked in the track's infield slammer, bright-eyed kids have mortgaged their souls to the military, yelping dogs discovered sanctuary, golf tournaments waged, nude spectators stormed the track, flea markets pitched their tents, lunatics smuggled their street cars on the speedway and killed themselves, biplanes landed and took wing, tornadoes unleashed their dark vortices, conflagrations erupted, human ashes spread, trainloads of track dogs consumed, and rivers of beer gulped and pissed into oblivion.

Sound like fun? Evidently, some people think so. Why 425,000 or so Indy customers devotedly shoehorned into the IMS's 224 infield acres for one May day in 2002 nevertheless remains among the world's major unsolved mysteries, ranking right up there with the identity of the Dinnertime Bandit. No less than His Excellency, Andy Granatelli the high priest of petroleum enhancers and an enigma in his own right, was at something of a loss to characterize Indy, if not to explain it. Andy articulately identified it, however, as "a Memorial Day set piece of the purest Americana," rightly averring that "Indy is corn. It is fried chicken and beer and box lunches and old racing friends and enemies. . . . It is the blare of bands. The only place in the country where 'Back Home Again in Indiana' gets top billing over 'The Star Spangled Banner.'" Indy, he continued, "is a special brand of hypnotism, and it sets up an impossible dream . . . I love it; I hate it."

This sportsman eagerly awaits the onset of the 1991 500-mile race at Indianapolis. He appears to have been chained to his post. *John Mahoney*

No question. It's all an exercise in diabolic pop psychology. Pageant planners eventually figured out that a few folks of more or less sound mind viewed auto racing, all 500 miles of it, as monotonous, loud, pointlessly violent, and (above all) confusing. Dave Walsh, sports editor of the International News Service, opined in the 1920s that although you don't have to be crazy to drive a race car, it helps. Three generations later, eccentric, bow-tied publicity man Gaylord "Snappy" Ford retorted that racers were "not half as nuts" as some spectators. Be that as it may, some still see car racing as patently insufficient as nourishing sustenance for soul and spirit. Not everyone is there to view an auto race. The occasion cries out for more old fashioned midwestern wizz and vinegar, something to gussy up an auto racing marathon, to wit: a cathartic squadron of chocolate soldiers, cadenced drummers, tubas, pennywhistles, cymbals, motorcycle stunt riders, bozos who refuse to sit down, stirring marches, wafting balloons, billowing flags, cannonballs, drum and bugle processions, sailors, marines, boy scouts, tinhorn politicians, kilted bagpipers, apocalyptic preachers, television trash, aerial explosions, half-naked girls, honking horns, drunks, rhinestone cowboys, free-falling parachutists, solemn encomiums, deafening aircraft flyovers, barking dogs, and in 2001, "a rappel demonstration," meaning, as nearly as we can determine, a person sliding down a rope.

Collectively they elevate the spirit and arouse, ignite, and invigorate even the deadest of souls. Driver Edward Julius Sachs, be he genius or fool, mystic or nimble-witted jester, was so impossibly overwhelmed by Indy's race day arousal that in a moment of abandon he commandeered a drum major's baton, and with Sachsian aplomb strutted smartly uptrack with a full marching band close at his heels. Sachsie, never one to mask his emotions, unabashedly admitted that he never survived a pace lap without unbridled, epiphanous tears of joyous fulfillment coursing down his face.

"There are a few," an anonymous scribe said of Indianapolis 500 grandstanders, "who look upon the contest as a scientist might watch the antics of a medicated guinea pig." Even before there was a 500-mile race, one observer referred to auto races at the Speedway as a "three-day racing carnival." It was not until 1923, however, that the Speedway devoted any attention in its race-day program to hyping its burgeoning appetite for sideshow entertainment. That was the year it trotted out an in-your-face 1,500-piece band composed of fifty smaller musical units prepared to uncouple and meander through the crowd at whim and will like wandering minstrels, regaling any who might bend an ear. "College, Industrial,

Fraternal, Civic, Soldier, Municipal, and even High School bands," a program notice read, "gather for this enormous tournament of music. Led by a color guard of United States Marines the band parade is one of the most stirring, patriotic and commemorating scenes that will be held anyplace in the world today."

A year hence, a writer bearing the unlikely name of Russel Seeds cited Speedway president Jim Allison's apparently off-the-record remark about the problem of unresponsive race spectators. "We've got to do something to make 'em sit up," Allison snorted. "If the thing is going to be a funeral, let's take a shot at first class music and flowers." Back in 1922 the Speedway had, in fact, published a sketch of a racer sharing a cordial cigarette interlude with the Grim Reaper allegorically depicted as a gowned skeleton.

On the brighter side, what purported in 1927 to be the "largest band in the world" passed in review before Sgt. Alvin C. York, whom Gen. John Joseph Pershing called "the greatest civilian soldier of the war." Paul Whiteman and his Old Gold Band jammed at the Speedway in 1929, after which the joint fell under full red-alert siege, with a deafening rollout of one multiple report bomb, two salute bombs, a parachute smoke bomb, an Italian flag bomb, a British flag bomb, a French flag bomb and finally an American flag bomb. Grandstand hayrakes went so battlefield ballistic that the track continued its blitzkrieg a year later, throwing in an artillery shell bomb, a multiple report flag bomb, and a comet flash bomb. Henceforth, race day has begun with a bang, when the threatening sound of an explosion signals the opening of spectator gates. In fact, by 1947 the track had appointed a short-fused incendiary guy named C. C. Naftzger as its own in-house bomber. If you heard an explosion, chances are that Naftzger had something to do with it.

It worked supremely well. *Chicago Herald-Examiner* sports editor Warren Brown proclaimed in 1932, the year that Karl C. Kraft's "Speedway March" first thundered across the acreage, that although he'd witnessed the Kentucky Derby, and the likes of Bobby Jones, Babe Ruth, and Red Grange in the fevered pitch of battle, he opted for the Indianapolis 500 entertainment package for what he called "the doggondest five hours or so . . . of never-know-what-will-happen-next." Indianapolis newspaperman Bill Fox, Jr. who acknowledged in 1931 that "The Indianapolis Motor Speedway has a passion for bombs," sarcastically advised in 1933 that the average spectator is one who "will love the big parade and bombs at the start," and then focus "attention on the track[,] ready to cheer the young man who will take such pride in beginning a checkered career."

It was commentator John Fitzgerald, however, who was among the first to apprehend the 500-mile race as unabashed theatrics in overdrive. "The largest band in the world plays the overture," he wrote in 1937, the race's silver anniversary. "The curtain is raised—the drama already at a furious pitch—a million thrills are being born on the huge stage. And the ending—that, my friends, is the part written by Destiny, revealed as the afternoon sun shines its brightest upon the Speed Spectacle." The audience, said scribe Tom Ochiltree deprecatingly in 1939, consists chiefly of "a democratic army of the shirt sleeve, pack-your-own lunch type. They are clerks, small store keepers, farmers and mechanics[,] and for them the whole thing is a combination community picnic and predated Halloween in county fair surroundings, multiplied a thousand fold." John Hillman rose fearlessly to the defense of the common man in 1947. "We're folksy people out here in Hoosierland," he noted. "We like picnics. We like reunions. We like an open house. And Speedway Day is all of these." In 2001 the Speedway went one better, by honoring "all the mothers at the track" on May 13.

After November 14, 1945, when Tony Hulman wagered his $750,000 on the then dilapidated Indianapolis Motor Speedway, the entertainment of choice commencing in 1946 became the Purdue University "All-American" marching band that in one manifestation or another had made a showing at every Indianapolis race since 1919, the year when, under the direction of Paul Spotts Emrick, it was at the forefront of an Indianapolis celebration marking the conclusion of World War I. The Purdue ensemble that turns up at the Speedway these days is approximately two-thirds of its full football season complement, since in May the university is not in session. What one sees are therefore volunteers with a penchant to entertain and be entertained. Early in the Hulman regime, the band occasionally broke ranks long enough to spell *Tony* race mornings on the main straight. Under the brutal heat of the 1953 race, three of Purdue's sixteen drum majorettes keeled over before they reached the starting line, but the show rolled inexorably onward. The Boilermaker band returned a year later to mellow the multitudes with a now-customary rendering of "On the Banks of the Wabash." Nobody's fool, Hulman knew from the outset that he was in the entertainment business. "He wants," wrote Bill Fox, Jr. in 1946, "everyone to have a good time at his race."

In 1954 when the gold and black marchers were under the direction

Representatives of the Purdue University Marching Band aboard a Chevy pick-up, 1957. *Purdue University Archives*

of Al G. Wright, and when some members of the fourth estate referred to Purdue quarterback Lenny Dawson as the "Golden Boy," a majorette named Juanita Carpenter assumed the inevitable nickname of "Golden Girl," a designation, so a Purdue spokesperson reminds us, that has "evolved into a movable crown" representing "the standard for excellence within the twirling community." The Purdue presence has been, at times, as breathtaking as the racing competition. An anonymous writer in 1962 aptly remarked on its "gold instruments sparkling in the brilliant sunshine and the sequin-costumed majorettes striving to out-sparkle them."

Egging the multitudes on with his customary brio since 1947 has been public address personality Tom Carnegie, a polio victim with a mellifluous, disciplined, somewhat arrogant baritone delivery. He's the "Heeeee's on it!" man, capable of inciting a cemetery into a square dance. Carnegie's partner-in-crime was fellow old-timer Jim Phillippe, another cunning public orator and former theatre director, who conceded that in his view, race day was "all show business." Phillippe died in the fall of 2003. If the two understood surprisingly little about auto racing, it did not show.

"Clusters of aerial bombs appear in four groups," journalist Russ

Members of the Purdue University Marching Band with perennial Indy 500 personality Jim Nabors. *Purdue University Archives*

Catlin noted on race morning in 1948. ''There is a flack pattern and one tri-motored plane deliberately flies through the bursts. Thousands of colored balloons are released [possibly reminiscent of the ascension balloons that wafted serenely above the Speedway in 1909], and the cars are pushed to the starting line. Goose pimples and jitters are contagious. . . . Time is near now, and motors are started as famed singer James Melton gives a slow version of 'Back Home Again in Indiana.''' Little, of course, jump-cranks emotions as vigorously as a sound rendering of that shopworn shibboleth, ''Gentlemen, start your engines,'' the origin of which has never been definitively established.

Ever in search of stunts with which to regale race-day throngs, the Speedway in 1949 extended an invitation to an automotive-minded horse that drove a van 300 yards up the main straight, cut a U-turn and motored back. But at least by 1950, the track presented a consistent race day format: a Marine color guard, a spirited rendering of ''The Star-Spangled Banner,'' a salute to fallen military personnel, and a series of eight more *de rigueur* detonations. By 1952 Morton Downey succeeded vintage car fancier Melton as warbler-designate of ''Back Home Again,'' and was in turn succeeded in that solemn duty by Dinah Shore in 1955, and ultimately by his nibs, the lovable Jim Nabors.

With a mind to getting the crowd in on the act, shrine potentate Worth Baker and former Indianapolis mayor Alex Clark in 1956 began organizing something called the 500 Festival that used the race as a convenient pretext for cranking up a social life in May, especially among citizens who didn't care a whole lot about car racing. They obliged everyone to dress in standard issue black and white, and turn out for such mandatory occasions as parades, balls, dinner parties, beauty contests, and convertible rides around the Speedway. The standing Festival joke is that someone arrived at the bright idea of topping off the month with a corking good auto race.

Until two or three years ago, race-day early birds awoke to the bracing big band strains of George Freije's dawn-busting All-Stars and their downbeat rollout medley of musical calisthenics. It was an orchestral introduction to what, for all its real and imagined faults, is still the planet's most prestigious automobile racing extravaganza. George and the boys caused the sun to rise over Indiana, and to set race day into motion. "The electricity in the air at Indy," two-time Indianapolis champion Arie Luyendyk observed, "isn't really found anywhere else." Added 1998 winner Eddie Cheever, "When you arrive here on race day . . . the place has warmth. It's got color. It's got movement in the stands." It has to be May, and it can only be at Indianapolis. It has to be a ritual of balloons and blitz, bombast, bullcrap, and bravura.

An oldtimer fondly remembered a burn-scarred dirt track veteran who towed a broken down thirties racing car to the Indianapolis Speedway shortly after World War II, on the off-chance that he might by some fluke compete in the 500-mile race, if only for a few sorry laps, until his engine exploded in a disgusting belch of oil-laden gray smoke. "He didn't run in the race," recalled the oldtimer, "but at least he drove on the *Indianapolis track*." For all the gentlemen who have ever started their engines, that feeling resonates.

Appendix

Winners of the Indianapolis 500

Year	Winner	Average Speed in M.P.H.
2004	Buddy Rice	138.518
2003	Gil de Ferran	156.291
2002	Helio Castroneves	166.499
2001	Helio Castroneves	141.574
2000	Juan Montoya	167.607
1999	Kenny Brack	153.176
1998	Eddie Cheever, Jr.	145.155
1997	Arie Luyendyk	145.827
1996	Buddy Lazier	147.956
1995	Jacques Villeneuve	153.616
1994	Al Unser, Jr.	160.872
1993	Emerson Fittipaldi	157.207
1992	Al Unser, Jr.	134.477
1991	Rick Mears	176.457
1990	Arie Luyendyk	185.981
1989	Emerson Fittipaldi	167.581
1988	Rick Mears	144.809
1987	Al Unser	162.175
1986	Bobby Rahal	170.722
1985	Danny Sullivan	152.982
1984	Rick Mears	163.612
1983	Tom Sneva	162.117
1982	Gordon Johncock	162.029
1981	Bobby Unser	139.184
1980	Johnny Rutherford	142.862
1979	Rick Mears	158.899
1978	Al Unser	161.363
1977	A. J. Foyt, Jr.	161.331
1976	Johnny Rutherford	148.725
1975	Bobby Unser	149.213
1974	Johnny Rutherford	158.589
1973	Gordon Johncock	159.036

1972	Mark Donohue	162.962
1971	Al Unser	157.735
1970	Al Unser	155.749
1969	Mario Andretti	156.867
1968	Bobby Unser	152.882
1967	A. J. Foyt, Jr.	151.207
1966	Graham Hill	144.317
1965	Jim Clark	150.686
1964	A. J. Foyt, Jr.	147.350
1963	Parnelli Jones	143.137
1962	Rodger Ward	140.293
1961	A. J. Foyt, Jr.	139.130
1960	Jim Rathmann	138.767
1959	Rodger Ward	135.857
1958	Jimmy Bryan	133.791
1957	Sam Hanks	135.601
1956	Pat Flaherty	128.490
1955	Bob Sweikert	128.209
1954	Bill Vukovich	130.840
1953	Bill Vukovich	128.740
1952	Troy Ruttman	128.922
1951	Lee Wallard	126.244
1950	Johnnie Parsons	124.002
1949	Bill Holland	121.327
1948	Mauri Rose	119.814
1947	Mauri Rose	116.338
1946	George Robson	114.820
1941	Floyd Davis	115.117
	Mauri Rose	115.117
1940	Wilbur Shaw	114.277
1939	Wilbur Shaw	115.035
1938	Floyd Roberts	117.200
1937	Wilbur Shaw	113.580
1936	Lou Meyer	109.069
1935	Kelly Petillo	106.240
1934	Bill Cummings	104.863
1933	Lou Meyer	104.162
1932	Fred Frame	104.144
1931	Louis Schneider	96.629
1930	Billy Arnold	100.448
1929	Ray Keech	97.585
1928	Lou Meyer	99.482
1927	George Souders	97.545
1926	Frank Lockhart	95.904
1925	Peter DePaolo	101.127

1924	L. L. Corum	98.234
	Joe Boyer	98.234
1923	Tommy Milton	90.954
1922	Jimmy Murphy	94.484
1921	Tommy Milton	89.621
1920	Gaston Chevrolet	88.618
1919	Howdy Wilcox	88.050
1916	Dario Resta	84.001
1915	Ralph DePalma	89.840
1914	Rene Thomas	82.474
1913	Jules Goux	75.933
1912	Joe Dawson	78.719
1911	Ray Harroun	74.602

All were 500-mile races except:

2004—450 miles, rain
1976—255 miles, rain
1975—435 miles, rain
1973—332.5 miles, rain
1950—345 miles, rain
1926—400 miles, rain
1916—only scheduled for 300 miles, not 500

As a general rule, the races have an obligation to be 51% completed. Hence, Indianapolis needs 101 of 200 laps completed to call it a race. If it's less than that, the race needs to be restarted at the earliest possible time.

The Indianapolis 500 races in 1942, 1943, 1944, and 1945 were not run due to World War II.

The races in 1917 and 1918 were not run due to World War I.

Index

About the Author

Terry Reed has written numerous articles in publications such as *Penthouse*, *Stock Car Racing*, *On Track*, and *Indy Car Racing*, with best-of-year winners in the American Auto Racing Writers and Broadcasters Association-refereed competition. His work has appeared in the *American National Biography* published by the Oxford University Press and in Microsoft Corporation's *Encarta* encyclopedia. Reed has published books on Truman Capote as well as playwright and *New Yorker* essayist S. N. Behrman. He holds a doctorate in Anglo-American literature.